Curriculum Leadership Development

A Guide for Aspiring School Leaders

Curriculum Leadership Development

A Guide for Aspiring School Leaders

Carol A. Mullen
University of Southern Florida

LEA

LAWRENCE ERLBAUM ASSOCIATES, PUBLISHERS

2007 Mahwah, New Jersey London

Copyright © 2007 by Lawrence Erlbaum Associates, Inc.
   All rights reserved. No part of this book may be reproduced in any form, by photostat, microform, retrieval system, or any other means, without prior written permission of the publisher.

Lawrence Erlbaum Associates, Inc., Publishers
10 Industrial Avenue
Mahwah, New Jersey 07430
www.erlbaum.com

Cover design by Kathryn Houghtaling Lacey

Library of Congress Cataloging-in-Publication Data

Curriculum leadership development : a guide for aspiring school leaders / Carol A. Mullen.
       p. cm.
Includes bibliographical references and index.
ISBN 0-8058-5931-4 (pbk.: alk. paper)
ISBN 1-4106-1467-0 (E-Book)
1. Curriculum planning—Handbooks, manuals, etc. 2. Educational
leadership—Handbooks, manuals, etc. I. Title.
LB2806.15.M85 2006
371.2′03—dc22
2006003212
CIP

Books published by Lawrence Erlbaum Associates are
printed on acid-free paper, and their bindings are
chosen for strength and durability.

Printed in the United States of America
10 9 8 7 6 5 4 3 2 1

Contents

List of Figures and Tables   vii
Preface   ix

I Trends and Issues in the Study of Curriculum Leadership   1

1   Changing Times for School Curriculum Leaders   3
2   Origins, Definitions, and Types of Curriculum   11
3   Process/Product Classification of Key Curriculum Thinkers   27

II Curriculum Leadership Cases for Schools and Faculties   57

4   Coping With Transitions as a New Site-Based
    Administrative Leader   59
5   Information Literacy Development for Students and
    Equitable Access   70
6   Inclusion and School Preparedness to Educate
    Students With Disabilities   84
7   Nurturing School Culture and Collaborative
    Curriculum as Campus Leader   97
8   Countering Interruptions of Teaching With
    Curricular Leadership   115
9   Reflective Analysis of National Board-Certified
    Teacher Mentoring Programs   132
10 Administrator Walk-Through as Instructional
    Aid for Classroom Teachers   149

11 Transformation of an Inner City Elementary School
     Into a Magnet School   162
12 Career Academy Trends in Modernizing Curriculum
     and Infusing Technology   177
13 Early Reading Intervention Through After-School
     Tutoring Programs   187
14 Curricular Effects of Looping for Students,
     Teachers, and Parents   202
15 Science Teachers as Curriculum Coaches of
     Language and Meaning-Making   214

           III University-Based Curriculum
                 Leadership Exercises   227

16 A Guide for Instructors, Coaches, and Future
     School Leaders   229
References   247
About the Contributors   262
Author Index   267
Subject Index   272

List of Figures and Tables

FIGURES

Figure 9.1   A teacher mentor–protégé mentoring cycle   138

Figure 11.1   Transforming a regular elementary school into a
              district magnet school   170
Figure 11.2   Fitting together the pieces of a thematic curriculum   174

Figure 16.1   Meditation on curriculum as growth and decay   245

TABLES

Table 3.1   Key Thinkers in Curriculum Studies   42

Table 7.1   Administrator School Culture Interview   101
Table 7.2   School Culture Survey of Teachers' Perceptions   105
Table 7.3   Elementary School and ESE Center Survey Results   108

Table 8.1   Letter Accompanying Teacher Survey "Factors
              That Interfere With Instruction"   120
Table 8.2   Factors That Interrupt Teacher Instruction   121

Table 10.1   Administrator/Teacher Mentor Walk-Through
              Reflection Sheet   153
Table 10.2   Comparing Formal and Informal Walk-Through
              Models   158
Table 10.3   Classroom Walk-Through Checklist   160

Table 13.1   Performance Data for Tutored Students
             and Control Group   192

Table 16.1   Curriculum Mapping of How Living Things Interact   240

Preface

Imagine you are a giant octopus—"an intelligent creature: In laboratory tests and aquariums, it has been able to solve mazes very quickly, unscrew jar lids to retrieve food inside the jar, and even mimic another octopus in a different tank" (National Parks Conservation Association, 2005, para. 1). One long-reaching arm gently holds a real-live school building filled with people, situations, and things. Curious, you remove the roof (easy as a lid) and, observing the dynamic action inside, witness busy interactions among students, teachers, and administrators. Many are engaged in reading, writing, building, testing, creating, speaking, and listening. You look long and hard, searching for *curriculum*—your arms touch on various aspects of curriculum, some tangible, others intangible—books, tests, classrooms, activities, discourse, interaction, experience, and more. You soon realize that curriculum embodies everything from within the school and without, and internal and external to individuals (see chap. 2 for origins and definitions of curriculum).

Although you grasp the visible or tangible aspects of curriculum, such as materials, activities, and equipment, you can see that it is challenging for school people to engage the beliefs, values, and biases of groups and individuals. All that is planned and unplanned, academic and nonacademic, intentional and hidden configures every student, teacher, and leader's experiences of the curriculum.

As an octopus, you encounter the pervasive forces of curriculum and leadership, and accountability and democracy. These all have a critical role to play in the making and remaking of the school's curriculum. Such national influences as federal laws and civil movements, as well as various state and local changes, shape how curriculum leadership and democratic accountability are expressed in schools. But to what extent are teachers and administrators aware of the impact of these forces within their own environment? By better understanding the workings of curriculum (formal and informal;

official and hidden) and leadership (role and function; disposition and aspiration), as well as democracy (justice, fairness, self-regulation) and accountability (responsibility, standards, objectivity), practitioners can become better informed about what they do and why, and learn about the possibilities for creativity, renewal, and liberation.

The theme of this book is curriculum leadership development for aspiring and practicing school leaders. I attempt to connect curriculum and leadership, and democracy and accountability, in ways that are instructive for teachers and administrators alike. Although numerous books present these ideas as important subjects in education, few relate them by exploring the tensions inherent in curriculum and leadership, and democracy and accountability for schools.

Also, many texts, although interesting and stimulating, do not highlight first-person accounts from experienced teacher leaders. Unlike previous texts, not only does *Curriculum Leadership Development: A Guide for Aspiring School Leaders* focus on curriculum and leadership development at the school level, it also offers educators' reflections on and analysis of real-life curriculum leadership situations. A group of 17 teachers and administrators provided cases depicting a range of issues relevant to curriculum leadership (Part II). Additionally, 253 master's papers, collected during my teaching from 2004 to 2006, were analyzed for relevance to this project. Some of these teachers view the high-stakes movement, and specifically the impact on leading and teaching, in positive terms. As one master's student claimed, "More and more each day, administrators are being held responsible for narrowing the test score gap between disadvantaged and advantaged students and for ensuring that all teachers are high quality" (course paper, 2004). Another expressed the value she placed on disaggregated test score data as critical information for improving her effectiveness in the classroom:

> The groups that are not achieving significant progress at my school are the Hispanic students and the Black males. High-stakes test scores serve as a great tool for seeing who needs more attention. As a teacher I can use my abilities to identify individual students in my class who need the extra help, but to know that a certain group as a whole needs more attention is very valuable to learn. (master's course paper, 2005)

Contrasting with this perspective, other graduate students who are educators have debated this stance:

> How can someone believe that through continuous pressures of testing that something good can actually come out of this? Instead of sacrificing the sanity of children and teachers, why aren't we trying to close the achievement gap through ongoing reflection, collaboration, and meaningful professional development? (master's course paper, 2005)

In Part I, two other scholar practitioners assisted me in providing an overarching curriculum framework for this book. Together, the large group of authors provide reflection on curriculum leadership from an inside-out perspective, sharing experiences in an authentic and meaningful way.

Moreover, I address theory in the form of salient theoretical, curricular, and pedagogical frameworks that underlie curriculum leadership. The issue of practice is paramount as well. Practical issues and concerns form the backbone of each contributor's chapter. Exercises appear at the end of all the case-based chapters (Part II) and within an entire section (chap. 16) devoted to instructional curricular tools for the university classroom.

READERSHIP OF THIS BOOK

If you are a graduate student in education (MEd, EdS, EdD, and PhD) who will guide schools in such curriculum leadership roles as assistant principal, principal, lead teacher, administrative resource personnel, and district coordinator, this book is for you. Advanced undergraduate students keen on becoming leaders will also derive value from this text. Another primary audience is the curriculum professionals (faculty, adjuncts, etc.) who teach practicing teachers. Other readers include curriculum developers and reformers, theorists, scholars, researchers, district leaders, and school consultants.

The disciplines that this book targets are curriculum and educational leadership, as well as school administration and teacher education, specifically courses aimed at developing the leadership capacity of new and experienced teachers. The text adopts a descriptive but rigorous qualitative approach that is based on case studies, action research, data, and reflection. Familiarity with basic curriculum concepts and/or practices would be helpful to your understanding.

ADDRESSING KNOWLEDGE GAPS

This book is grounded in current and relevant theory, research, legislation, and application in the closely related areas of curriculum leadership, development, and scholarship. Furthermore, links among curriculum development, constructivist curricula, and mentoring scaffolds are explicated. As a professor of educational leadership and policy studies and a scholar in the curriculum/leadership fields whose doctorate is in this combined area, I am uniquely qualified to address these gaps.

The gap specifically concerning curriculum leadership in educational research is discussed in chapter 1. A related gap concerns the voice of authority: Too many scholars and not enough teachers and leaders are writing the official narratives of curriculum planning, educational leadership, and standards-based change. In educational leadership, we need to move away from high-sounding abstractions to embrace research and action, and to better see schooling practices through the eyes of practitioners. In my text, a decentering of the professor as scholar is enacted without trading off my own expertise, analyses, and reflections. I aimed to bring forward the voice and curricular experiences of the professional student who is a seasoned teacher or beginning administrator. By doing so, this book aims to create spaces for the voices of curriculum in a new key (Pinar & Irwin, 2005). Detailed illustrations of practitioners' experiences as curriculum makers and action researchers are also provided. I have played a mentoring role by encouraging the writing and research of this group of graduate students and by being a proactive coauthor, turning students' preliminary ideas or rough notes into educational inquiries and by making detailed as well as extensive contributions to all chapters. In turn, two graduate students critiqued the entire book manuscript, reading it for accessibility to their peers. To clarify, the pronouns used in the coauthored accounts (Part II) emphasize "I" over "we" in order to shine light on the voices of the student contributors and the value I place on them.

In an instructional capacity with this group of authors and other students more generally, I have struggled to find appropriate and relevant textbooks for my master's courses, primarily Administrative Analysis and Change, Educational Leadership, and Foundations of Curriculum and Instruction. My students who are practicing teachers complain about texts that are too scientifically oriented and distant from their experience (technocratic and objective). They warm up to writing that deals with current issues that affect schools, embrace the inner curriculum (e.g., autobiographically grounded, reflective work), and deal with topics of immediate interest to them. Also, from my own point of view, new curriculum books should ground concepts of curriculum and leadership in experiential learning while promoting democratic action and critical thinking. Criticisms of the various books that I have adopted for my curriculum and leadership courses over the years led me to change the assigned books every semester, at times assembling reading packets in order to avoid textbook adoption altogether. Toward this end, I have been inspired to craft a text that would be well received by student populations like my own that also "pushes the envelope of their own thinking."

CONTENTS AND ORGANIZATION

This text has a dual focus: It features key issues that influence K–12 American public school curricular leadership *and* that are relevant to preservice leadership preparation. Curriculum frameworks are discussed from various democratic and accountability perspectives. Critical issues in school curriculum and practitioner development are addressed by insiders, and influential cultural forces, legislative changes, and societal trends are incorporated. This book also highlights processes involved in learning on the part of aspiring school leaders and teaching on the part of graduate faculty. Finally, it envelops the relationship between curriculum and instruction as in the case of public school curriculum that is aligned with high-stakes standards and student testing and is thus preset or mandated.

Part I defines curriculum leadership and the related concepts appearing in this book. Importantly, the voices of master's students are incorporated. Their analyses are not casual observations but rather evidence-based claims rooted in data that have been collected, interpreted, and discussed. Part I communicates the empowering role of practitioner as researcher and the promise of action research for incorporating theory and practice. It also sets the national, state, and local context of curriculum leadership by introducing relevant legislative and policy issues and trends in school curriculum.

This section also characterizes the curriculum leadership field through a kaleidoscope of curricular lenses—critical, cultural, personal, and, importantly, practical—and it includes origins, definitions, types, and classifications. The historical evolution of curriculum and the individuals who have influenced it are incorporated. An extensive chart outlining key curriculum thinkers and their contributions is included as a pedagogical or learning aid.

Part II is a series of coauthored cases written by aspiring and practicing leaders who are K–12 public school teachers as well as administrators. These all focus on curriculum leadership as personal and staff development. The scholarly cases examine a host of challenges to becoming a curriculum leader, whether as teacher or administrator, along with possible solutions. Issues include transitional realities of a personal and professional nature facing new site-based administrators; consciousness raising around interruptions to teaching and learning; literacy leadership as a key to curriculum redesign and school improvement; and national board certification and its role in supporting collaborative curriculum development and mentorship. The teacher authors have themselves selected these topics and issues for investigation. The 12 cases should be a great support to teachers and administrators searching for new curricular ideas and practices. Those who view curriculum as an abstract ideal forced on them by a central office or the state board of education (Mullen, 2003, 2004a) could also benefit from the self-empowered, proactive leadership stance of the authors, a group of practicing teachers.

Part III covers instructional curricular tools for university instructors that curriculum leaders can adapt to the school-and-district context. Through a variety of artistic and scientific strategies, you will learn to relate your personal philosophy and values to curriculum and leadership.

DISTINCTIVE FEATURES

- *Case Studies*—As Shapiro and Stefkovich (2005) aptly observe, cases are popular in education; they also promote pedagogical engagement and are seen as assets in textbooks. Each of the book's case studies is accompanied by reflective inquiry exercises.
- *Student/Teacher Voice*—The voices (writings) of aspiring and practicing school leaders (graduate students) are heard throughout Parts I and II in the form of cases, reflections, and quotations.
- *Practical, Reflective Activities*—See earlier, "Case Studies." Examples of such questions appear at the end of all chapters in Part II and throughout chapter 16.
- *Instructor-Led Classroom Exercises*—Journaling a philosophy of curriculum statement, defining key terms, initiating curriculum leadership, and devising curriculum timelines are examples.

TEACHING NOTES TO THE INSTRUCTOR

This guide can be used as a core or supplemental education textbook for curriculum and educational leadership courses at the master's or doctoral level. It can also be used in critical pedagogy, feminist, and philosophy of education courses and to assist faculty, including adjuncts, curriculum researchers, and thesis/dissertation supervisors and candidates. Finally, it can serve as a support for staff/personnel development in schools.

Course Relevance

Graduate courses in educational leadership for which this book is ideally suited include:

- *Master's level*—Administrative Analysis and Change, Case Studies in School Administration, Principalship, Educational Leadership, Foundations of Curriculum and Instruction, School Curriculum, School Curriculum Improvement.
- *Doctoral level*—Graduate Seminar, Issues in Curriculum and Instruction, Selected Topics (e.g., Curriculum Leadership, Supervision, Mentoring, Philosophy).

ACKNOWLEDGMENTS

I appreciate the caring, democratic modeling of curriculum leaders Dean Colleen Kennedy, former Associate Dean for Academic Affairs Carine Feyten, and Associate Vice President for Academic Affairs Judith Ponticell of the University of South Florida's (USF) College of Education. I thank William A. Kealy, Associate Professor of USF, for producing the digital renderings of the images exhibited herein. I am indebted to Lori Kelly, Lawrence Erlbaum Associates' (LEA) Textbook and Journal Marketing Manager, who, as my acquisitions editor, spent time discussing my ideas for this book at the 2005 meeting of the American Educational Research Association in San Diego. The LEA publishing team was conscientious and professional in the work carried out, and the two cycles of external reviews were handled in a timely manner. I also appreciate the critical reading of the book manuscript that Carol Burg and Janice Hutinger, my doctoral students in educational leadership at the USF, completed during its drafting. I am most grateful to the group of graduate students who contributed original works in partnership with me—the cases are the heart of this "octopus." Finally, in accordance with the University of South Florida's rule 6C4-10.109.B-6, I am confirming that the opinions stated in this book are my own, not the University's.

I

Trends and Issues in the Study of Curriculum Leadership

1

Changing Times for School Curriculum Leaders

Carol A. Mullen

As curriculum leaders, we are called [on] to be "cathedral builders." ... We no longer have a direct impact on the students in our buildings the way we did as classroom teachers. Instead, the way we increase the level of achievement for our students is through the things we do to increase the ability of our teachers to "see" a school that could be and their competency to meet that challenge. It will demand all that is within us—intellectually, physically, and ethically. But such is the calling of a cathedral builder.

—Retired elementary principal and superintendent
(Schermer, 2005, p. 5)

Real change is not easy—it is nonlinear, multifaceted, uncertain, and even chaotic at times (English & Larson, 1996; Hargreaves & Fullan, 2000). The role of teaching and administering, managing, and leading had dramatically changed over a short time: "... the emerging competitive marketplace in education, with its reliance on test scores as the arbiters of "quality," has elevated curriculum leadership to the forefront in determining effective curriculum practices in schools" (English & Steffy, 2005, p. 425). Along with other actions taken, democratically accountable curriculum leaders are changing the status quo by

- turning inequitable power structures and relationships in their own school communities into different and promising social relationships;
- promoting instructional competence and preparing their faculties to improve the academic performance of all students;

- transforming autocratic decision making into shared governance through distributed leadership strategies that engage teachers and students;
- developing the capacity of staff to think critically and expand professionally while satisfying school goals.

In discussing professional development as a tool for change, since the 1990s research has shown that teacher learning can have a positive effect on student achievement where it focuses on curriculum. Specifically, teachers are more likely to change their practices when their in-service training, for example, clearly connects curriculum to subject matter content, curriculum materials and instruction, and standards and assessments (Research Points, 2005).

Who better to turn to for insight into such changing agendas than the insiders themselves? Practitioners who are highly capable in their multiple roles make excellent informants. As stated by master's students in an educational leadership course I teach,

> Principals who pursue site-based management must respond positively to the change from autocratic decision making to collaborative decision making. Site-based management of schools will be effective only if administration integrates high-quality performance in diverse dimensions of the role as curriculum leader— mentor, evaluator, politician, manager, and cultural expert. (Anonymous, course paper, 2005)

Teachers and principals who study the issues they identify as important not only speak as informed authorities, but also as action researchers seeking to make a difference.

This book brings together just such an exemplary group of emerging leaders, empowered here through the lenses of action researcher and scholar practitioner. Action researchers "want their research findings to have an impact on the situation or context as the intervention takes place, and [action research] sees the practitioner as researcher" (Robertson, 2005, p. 76). Scholar practitioners "use theory to inform their practice and allow their reflections upon their practice to inform theory." Their reflections can be "non-critical or critical, or critical in the traditional or radical sense" (Horn, 2002, p. 101; for an essay on this subject, see Mullen, 2005b). With support from insiders, then, *Curriculum Leadership Development* depicts the interiority of present-day schools, displaying the shifting ideologies and evolving practices of educators. Clandinin and Connelly (e.g., 1992, 1995) have long credited teachers as a group with personal and professional knowledge worth mining. In my experience, practitioners who study in higher education degree programs while attending to their school responsibilities are especially capable of sparking and sustaining constructive dialogue about curriculum and its multifaceted nature (Mullen, 2004a, 2004b). Leadership aspirants are now seen as curriculum leaders. Agreeing with this assessment, a doctoral student/veteran teacher who is currently preparing for site-based administration, wrote,

> Without a strong curriculum foundation and awareness of new leadership styles (e.g., knowing how to engage in shared leadership and mentor staff), aspiring school leaders may not experience success. There is an implied importance that these two major components be built into all administration preparation support programs. However, based on my own experiences new teachers see the need for these to be incorporated into university programs and hence in their own administrative background. (Anonymous, course paper, 2006)

Learning what these insiders know and experience will enrich the collective wisdom of teachers, principals, professors, and policymakers. Toward this end, I have guided my contributors to work closely with me and one another on producing scholarship around these questions:

1. What does the concept of curriculum leadership mean to you, and how do you make sense of it in practice as an action researcher?
2. What do you believe are the flagship curricular questions and challenges facing schools and society today?
3. What changes in the role of curriculum leaders most affect teachers and principals personally as well as professionally?

The 17 school-based contributors address this general framework in their scholarly cases (Part II). Many other teachers studying at the University of South Florida also provided reflective statements and tool-kit ideas included as data sources in Parts I and III. Major areas highlighted through action research (data collection and analysis, and interpretation and discussion) are administrator coaching, curricular interruptions, high-stakes testing, literacy leadership, magnet academies, student progression, teacher certification, technology leadership, transitional leadership, school culture, site-based leadership, and special education.

One lesson learned from these studies is that despite the narrow legislative treatment of curriculum as high-stakes testing outcomes, at least some practitioners conceive of curriculum in nontraditional or broad and humane terms. They have explored how curriculum is planned, enacted, experienced, and assessed within teaching/learning spaces that stretch beyond the classroom. For this group of aspiring leaders, curriculum development is a comprehensive school-wide improvement process that comprises effective program design and teaching strategies.

Yet another lesson learned is that curriculum, as a multifaceted, holistic concept, should not be equated with student achievement, test scores, grades, prepackaged curriculum materials, academic or professional standards, policies, guidelines, or tests. As a group, we recognize that each of these areas has become a crucial part of the whole within today's national policy climate. Finally, curriculum is not restricted to the academic domain by the authors either, as we recognize its personal, professional, and political dimensions.

Importantly, the contributing authors together expose hidden aspects of the curriculum of schooling by examining "what is *not* being taught" (Poeske, Stober, Dyson, & Cheddar, 2005, p. 45) to many aspiring and practicing teachers in such areas as information literacy (chap. 5) and classroom interruption (chap. 8). As concerns school leadership, they also examine what is *not* sufficiently modeled by "cathedral builders" in such domains as inclusive settings for students with disabilities (chap. 6). They are not blind to "the hidden curriculum of domination" and the tendency of school cultures to perpetuate "the classical canon and [the] meanings and knowledge that have stood the test of time" (Poeske et al., 2005, p. 44), yet each holds onto shared values, communal cultures, and curricular cohesion. And they understand that what appears fundamentally rational and knowable, as in the case of academic and professional teaching standards, is often rife with uncertainty and tension at the level of local implementation.

The reader will see that a spirit of hope and possibility, enthusiasm and even empowerment characterizes these developing leaders' attitudes toward educational change. This is testimony to the fact that although "curriculum decisions made at the local level have been vastly reduced since the 1960s as federal and state constraints on local policymaking have increased, ... *local decisions are still important*" (Marsh & Willis, 2003, p. 16, emphasis added).

BACKGROUND

The empirical cases selected for this book represent issues similar to those that practicing teachers in my graduate classes have generally addressed. This makes the cases appearing here all the more relevant because the topics selected for inquiry are not unique—curriculum leaders should already be familiar with all of the core issues presented and aspiring leaders should be making every concerted effort to become so. However, the approach taken to each issue, the observations made, and the personal writing style and voice of each writer carry that individual's unique stamp.

It only stands to reason that this volume does not exhaustively depict all priorities for school leadership today, including excessive site-based leadership turnover, and school safety and student discipline, including zero-tolerance policies, and leadership preparation through universities and schools. (Other publications of mine cover these particular issues, see, e.g., Mullen, 2004a, 2004b). Further, even though diverse educational meanings and situations are depicted in these pages, it is simply not possible to cover all facets of curriculum in a single text. What one person would consider a legitimate example of curriculum, another would not. We have not intended to focus on particular aspects of the curriculum while shutting out others, a problem that Marsh and Willis (2003) say pervades curriculum texts. A combination of space constraints and enthusiasm for certain topics has resulted in the selections made. As mentioned in the preface, all of the author chapters appearing in this book were jointly produced with me in 2005; my own conceptual input and scholarly writing and research significantly influenced each.

CASE STUDY

For this book, four major bodies of literature—school curriculum, school improvement, teacher development, and administrative leadership—were consulted, in addition to many specialized topics, such as inclusion, technology leadership, and school culture. Together, these navigational guides supported the development of the practitioners' case studies and the kaleidoscope we present.

To clarify, what is case study? Narrative research in the form of case study has become an honored tradition within the human and natural sciences. It serves as a proven reflective tool that connects knowledge with practice for school personnel eager to make sense of often fast-paced situations. Case studies, unlike cases, are more than school stories. These empirical, narrative treatments of research blend story, data, and analysis for eliciting insight into salient issues and circumstances (Merriam, 1998; Mullen, 2004b). At the same time, the importance of sharing personal and professional experiences is celebrated; by doing so, we gain "access to new stories, new wrinkles in established patterns; in other words, new sources of meaning" (Kenyon, 1996, p. 32). Gardner (1991) connects the value of storytelling to the lives of administrators and other curriculum leaders: "Leadership is a process that occurs within the minds of individuals who live in a culture—a process that entails the capacities to create stories, to understand and evaluate these stories, and to appreciate the struggle among stories" (cited in Sergiovanni, 2000, p. 169). By understanding and evaluating our stories, we become empowered to change those that can help bring coherence and continuity to our experiences (Clandinin & Connelly, 1992, 1995).

For teachers who aspire to lead schools, the case study method offers an outlet for meaning making as well as a strategy for framing issues and learning skills, and within a relatively short time frame. Clinical or field-based internships are often the curriculum students prefer; however, this option is not always realistic for part-timers and understaffed programs (Mullen & Cairns, 2001). Besides, action research is not a substitute for the internship, as it has its own unique rewards. In becoming action researchers with a public voice, teachers learn how to conduct inquiries in areas of interest, complete with results, by bringing together scholarship and ideas with data and analysis.

Schools need internal experts who know how to collect and analyze data, substantiate assertions with evidence, and convincingly report results to their public constituents. Such scholarly activities have, in fact, become performance indicators of outstanding school leaders (Lortie, 1998). As revealed in chapter 2, practitioners who can identify biases and the hidden curriculum as well as test assumptions implicit in policy and change models (e.g., zero-tolerance policies make schools safer) can help transform their immediate school communities.

CONTRIBUTOR PROFILES AND WRITING PROCESS

This book's master's and doctoral writers are a diverse group of males and females (though they are predominantly White, like the educational leadership field itself) in their 30s, 40s, and 50s who have worked in various states and countries. Everyone holds responsibilities as teacher mentors, lead teachers, department heads, and directors. They are also specialists in technology, reading, mainstreaming, and other areas at their schools and possess certifications in specialty areas as well as university degrees. These writers all aspire to be educational leaders, typically principals, and, to a lesser extent, professors; superintendent is a more remote possibility.

For their chapters, the contributors chose topics of genuine interest for which they had unresolved questions. They felt motivated to make selections that could prove informative for their administration and stakeholder groups, as well as policymakers. They offer perspectives on their topic that accommodate the views of stakeholder groups and promote personal reflection. These writers collected data by designing their own research instruments in close consultation with me and engaged students, teachers, administrators, parents, or recognized experts in their research explorations. Although some opted to conduct formal conversations or taped interviews, others distributed original surveys and analyzed school and policy documents. They all obtained official permission for conducting their research and used anonymity to protect their participants and school contexts.

The chapters were launched with a written proposal, and subsequent drafts ensued in which I provided ongoing, intensive feedback and writing. Peers also provided input and critique. Students were guided through the steps of creating research instruments, resolving study obstacles (e.g., unreturned phone calls), and electronically sharing information and texts. Other specialized, interactive activities provided further support. One such support system featured conventions and alternatives for analyzing the data collected, as students would feel at a loss when it came to interpreting interview transcripts, completed surveys, and more.

The writers used the three questions framed at the outset as a guide for probing issues of curriculum, leadership, and curriculum leadership. As a writing scaffold, they also followed my case study model for guiding scholar practitioners' action research (see chap. 16; for an elaboration, consult Mullen, 2004a, 2004b). This template blends research and story by privileging neither over the other, and it was designed for the purpose of application as well as flexibility.

This model helped clarify what case study means (and does not mean). Short, nonanalytical vignettes were distinguished from research-based case studies. In order to learn about how they differ, the writers read abbreviated cases (e.g., *Journal of Cases in Educational Leadership*; see www.ucea.org/cases) and case studies. Although school stories are vital to the case study method, they are developed with data, analysis, and insight.

PARTING THOUGHT

Many compounding sources outside the immediate jurisdiction of schools shape its curricular directions and expectations for site-based leadership. Policymakers, university educators, and other nonschool groups, such as business executives, generate targeted areas for reform. Unless practitioners publicly communicate priority issues and methods for guiding schools, it will remain within the purview of outsiders to decide what they should think, know, and be able to do. Even when liberal educational researchers such as Michael Apple, Henry Giroux, Patti Lather, Peter McLaren, and William Pinar argue for a revolutionary pedagogy on behalf of schools, our academic discourse tends to bypass practitioners and their world. By going directly to the practitioner, a primary source of school reform, issues are heard by schools at an unprecedented level. Here we expose you to the thoughts and writings of others like (and unlike) yourself who are in similar (and dissimilar) situations so that you can more readily make authentic connections and new discoveries.

REFLECTIVE, PRACTICAL ACTIVITIES

- What do you see as the major changes or influences affecting public schools today from your own perspective as an administrator, teacher, parent, or community member?

- Describe the most challenging or controversial curriculum change process in your school or district. What made this process so difficult? What steps were taken to resolve the issues?
- At your institution (e.g., school site, district office, university) address what strategies are currently being used to support the success of aspiring and practicing school leaders in their changing roles as they grapple with the cultural, economic, political, and social elements of schooling.
- Give examples of these curriculum leadership roles—mentor, evaluator, politician, manager, and cultural expert. You can expand this list. Rallis and Goldring (2000), for example, in describing the multiple roles of dynamic principals add facilitator (facilitates teacher leadership), balancer (balances the messages of school and community), and flag bearer/bridger (coordinates the inner life of the school with the outer world).

2

Origins, Definitions, and Types of Curriculum

Carol A. Mullen

The definition of curriculum as a structured series of learning opportunities highlights the constructed nature of the curriculum based on a conception of knowledge—its organization into disciplines—and learning theory. It also serves to draw attention to the curriculum as a values-driven *selection* of material or course content that operates to both include and exclude certain traditions of knowledge, particular perspectives, and sets of values.

—Critical theorists (de Alba, González-Gaudiano, Lankshear, & Peters, 2000, pp. 10–11)

ORIGINS AND DEFINITIONS OF CURRICULUM

No single definition of curriculum accommodates all perspectives and priorities. In fact, more than 120 definitions appear in the literature (Marsh & Willis, 2003). By going beyond defining curriculum to grapple with its range of meanings, you can develop richer insight and potency as a leader. Resist seeing curriculum strictly as something fairly obvious and straightforward, such as a school or district document or set of standards that gets implemented. Instead, envision curriculum as a "text" to be analyzed. In the broadest sense, just about anything can be considered text. Your situations, events, and dreams, even your own life experiences, can be viewed as text, that is, as material worthy of interpretation. In other words, you can analyze curriculum just as you would books, film, and other texts (Connelly & Clandinin, 1988), or culture, people, and incidents. As you know, your intellectual and intuitive, if not "sleuthing," powers are indispensable when it comes to making sense of the world around you.

Curriculum, like anything else, can have a limiting or developmental impact on people's lives (Pinar, 2005b). For example, out-of-date curriculum books restrict students' comprehension and meaning-making. Similarly, those that present curriculum from only a historical light exclude contemporary understandings of curriculum that incorporate political, institutional, phenomenological, aesthetic, and other lenses. Curriculum has expanded meaning as one engages in acts of deliberation, discourse, and reflection. When singular lenses *are* used, these must be explained, or even outright interrogated as a way of dealing with one's implicit biases. Positions that show support for, and critique of, the No Child Left Behind Act of 2001 (NCLB; U.S. Department of Education, 2002) surface in this book.

How would you respond if you were asked to provide a definition of *curriculum* at a staff development meeting, retreat, graduate course, or another context? Would you simply share that curriculum is a course or program of study, or would you feel prepared to discuss it as carrying personal and political values. As curriculum scholar Brubaker (2004) reveals, in educational circles we can expect to experience the neutralization and depoliticization of curriculum. But even the activities created by teachers for students are not neutral—they are value-laden in that they reflect "the ideas, perspectives, and skills deemed most worthy of an education" (Henderson & Hawthorne, 2000, p. 3). Curriculum is a powerful tool for influencing people's thoughts on just about any subject.

Curriculum, derived from Latin, means "race-course," "the race itself," or "career" (Bobbitt, 1918/2004; Connelly & Clandinin, 1988). Over the decades, this word has accumulated numerous connotations and distinctions: a single course (syllabus); a course/program of study (a printed list of subjects and curricula at schools and a catalog for diploma and degree programs at higher education institutions; see Brubaker, 2004); and, importantly, the lesson plans created by teachers and curriculum developers. Along with district coordinators, site-based curriculum leaders (i.e., principals, teachers, and administrative resource personnel) can expect to have to follow the school district's learning objectives, benchmarks, and program designs that correspond to governmental policies and standards, such as the U.S. Department of Education's (Oleson, 2005).

Outer curriculum has been coined (Brubaker, 2004) to describe external forms of and pressures on curriculum. An oppositional force, *inner curriculum*, emphasizes what is personally, interpersonally, and perhaps cooperatively learned within educational settings. Although in constant tension, the inner and outer curricula can serve as productive springboards to one another, especially when both forces are viewed as "organic and growing, and thus subject to change, rather than static and fixed" (Brubaker, 2004, p. xviii).

Leading curriculum scholars (e.g., Connelly & Clandinin, 1988) have developed their own language for describing this dialectic (such as personal practical knowledge versus policy conduit), partly in an effort to encourage curriculum planners to create their own curriculum or interpret existing mandates. A more conservative position is that "the best curriculum work integrates curriculum functions at several levels—state, district, school, and classroom" (Glatthorn, 2000, p. 25). In this picture, school teams develop curriculum that builds on the district's "mastery core," supplements the mandated program with courses for special-needs populations, aligns the curriculum, and monitors its implementation and results (Glatthorn, 2000). All of this must be funneled through classroom teachers, who influence what is taught and how (Walker, 2003). English and Larson (1996) say that "three forms of curriculum are at work in schools"—"formal, informal, and hidden curricula" (p. 9). What follows is a paraphrase (from pps. 9–10 in the original source) of each form.

Formal curriculum is developed by influential bodies (state boards of education, accreditation associations, or national associations) from outside the school environment. This officially sanctioned, top-down curriculum will be developed, implemented, and monitored. Although not developed demographically with local schools, this curriculum is, in many states, locally endorsed and sometimes designed.

Informal curriculum is manifest in the values implied in the selection of curriculum content and in the socialization patterns within schools. In the first instance, religious conservatives react to the fact that "scientific creationism" is omitted from the science curriculum and the study of evolution. In the latter case, student groups based on volunteerism are a common practice that can prove detrimental where learners seek homogeneity or thwart diversity.

Hidden curriculum is "latent but present" in the school routines that students experience; these can vary from one country to another. "Implicit cultural values" are unconsciously transmitted and taught by teachers and other educational groups. For example, in Westernized countries, it is assumed that students must complete one task before embarking on another. More invasive examples of the hidden curriculum involve gender-based assumptions about girls and boys, and racial stereotypes about different ethnic groups.

Other meanings of *curriculum* include all of the planned and unplanned experiences (or general and directed learning) of children in the classroom and extracurricular, cocurricular, and out-of-school curriculum. Curriculum, in the broadest sense, then, concerns all of the experiences that an individual has, both directed and spontaneous, as well as the intended or formal experiences associated with educating and shaping the abilities of students. Nontraditional definitions of curriculum assume a broader and deeper view of experience in relation to schooling or life (Connelly & Clandinin, 1988). Increasingly, the aesthetic (Eisner, 1996), legal (Janesick, 2003), and moral (Pinar, Reynolds, Slattery, & Taubman, 1995/1996) aspects of curriculum development exist in tension with accountability issues, particularly educational standards, high-stakes testing, and authentic assessment (Flinders & Thornton, 2004a, 2004b).

Although some scholars claim curriculum is about what is taught (e.g., Janesick, 2003), most say that curriculum is actually the definition of *instruction*, as curriculum focuses on what is learned or experienced (e.g., Brubaker, 2004). Many would agree, however, that curriculum is about both, that is, what is taught *and* learned (English & Larson, 1996). The unstudied, or null, curriculum (issues not covered in the official school [or other] curriculum) and hidden curriculum (a by-product of the null curriculum, as well as covert or ideological messages underlying the overt curriculum) offer invaluable frames of reference for improving education (Pinar et al., 1995/1996; see also Jackson, 1990/2004).

The hidden curriculum exerts a powerful influence in how we think and act. Examples in our learning and environment include "unacknowledged attitudes, beliefs, codes of conduct, and conventions for social relationships" (Marsh & Willis, 2003, p. 11). According to curriculum theorist Jackson (1990/2004), three forces—"the crowds, the praise, and the power" (p. 99)—constitute the hidden curriculum that students, teachers, and administrators alike must master. Jackson associates this idea of the crowd with "institutional conformity" and "intellectual prowess" (p. 99). As he explains, educational rewards go to those students who are not just bright but also conform to the rules of their classroom, school, and society. In fact, we have always known that "good behavior pays off" (p. 100)—students who violate institutional rules will have greater difficulty succeeding than those who have intellectual deficiencies, he claims. Jackson speculates that "the same strengths that contribute to intellectual achievement [may] also contribute to the student's success in conformity to institutional expectations" (p. 100). We see this dynamic at work in many respects, including when bright and talented students adapt well to tests for which they have not studied or do not know the material. No doubt, this situation raises uncomfortable questions about the value of high-stakes tests for measuring intellectual ability given the contaminating variable of, to use Jackson's word, "test-wise" capability.

Although the importance of becoming or feeling part of "the crowd" is not something that Jackson pursues in his essay, this vital subject is worth exploring. This revolves around the idea of fitting in, a hidden but essential part of any school community. As a general rule, youngsters who are perceived as insiders because they have friends, belong to teams and clubs (often cliques), and are well liked, for example, tend to flourish over those who for one reason or another are seen as outsiders, may be disliked or ridiculed, even bullied, and hence isolated. Violence, known to ensue in such cases, was epitomized by the 1999 student-led shootings at Columbine High School, Colorado. In the aftermath, the reality of social cliques in high schools was a frequent topic of discussion. Many argued that the [perpetrators'] isolation from the rest of their classmates prompted feelings of helplessness, insecurity and depression, as well as a strong desire for attention (*Wikipedia,* 2005, p. 6).

In the case of such unstudied or null curriculum, nontraditional and controversial issues in particular are simply omitted from student learning. Regarding the hidden curriculum, messages are sent to and from students that legitimate certain perspectives over others. As one prevalent example, "it is still tacitly assumed that everyone is heterosexual until proven otherwise," Thornton (2003/2004, p. 307) explains. This entrenched bias reinforces the archetypal norm of "heteronormativity," which undermines an inclusive curriculum and encourages stereotypes. Similarly, "we–they" attitudes that permeate mainstream schooling generate a climate in which multiethnic education is difficult to study and appreciate (Thornton, 2003/2004).

A similar, especially powerful notion, the evaded curriculum, also concerns "matters central to the lives of students and teachers but touched upon only briefly, if at all, in most schools" (American Association of University Women [AAUW], p. 215). Examples include gender bias, sexism, racism, sexuality, and sexually transmitted diseases, as well as "the functioning of bodies, the expression and valuing of feelings and the dynamics of power" (pp. 215–216). Children and adolescents often deal with sexuality, disease, emotion, and other sensitive issues privately, not as part of a school's formal educational discourse.

Finally, the following eight definitions of curriculum underscore the teacher or leader's role in its development. At one extreme, curriculum is concerned with how students experience life within and beyond the classroom and for the entirety of their lives and, at the other, it is focused strictly on planning and design as straightforward activities.

1. Curriculum is such "permanent" subjects as grammar, reading, logic, rhetoric, mathematics, and the greatest books of the Western world that best embody essential knowledge.

2. Curriculum is those subjects that are most useful for living in contemporary society.
3. Curriculum is all planned learning for which the school is responsible.
4. Curriculum is all the experiences learners have under the guidance of the school.
5. Curriculum is the totality of learning experiences provided to students so that they can attain general skills and knowledge at a variety of learning sites.
6. Curriculum is what the student constructs from working with the computer and its various networks, such as the Internet.
7. Curriculum is the questioning of authority and the searching for complex views of human situations.
8. Curriculum is all the experiences that learners have in the course of living. (Marsh & Willis, 2003, pp. 9–10)

CONTINUING INFLUENCES AND CURRICULUM TYPES

Franklin Bobbitt's early 20th-century work *The Curriculum* (1918) and Ralph Tyler's *Basic Principles of Curriculum and Instruction* (1949), both efficiency-based, continue with potency as curriculum forces today. In fact, the behaviorist treatment of curriculum as a taxonomy (classification scheme) that emphasizes objectives, design, implementation, and evaluation, as well as measurement, training, and testing, has been revitalized through standardized testing policies and pressures (Flinders & Thornton, 2004c; Mullen, 2005c). However, critical curriculum theorists (see Pinar et al., 1995/1996) vehemently believe that "writing behavioral objectives, evaluating with standardized texts, presenting material in linear, lock-step fashion, expelling unruly students" are all solutions that have failed (p. 8). They urge educators to avoid treating curriculum as a gadget in need of fixing and to apply "disciplined understanding" to what is at stake.

Popham (1972/2004) classifies curriculum objectives in three primary domains—cognitive, affective, and psychomotor. The cognitive domain dominates such mechanisms as national educational reform legislation (e.g., the NCLB Act). For example, high-stakes standardized testing now governs the landscape of school curriculum, significantly reshaping how American schools approach teaching and learning. However, such reductionism disregards holistic approaches to the official curriculum. Inattentiveness to the affective (e.g., responding) and psychomotor (e.g., perception) domains of teaching and learning, for example, alter the overall educational process. As

Eisner (2001/2004) asserts, "For describing some features of the world, including the educational world, [quantification] is indispensable. But it is not good for everything, and the limitations of quantification are increasingly being recognized" (p. 298). In other words, the cognitive focus within schools and states on quantifying—that is, counting and measuring student, school, and, most recently teacher, success via test scores—has put into jeopardy all nonquantifiable aspects of the curriculum.

Consequently, curriculum leaders should be aware of which objectives, domains, and subjects are valued at the district, state, and federal levels. They also need to know which are being bypassed or even evaded in the current testing milieu that values measurable standards and outcomes. School leaders can discover this bias in the testing climate and work toward overcoming it, possibly by dialoging with the teachers and other professionals in their school and district, reading the educational literature to access empirical arguments and evidence-based claims, contacting their education state representative to ask questions, or joining a decision-making curriculum program or panel. By talking with students, parents, researchers, and community leaders, they can also find out how ethnic individuals or groups experience the testing bias and what can be done to remedy this problem. The goal is to create equitable testing conditions for all children and adolescents, not to perpetuate the biases inherent in nearsighted testing policies and procedures.

Preparation for life is another continuing influence on the curriculum, one that Bobbitt (1918/2004) spearheaded by turning curriculum-making into a scientific endeavor. In his own words, curriculum "is that series of things that children and you must do and experience by way of developing abilities to do the things well that make up the affairs of adult life; and to be in all respects what adults should be" (p. 11). In contrast, Dewey (1929/2004), in his famous essay "My Pedagogic Creed," argues that "education [and, hence, curriculum] is an organic, experiential process of living and not a preparation for future living" (p. 19). The idea here is that teachers and leaders are responsible for enabling students to experience "genuine reality," defined as "forms that are worth living for their own sake" (p. 19).

"Mindful curriculum leadership," as Schirduan and Case (2004) say, is a "pedagogically centered curriculum practice" (p. 87) in which the well-being of the child as learner is the school's focus (see also Henderson & Hawthorne, 2000). Interestingly, Kliebard's (1975/2004) essay on scientific curriculum-making comments on this "subject of education as preparation," saying that this notion has become "ingrained in curriculum thinking today" (p. 39). Specifically, it has become "the job of curriculum planners to anticipate the exact skills, knowledge and—to use today's most fashionable term—'competencies' that will stand one in good stead at an imagined point in the future" (p. 39). This notion of education as preparation plays a role in this book, particularly as concerns the role of technology leadership for schools (see chap. 12).

Predictions based on what students will need to know and be able to do continue to form the basis of curriculum planning today. Preservice teachers and leaders experience accountability that is now securely predicated on measurable, performance-based criteria (Mullen, 2004a). But curriculum leaders and graduate faculty need to understand perspectives on and methods of learning and assessment that have been omitted from the official curriculum. Children and adults alike have the right to a well-rounded education. Finally, because the field of curriculum is still relatively young, another continuing influence on school curriculum is change. In its dynamic state of development, curriculum study has been interpreted from many perspectives. Leading education researchers provide a multidimensional view of curriculum, indicating that it can and should be interpreted from historical, institutional, scientific, managerial, feminist, critical, political, racial, gender, phenomenological, postmodern, autobiographical, aesthetic, theological, and spiritual perspectives (Flinders & Thornton, 2004c; Pinar et al., 1995/ 1996; Slattery, 1995).

Nontraditionalists or liberals argue against the alignment of curriculum with high-stakes testing and the cognitive domain of curriculum. For example, Schirduan and Case (2004) believe that elementary curriculum leaders should be taking into consideration multiple intelligences as a major curricular strategy for building bridges between students' strengths (e.g., science) and weaknesses (e.g., reading; chap. 6 addresses this topic.) They say that principals should encourage classroom teachers to adopt "curricular strategies that enhance academic and positive self-concept levels in students with ADHD [Attention Deficit Hyperactivity Disorder]" (p. 88), especially as 50% of this population experiences school failure.

Curriculum Leaders and Curriculum Leadership

Curriculum leader, a primary force denoting highly effective leadership in this book, is defined as the individuals "and the organizations they are part of, and the activity they are engaged in" (Gross, 1998, p. xii). Importantly, Gross indicates that *curriculum leader* and *curriculum leadership* both refer to active participation "in moving schools forward to provide a learning program that is vigorous and relevant in preparing students for a successful future and that demonstrates results over time" (p. xii). At the school level, curriculum leaders are principals and assistant principals, as well as teachers, teacher mentors, administrative resource personnel, and curriculum developers and reformers; besides being scholars, researchers, and consultants, they are employed within school districts. Curriculum leaders also work at places remote from schools, within districts, universities, associations, and legislatures. Glatthorn (2000), however, emphasizes the value of functions, not roles; by being goal-oriented, curriculum leaders rise above routine tasks, with the "ultimate goal" of "maximizing student learning by providing quality in the content of learning" (p. 24).

The teachers contributing to this book convey an image of administrative leaders who effectively lead 21st-century schools as being aware of a range of important issues. A group of leading researchers who educate future teachers and leaders also think of site-based curriculum leadership as comprehensive in nature. Its multifaceted character features such challenging and enduring issues as

> Educational excellence, student achievement and performance, advances in assessment, knowledge bases and procedures for implementing a constructivist and collaborative curriculum, classroom climates for learning, delivery systems and methods for learning, conceptual development across the disciplines, and the use of technology. Dimensions of multiculturalism, inclusion, justice, and fair play [are] regarded as curriculum concerns. (Bernhardt, Hedley, Cattaro, & Svolopoulos, 1998, pp. 2–3)

The teacher authors also identify these as leading areas of school improvement that matter not just to today's administrators, but also to educators like themselves. Some of their cases pursue the contextual and environmental factors that support such issues as student achievement and school performance. For example, chapter 8 is a study of the daily bombardment of forces that interfere with a teacher's ability to carry out her efforts to provide quality instruction to the students in her care. Another (see chap. 4) grapples with transitional challenges facing new administrators for whom such goals as educational excellence are compounded by the uncertainty they feel and the accelerated learning they experience.

As you can see, highly effective curriculum leaders are deeply engaged, committed individuals. They attempt to transform the conformist culture of their schools, partly by confronting the tendency of its members to resist change. They undertake this great challenge through a number of interrelated processes. But first they must understand that curriculum is not simply a binder of materials sitting on their desk waiting for their appraisal or a reading (or any other) program to be implemented in a teacher's classroom or across the school.

Change agents probably view curriculum in holistic, not fragmented, ways, a position that echoes Schwab's (1969) legendary position: "Curriculum in action treats real things: real acts, real teachers, real children, things richer and different from their theoretical representations" (p. 35). A list of "real things," or modern day activities, includes "alter[ing] modern educational structures as necessary [and tackling] fundamental issues of educational service without being sidetracked by institutional maintenance concerns," meaning mindful curriculum leaders do not "fiddle while Rome burns" (Henderson & Hawthorne, 2000, p. 53).

Among the "real things" that might count for Schwab are the many qualities that exemplary curriculum leaders demonstrate. These include the ability to "maintain good working relationships," "sponsor productive interactions," "initiate and sustain dialogue,"and "inspire excellence" (Walker, 2003, pp. 205–207). Glatthorn (2000), who studies principals in the role of curriculum leaders, explains that those who are strong and effective have an "active *initiating* style" (p. 25) in all of the major areas of the school (e.g., development of policies and goals; modeling and monitoring of high academic achievement for students; solicitation of input from faculty on various matters). Focused on school-wide improvement, they exhibit these "enabling behaviors": "(a) facilitating communication, (b) creating a positive, open climate, (c) building a vision with the staff, (d) developing staff through involvement, and (e) being an effective and positive role model" (p. 28). Such holistic frameworks of qualities extend well beyond the assumption that it is enough for leaders to help educators select, develop, and implement curricular materials. It also reaches past a leader's ability to spearhead the adoption of a new curriculum. However, even this is not as easy as it sounds, as "adopting a new program requires preparation, faculty acceptance, community acceptance, and resources—just to start" (Gross, 1998, p. 34).

Henderson and Hawthorne (2000), along with Slattery (1995), add the crucial notion that because curriculum leaders are inclusive of varied forms of schooling experience, they accommodate the aesthetic, intuitive, and visual; also, because they are culturally oriented, they consistently respect diversity, encourage civility, and promote equity. Such individuals are, to return to an earlier topic, proactive when it comes to eradicating "overt and embedded forms of bias related to gender, race, class, sexual orientation, and other significant human differences," all in an effort to create a "pluralistic, democratic society" within their own school community or elsewhere (Henderson & Hawthorne, 2000, p. 54).

Schermer (2005) playfully suggests that because all curriculum leaders hold a formal leadership role, they are cathedral builders. This experienced principal and superintendent asks, "What image, symbol or metaphor [will you] create for the cathedral you are building? Stage manager? Orchestra conductor? Military general? Animal trainer? Football coach?" (p. 3). It is up to these leaders to decide how they will approach this role as they "go about the curriculum construction business" (p. 3).

Curriculum leaders' mental images will differ when it comes to such issues as human inequities or outdated programs and lax standards. New administrators who are change agents will have low tolerance for teacher apathy and other pervasive school problems. They redefine not only their responsibilities but also their approach to individuals and groups, structures and systems. "From controllers of teachers' instruction to involvers of teachers in decisions about curriculum and instruction" (Schermer, 2005, p. 4), the collaboratively oriented curriculum leader engages teachers in conversations about their work and the world outside their classroom. They are committed to stimulating the development of professional learning communities and all individual teachers. Such leaders care about having current and relevant learning programs in place—they want *all* of the students within their charge to be academically successful lifelong learners who are well prepared for post-secondary education or work. They also avoid making quick, uninformed decisions that could adversely affect the people in their building. Moreover, such leaders are data oriented in their decision making, meaning that they use multiple forms of information to help them figure out what is needed within the school's curriculum, as well as what is working and what may need changing. Some practitioners who write on this topic see the NCLB Act as a useful guide and hence basis for best practices and school improvement, arguing that it has raised the bar on effective instruction and student performance. Maintaining "good data on student achievement [in order] to see if progress is or is not being made for all of [your] subgroups" (e.g., Oleson, 2005, p. 2) is essential to this practice. The provisions this legislation provides for "'annual testing in every grade'" could give teachers "'the information they need to ensure that every child will reach academic success'" (Chen, Heritage, & Lee, 2005, p. 310).

Chen and colleagues (2005) draw a parallel between the NCLB's focus on the planning and evaluation of children's learning and Dewey's belief that strong teachers understand grading and promotional practices with reference to a common standard. However, this research evaluation team from the National Center for Research on Evaluation, Standards, and Student Testing (CRESST) stresses that Dewey was referring to an altogether different context—the continual interpretation of children's needs, capacities, and habits that necessitate frequent, detailed assessments. In contrast, the priority that the NCLB gives to annual testing probably makes it an information-poor vehicle for understanding student achievement and for guiding instruction.

Hence, leaders who function as effective and mindful curriculum makers facilitate testing environments supported by multiple, preferably fine-grained assessments and ongoing curriculum improvements. But even this is only a part of their role (Mullen, 2004a). Illustrating Schwab's (1969) notion of the practical-in-action, principals and teachers who turn routine tasks into opportunities for highlighting the curriculum stand out. They might seize a moment while monitoring the hallways or cafeteria to ask what projects students are working on and what they are learning (Glatthorn, 2000), or how they are making use of the media center's resources and other support systems (see chap. 5).

As another instance of the practical-in-action, many early-career assistant principals (Oliver, 2003, 2005) from California and principals from Florida (Mullen, 2004a) have reported greater value for instructional supervision than other dimensions of the work, including organizational management. Current North American studies (e.g., McCarthy, 1999) and educational legislation (e.g., *A Nation at Risk*, National Commission on Excellence in Education [NCEE], 1983) reinforce that instructional supervision—seen in this book as a function of curriculum leadership—has become a top priority for schools and focus of principalship preparation. The move toward curriculum as instructional supervision/coaching, with emphasis on student learning through teacher–teacher mentoring (see chap. 3) and principal–teacher mentoring (see chap. 6), potentially signals a new culture of curriculum. It may be that for the most effective curriculum leaders, instructional supervision is not viewed as somehow separate from organizational management, school–community relations, and other domains of the job. A seasoned elementary principal from Alberta, Canada was described as having a holistic view of curriculum:

> For him, everything is about teaching and learning, no matter the situation or the individuals involved—sometimes one plays the role of teacher, sometimes learner, but [we] are always positioned somewhere along this continuum with teaching at one end and learning at the other. (Dick, 2005, p. 114)

Conceivably, at a time of economic expansion and growth, the primary concern of an organization should be personnel—finding appropriately and highly qualified persons to accomplish the work of the organization. However, the value placed on curriculum development and specifically instructional supervision has nonetheless been sustained for some school principals, despite budgetary restrictions. Nevertheless, studies report mixed results. First, in many school systems, managerial tasks are emphasized over mentoring ones, especially for "subordinates." Oliver's (2003) survey-based study of assistant principals in Orange County, California, found that although principals focus more on "leadership activities associated with instruction and programs," assistant principals are usually allocated "management-oriented tasks" (p. 38). Second, even high school principals have been found to spend far less time on "program development" than they expected.

Glatthorn (2000) elaborates, stating that "even when principals are generally aware of their curricular responsibilities, they have difficulty finding the time to execute the role" (p. 24).

Curriculum leadership involves new administrators in such practical areas of school administration as faculty hiring, classroom management, teacher–student interaction, whole-school ownership of instructional support, diversity and security agendas, and standardized test interpretation (Mullen, 2004a). Further, curriculum leaders generally model a climate of academic achievement, especially vital within disadvantaged sites, in the following ways: classroom visits; curriculum assistance; one-on-one and small group discussions (including feedback on lessons); technology infusion; computer-based learning in laboratories; and test and assessment training (e.g., on statewide public school tests; McCarthy, 1999; Mullen, 2004a). New and experienced teachers who teach to the test as a strategy for avoiding poor student scores and public humiliation should be encouraged to transcend this inclination (Amrein & Berliner, 2002). Leaders need to communicate the message to their staff that it is important not to sacrifice their ideals. We all must endeavor to foster a meaningful, well-rounded curriculum.

Clearly, mentoring approaches to curriculum leadership are to receive strong support, but remember that they can be empowering or technocratic. Lead teachers, like other curriculum leaders may see curriculum as a process or product, and as a source of liberation or as a means to an end. As technocrats, they equate curriculum strictly with hands-on application, helping beginning teachers in their coaching role to facilitate the "curriculum in use" (Posner, 1992). Unfortunately, this familiar practice is often bereft of critical thinking and philosophical dialogue. In this situation, the mentor–mentee pair, although engaged in observations and discussion, would miss two major domains for stimulating reflection and action: situating and analyzing theoretical perspectives on the curriculum and re-examining and critiquing the curriculum (Mullen, 2005c; see chap. 10 on reflective mentoring approaches to administrator walk-throughs). Chapter 6 provides a provocative treatment of the general education curriculum.

BACKGROUND OF CURRICULUM LEADERSHIP

When did the concept of curriculum leadership first materialize? Based on my 2005 search efforts, it did not appear until fairly recently. English and Hill's (1990) book on restructuring describes curriculum leadership as the jurisdiction of the principal who, as the organization's head, must be a "master generalist," "one who knows curriculum management and change process *for the entire school*" (p. 6). More recent conceptions of curriculum leadership appear in Bernhardt et al. (1998) and Gross (1998). After investigating research-based Internet databases and "Googling," I learned that only a few writings on this topic exist. Glatthorn (2000) confirms that although much literature deals with instructional leadership only a paucity of studies focus on the practitioner's role as curriculum leader.

The now somewhat outdated term *curriculum administration* (e.g., McNeil, 1965) has enjoyed a longer history. Like curriculum leadership, curriculum administration is not typically defined, and so inferences must be made about its meaning and value from the statements and examples authors provide. From this inferential process, I can see that curriculum administration, similar to its newer counterpart curriculum leadership, is philosophically aligned with an accountability framework that promotes a means–end attitude toward education and with a democratic framework. Democratic curriculum leaders do not value standardizing educational experiences, with the intention of comparing schools and states based on student test scores. According to Pinar (2005b), they are oriented very differently, keen to foster intellectual and spiritual study as the basis of student learning and the development of students as "self-reflective and politically engaged citizens" (p. 77).

Perhaps surprisingly, even texts that have *curriculum leadership* in the title do not overlap with my own. Take, for example, Bernhardt and colleagues' edited volume *Curriculum Leadership* (1998). Its focus on collaborative leadership and constructivist curricula overshadows that of curriculum leadership, even though it does provide a list of key issues. As another point of consideration, *Transformative Curriculum Leadership* (Henderson & Hawthorne, 2000) modifies the concept of curriculum leadership with transformation. The latter concept is prioritized over the examination of curriculum leadership itself. Henderson and Hawthorne relate transformative teaching and curriculum but with ideas that, although relevant, are not directed to or verified by prospective or practicing school leaders. Although cases involving teacher leaders are provided within this volume, the one chapter relevant to my own book, "Becoming a Transformative Curriculum Leader," contains a single case. Moreover, a curriculum director of an educational service center—remote from the population that I represent—wrote it.

Brubaker's *Creative Curriculum Leadership* (2004) is an autobiographical text that stresses the relevance of the inner, or personal, curriculum in confronting the outer curriculum. Teachers and aspiring principals are its central audience. The author, not these practitioner populations, wrote the short cases. In contrast, my own book provides detailed cases that students have themselves coauthored. Although Brubaker's book is engaging, I incorporate student voice and scholarly rigor in a greater range of important topics, and in such forms as multiple frameworks and educational inquiry.

In *Teachers as Curriculum Planners* (Connelly & Clandinin, 1988), scholarly and practical ideas are launched for exploring one's experience and situations as a curriculum maker. Interestingly, the research of Connelly and Clandinin is not cited in the Brubaker text, even though they did much to spearhead the concept of the inner curriculum through their narrative inquiry model.

High-stakes standardized testing has changed the climate of public schools since 1988 when the Connelly and Clandinin text was published. Even Glatthorn's (2000) more recent book, *The Principal as Curriculum Leader*, is already to some degree outdated. It was published before the NCLB Act appeared and before culminating governing forces changed how curriculum is conceived, developed, implemented, and assessed. Also, Glatthorn's book omits a view of the inner curriculum and its subjective, interpersonal, communal, and mentoring aspects in favor of a more technocratic, objective, and technical view. Although the Glatthorn book serves as a valuable resource for researchers seeking to know such things as the distinction between the taught and learned curriculum, it lacks descriptive and aesthetic devices, including tools for reflection, such as discussion questions, cases, exercises, and more. This text focuses on practicing principals, unlike my own which is for aspiring and beginning school leaders.

NEW TRENDS IN CURRICULUM LEADERSHIP

A recent trend in curriculum studies involves modifying curriculum leadership with descriptors that highlight its varying functions and aims. With this linguistic tool, writers reveal their philosophical orientation, just as they have been doing for some time with the concept of curriculum. Such qualifiers as *transformative* and *creative* are popular; additional modifiers of curriculum and curriculum leadership are *democratic, collaborative,* and *critical*—all a lens for focusing the leadership and direction of schools in particular ways. Henderson and Hawthorne (2000), for instance, describe successful teachers and administrators as leading the development of their professional cultures through such collaborative means as "collegial reflective inquiry" (p. 58). Brubaker (2004) uses creativity to give meaning to the kind of curriculum leadership that is personal and reflective, and political and ethical. Creative curriculum leaders, he says, "recognize the distinction between bureaucratic and professional decision-making frameworks while at the same time attending to [their] moral compass" (p. 153). However, acknowledged is the "mighty struggle" this involves, given the pressures of high-stakes testing and top-down curriculum mandates (Brubaker, 2004, p. 153).

FINAL THOUGHTS

As revealed in this chapter, the curriculum field is known for its enduring issues and debates, characterized by lively, even "contentious discourse and outright disputes" (Flinders & Thornton, 2004a, p. xii). Importantly, the study of curriculum prospered when there was no national agenda to make schools accountable to standardized testing and no federal support for research and development. Its study will continue to flourish during these changing times for school leaders and despite restrictions on the value, meaning, and breadth of curriculum. Curriculum scholars and leaders endorse or critique intellectual traditions and trends. The dynamic activity this generates today reveals the increasingly complicated role of administrators and teachers in straddling these two worlds.

REFLECTIVE, PRACTICAL ACTIVITIES

- Based on your reading, develop your own list of definitions and examples of the traditional curriculum and the hidden curriculum.
- Using the set of eight definitions provided by Marsh and Willis (2003), identify those that you most strongly identify with and provide a rationale for your choice. Also consider problems posed by each of the definitions—for example, do some seem to suggest that the school has no special responsibility for school curriculum while others imply that what is planned is what is learned, failing to acknowledge that unplanned experiences can exert an even more powerful effect over what students learn?
- Speculate on the school of the future and its role in curriculum making. Will curriculum be found in "traditional classrooms? Computer laboratories? Community resource centers? Workplaces? Homes?" (Marsh & Willis, 2003, p. 11). Explain your response.
- What are the major future roles for curriculum leaders who are teachers? As ideas, consider "information-giver; subject matter specialist; motivator; gatekeeper; resource person; counselor, mentor" (Marsh & Willis, 2003, p. 11). Again explain your response.

3

Process/Product Classification of Key Curriculum Thinkers

Cameron Spears
Carol A. Mullen
Darlene Y. Bruner

FASHIONING FLINT FOR CURRICULUM MAKING

Education has been part of the human experience for at least 300,000 years (Hopkin, 2004). Clearly, early learners did not have school boards, high-stakes standardized testing, or any of the other advances (some might say "baggage" or even "weaponry") associated with contemporary education. However, our ancestors from around the world did at least have a simple curriculum that shaped their thinking, and work and life.

Since the earliest days of curriculum, its developers had to make choices. When fashioning flint blades, makers of this tool obtained flint buried beneath the ground. In contrast, flint that was laying on the surface of the ground was considered inferior. Although the learning that took place

300,000 years ago is radically different from the learning that occurs today in American schools, they overlap in many ways. For example, a particular individual or group might be responsible for developing the curriculum. In the early case, it might have been an elder, the "smartest" member of the group, or simply the person who had investigated blade-making, concluding that mined flint is superior. In the modern case, curriculum developers might be you or a committee, consultant, consortium, or any other stakeholder group or decision-making body.

In these early and modern cases differences of opinion about what constitutes a "good" curriculum can be imagined or identified. For example, in prehistoric times, one person might have believed that the best flint could only be found 3 feet deep, whereas another might have felt strongly that usable flint could only be found at depths of 6 feet or more. Similarly, there may have been nonuniformity about how the curriculum was best delivered: One thinker might have advocated teaching the young members by *demonstrating* the correct method of mining flint, while another might have preferred *directing* the youth to mine it by themselves. In fact, differences in curricular viewpoints such as these could have led to splintering or factions. In other words, a curriculum developer might have started a new "school" to counter the teachings of "the wrong way" and thus anoint "the right way." Perhaps certain attitudes toward education have actually undergone little change over the course of 3,000 centuries.

One significant difference between prehistoric and modern education is that ongoing effort has been made since the 1970s to identify, record, and promulgate curricular theory and best practices. These chroniclers, often original thinkers themselves, have attempted to build, whether descriptively or critically, on the work of others. Their efforts have enhanced historical appreciation and deepened curricular understanding. For example, while developing concepts of such magnitude today as narrative inquiry, stories of experience, and personal practical knowledge, Clandinin and Connelly (e.g., 2000) use as their intellectual scaffolds the pioneering works of John Dewey, Elliot Eisner, Nel Noddings, William Pinar, and Joseph Schwab, among others.

The highest achievers—those recognized for having made the most significant contributions to the curriculum field—sometimes earn membership in an elite group we call key thinkers in curriculum (Table 3.1), or simply key thinkers. These educators, philosophers, and scientists were not content simply to think and write about existing educational (and related disciplines) theories and practices. By inventing or defining new intellectual, curricular paradigms, artistic and scientific curriculum makers alike (e.g., Dewey, Eisner, Maslow, Pinar, Skinner) actually exceeded this goal.

METHOD: IDENTIFICATION AND CATEGORIZATION OF KEY THINKERS

We have developed this discussion around Table 3.1, an elaboration of a list entitled "Names to Know in Curriculum Study," from which it was partially derived (see Wiles, 1999, pp. 6–9). Also consulted were Flinders and Thornton's *The Curriculum Studies Reader* (2004c), a compendium identifying highly influential curricular thinkers and their well-known works, in addition to the online, searchable index Thinkers: Infed.org (http://www.infed.org/thinkers/index.htm, 2005). This compilation of more than 90 thinkers attempts to cover contributions central to "the development of the theory and practice of lifelong learning and informal education" (para. 1). Finally, as the next section explains, we have adopted the dichotomy of *process-leaning* and *product-leaning* in order to distinguish one key thinker's contribution from another's.

By categorizing the key curriculum thinkers in the social and behavioral sciences one by one, rich insights can be entertained. Toward this end, we offer a start that aspiring leaders and other readers can expand on to create an exhaustive synthesis of the curriculum literature and a more complex conversation. Because the field of curriculum is so broad and in flux due to its dynamic state of development (Pinar, 1995/1996), different key thinkers are identified while others are omitted. This reality, which may be both a limitation and a reflection of the changing field itself, characterizes this chapter. Moreover, various methods can be applied for categorizing each thinker.

In order to learn about some of the key thinkers' contributions to curriculum, it makes sense to identify commonalities and dissimilarities. With reference to William Pinar's (1995/1996) characterization of the curriculum field, we can identify not only different key thinkers but also various ways in which they might be categorized. For instance, they might be arranged chronologically, so that lineages, networks, and trends over time (as well as the possible influences of when particular key thinkers lived while doing their work) become apparent. One might base a classification scheme, as shown in Table 3.1, on a key thinker's philosophical/psychological foundation. Specifically, as we have found, a schema such as this can help with trying to figure out how a key thinker fits into the "higher order" of the social and behavioral sciences. Table 3.1 provides additional options for those interested in identifying similarities and distinctions among the key thinkers by noting, for example, each individual's educational purpose, principles, content area, and time frame. Readers are encouraged to critique the schema presented in the chart and add other key curriculum thinkers.

Some readers might question the inclusion of B. F. Skinner, Carl Rogers, and possibly others in our analysis, as they, although certainly intellectual luminaries, were not affiliated with curriculum studies. Our addition of these individuals is by design; their thoughts and writings related to *learning* have ubiquity as foundation pieces with momentous influence on generations of scholars (educational and otherwise) and the curriculum field itself. Those who doubt the relevance of Skinner, for example, need only cursorily read his research to encounter theories on learning, instruction, and education, as well as curriculum. Indeed, Skinner has been recognized not only as a foundational behaviorist but also as a major curriculum theorist (see, e.g., *History of Curriculum*, 2002). A similar rationale convinced us of the necessity to include Rogers, whose thoughts on learning in therapy and education, along with his writings on the freedom to learn, provide an intriguing link to the traditional study of curriculum. Finally, it should be noted that the curriculum field is sufficiently broad to allow (perhaps even invite) inclusion of theorists who otherwise may be considered "outsiders." Such an effort pushes against the edges of what we presume to know about our own discipline, interrogating behaviorist and postmodern mindsets, among others, that tend to exclude or override the other.

Synthesizing a New Curricular Taxonomy

Still another way to classify key curriculum thinkers, in accordance with those selected for adaptation here, involves a modified version of Smith's (2000) taxonomy. Mark Smith, a specialist in the field of informal education and lifelong learning, is the Rank Research Fellow and Tutor at YMCA George Williams College, London and Visiting Professor in Community Education, University of Strathclyde, Glasgow (see http://www.infed.org/hp-smith.htm). Along with a small group of affiliated educators, this scholar identifies "four ways of approaching curriculum theory and practice" (para. 4):

1. Curriculum as a body of knowledge to be transmitted.
2. Curriculum as an attempt to achieve certain ends in students—product.
3. Curriculum as process.
4. Curriculum as praxis (action or practice; para. 4).

The commonalities between Items 1 and 2 (body of knowledge and product) should be noted, as well as those unifying Items 3 and 4 (process and praxis). The first two refer to the "what" (or product) associated with curriculum theory and practice, whereas the last two embrace the "how" (or process).

Reflecting on these commonalities and distinctions, we have collapsed the four groups into two, allowing us to classify the key thinkers. A scheme such as this both simplifies *and* problematizes the task of categorizing the key thinkers in curriculum. Although this modernist, reductionistic strategy may help to illuminate relevant theories and insights, it should also stimulate readers' questions about what may be compromised or even lost in the process. Treading carefully, we define and present two categories that will serve as an overarching structure for this discussion: *product*-leaning key thinkers and *process*-leaning key thinkers.

KEY THINKERS IN CURRICULUM

Table 3.1 represents 26 individuals who have made significant contributions to curriculum or the foundations on which curriculum depends. Some are recognizable mainly to those in the field of curriculum or education more broadly, whereas other names will be familiar to nearly any educated person.

Across a diverse cross-section of highly influential scholars in curriculum, we next examine selected thoughts, concepts, and quotations, placing each key thinker into the product or process category. Further, examples of theory or practice from key thinkers illustrate the fact that even seemingly disparate theorists can often be harmoniously leveraged into a single curriculum, albeit cautiously and only for limited occasions within a given curriculum. A second theme we address involves how certain teachers may perceive some types of curricula as oppressive where the freedom they (and their colleagues and students) cherish is limited. An explanation is proposed that may spark understanding of why certain teachers favor one category of key thinkers over another.

In order to gather a subset of key thinkers from Table 3.1, trial-and-error methods were exercised, leading to criteria for selection. Notably, we identified theorists sufficiently diverse to allow us to "juxtapose different, often opposing points of view" (Flinders & Thornton, 2004a, p. ix). Similarly, our "heuristics" or discovery processes had to yield individuals with "enduring curriculum scholarship … that will help us link the field's past and present" (p. ix). Simply put, we devised a product/process curriculum continuum and located theorists on it, some at opposite ends. We also include theorists from the past and present. Finally, in order to provide some measure of balance to our analysis, we chose theorists who presented their philosophical/psychological foundations in a mainstream (i.e., less extreme or radical) fashion.

Next, we prepare the framework for this analysis. Briefly discussed is each key thinker in the context of the particular category: The first group of key thinkers includes those whose theories are product-leaning in nature, whereas the second consists of those whose theories are process-leaning. A third category (a hybrid of the two) is used as needed for certain key thinkers, especially those from outside the field of traditional education, that is, psychologists, animal behaviorists, among others.

Product-Leaning Key Thinkers in Curriculum

Franklin Bobbitt (1918) is credited with having literally "written the book" on curriculum. The seminal work he produced is titled simply *The Curriculum*. When discussing this period of Bobbitt's life, Flinders and Thornton (2004b) declare, "He is an apt starting point for tracing the development of professional curriculum scholarship and practice in the United States, as the essentials of his approach to curriculum have been dominant in practice ever since" (p. 2). Bobbitt (1918/2004) himself declared his influential work "a first book in a field that until recently has been too little cultivated" (p. 10), while Flinders and Thornton (2004b) both affirm and temper this claim: "Although it is not self-evident what constitutes the 'first' curriculum textbook, Bobbitt's claim is often conceded" (p. 2).

Bobbitt relied on scientific method for deciding what to teach (not how to teach it); thus, he clearly belongs in the product-leaning category. Although much of his curriculum centers on what is often considered training, at least in Bobbitt's case the training can be thought of as a stepping stone to intended outcomes. Specifically, students in Bobbitt's (1918/2004) system were being prepared to take their place to deliver "what ought to be in these difficult fields" (p. 16). Bobbitt demonstrates his product-centric position:

> The first task of the scientific curriculum-maker is the discovery of those social deficiencies that result from a lack of historical, literary, and geographical experiences. Each deficiency found is a call for directed training; it points to an objective that is to be set up for the conscious training. (p. 15)

In many ways, Ralph Tyler is an archetype of product-oriented curriculum. Tyler's (1949) seminal work *Basic Principles of Curriculum and Instruction* devotes many pages to guidance on the proper form of instructional objectives, as well the development of heuristics to obtain these objectives. One statement from this text encapsulates his beliefs, also clarifying where he resides with respect to the product/process dichotomy:

> Because the real purpose of education is not to have the instructor perform certain activities but to bring about significant changes in the students' patterns of behavior, it becomes important to recognize that any statement of the objectives of the school should be a statement of changes to take place in students. (p. 44)

Curriculum is imagined here as a behavioral force that promotes one-way change, and from the outside in, through a planned set of dynamics that focuses on the curriculum as product, the learner as object, and the instructor as mediator.

Process-Leaning Key Thinkers in Curriculum

We obviously spend much more time in this section, recognizing the apparent bias toward process-leaning curriculum of educational theorists and ourselves. Curriculum theorists, John Dewey, and many leading contemporaries, such as Tom Barone, Jean Clandinin, Michael Connelly, Norman Denzin, Maxine Greene, William Pinar, and Patrick Slattery, have all articulated how a product-centric position on learning gives master teachers an unreasonable degree of control over students' capacity to engage in meaning making, and to be creative, collaborative, and empowered. An exclusive, non-negotiated focus on product, then, standardizes and compartmentalizes, through such means as high-stakes testing and bureaucratic rules, curriculum and the richness of learning as growing, creating, being (Dewey, 1938; Pinar et al., 1995/1996).

John Dewey can be thought of as exemplifying the process-leaning key thinker. With little difficulty, one encounters discussions of Dewey's pervasive influence to the effect that he has made "the most significant contribution to the development of educational thinking in the twentieth century" (as cited in Smith, 1996/2000, para. 1). Similarly, Neill (2005) asserts,

Dewey is lauded as the greatest educational thinker of the 20th century. His theory of experience continues to be much read and discussed not only within education, but also in psychology and philosophy. Dewey's views continue to strongly influence the design of innovative educational approaches, such as in outdoor education, adult training, and experiential therapies. (para. 1)

Many examples can be cited from Dewey's writings that demonstrate his process-leaning thoughts on education and psychology. A quotation that captures Dewey's tendency toward favoring process (practice) over product (outcome) is from what many identify as his defining work, My *Pedagogic Creed* (1929/2004): "The question of method is ultimately reducible to the question of the order of development of the child's powers and interests. The law for presenting and treating material is the law implicit within the child's own nature" (p. 20). Dewey's experiential theory contrasts sharply with an outcomes-based theory in which the intended goal is for every student to achieve the same learning objective. He supported a dynamic and wide-ranging set of outcomes for the students based on their "powers and interests" combined with the learning conditions set by teachers, as well as those facilitated by schools and society.

James Conant, in his seminal work The American High School Today (1959), makes a strong case for process-oriented changes. In this frequently cited piece, Conant presents results and recommendations from his study of "high schools with a high degree of comprehensiveness" (p. 13). This researcher defines comprehensive high school as "a high school whose programs correspond to the educational needs of all the youth of the community" (p. 12).

Conant's original academic role was as a chemistry professor, and later department chair, at Harvard University. These credentials might lead one to look for Conant on the product-leaning, rather than process-leaning, list. However, his eventual position as president of Harvard University, in addition to his proposals regarding the American high school, may have solidified his role among the process-leaning key thinkers. Conant's (1959) comprehensive list of "recommendations for improving public secondary education" comprised 21 items, all or nearly all of which were treated as process oriented. Examples include "individualized programs," "homerooms," and "special consideration for the very slow readers." Conant's writings concerning the improvement of public secondary education are rich in the language of process and practice. In the "individualized programs" case, Conant asserts, "It should be the policy of the school that every student has an individualized program; there would be no classification of students according to clearly defined and labeled programs or tracks such as "college-preparatory, vocational, commercial" (p. 46). When depicting the details of his homerooms recommendation, he declares that "homerooms should be organized in such a way as to make them significant social units in the school" and "sufficient time should be allotted to the homeroom so that students may use this period to develop a sense of community interest and to have practice in a small way in representative government" (p. 74). Finally, Conant exposes his process-centricity when establishing the need for special consideration for slow readers, as in: "those who are well informed about the teaching of reading emphasize that the development of reading skill must be a continuous process throughout the school years" (p. 56).

Elliot Eisner supports a process orientation toward theory and practice, but differently. In his often-cited work The Enlightened Eye (1991), this pioneering arts-based educational researcher draws attention to the issue of human qualities and in situ writing, placing value on the artistic imagination that brings to life vicariously lived experience. Along these lines, Eisner (1991) writes:

> Schools also have moods, and they too display scenes of high drama that those who make policy and who seek to improve practice should know. The means through

which such knowledge is made possible are the enlightened eye—the scene is seen—and the ability to craft text so that what the observer has experienced can be shared by those who were not there. (p. 30)

Eisner also shares his now-classic views on one of the critical distinctions between quantitative and qualitative inquiry—"stating versus expressing meaning" (p. 31). Parallelism can be drawn between this notion and "process versus product" concepts of curriculum. *Expressing meaning* is similar to *process,* as both acts conjure a certain amount of flexibility, variability, and freedom. By contrast, *stating meaning* connotes *product,* as both often imply concreteness, rigidity, and nonmalleability.

One can infer that William Pinar's (1978/2004) contribution to the ideology of reconceptualization (sociopolitical emancipation) supports process-leaning curriculum, evident in such ground-breaking essays as "The Reconceptualization of Curriculum Studies." (This work was originally presented at the American Educational Research Association's annual meeting in 1977, later published in the *Journal of Curriculum Studies,* and then reprinted in Flinders and Thornton's [2004c] compendium of highly influential writings in curriculum.) Pinar believes that the functions of curriculum need rethinking along with the conditions of schooling that can lead to the emancipation of students and teachers alike. *Reconceptualization* is an intellectual "movement" formed in reaction to the apolitical and ahistorical stance of the status quo perpetuated by traditionalists and conceptual empiricists (technical rationalists). *Technical rationalism* focuses, we assume, on product-leaning curriculum, evident where school practices emphasize matters of "design, change (behaviourally observable), and improvement" (p. 150), including, by way of extension, product.

Pinar's (e.g., 1978/2004) curriculum theory delineates three types of "movements" as characterizing the curriculum field: traditionalism, conceptual empiricism, and reconceptualism. Although reconceptualists pursue perspectives on curriculum and research that are "politically emancipatory," they are nonetheless tolerant of different viewpoints:

We are not faced with an exclusive choice: either the traditional wisdom of the field, or conceptual empiricism, or the reconceptualization. Each is reliant on the other. For the field to become vital and significant to American education, it must nurture each "moment," its "internal dialectic." (p. 155)

One of the most prolific and influential individuals in our list of key thinkers is Jean Piaget. It would not be an overstatement to say that Piaget devoted nearly all of his life to processes involved with learning. He can thus be classified as a process-leaning key thinker. In his seminal work *The Origins of Intelligence in the Child* (1952), he lays the framework for six stages of development, beginning with "elementary sensorimotor adaptations" (p. 21) and concluding with "invention of new means through mental combinations" (p. 331). Piaget's writing, steeped in psychological theory, directly applies to curriculum and specifically the process-oriented domain.

Abraham Maslow, in his defining work *Motivation and Personality* (1954), presents his then new theory of human motivation. Its basic tenets are widely familiar in the social sciences today, influencing even the world of pop psychology. The taxonomy of "basic," "lower," and "higher" needs comprise a set of hierarchical prerequisites for learning that many teachers and students presume to be self-evident. Maslow's writings on motivation, which concern processes and transitions, often attempt to explain human behavior (e.g., "The child who pulls the clock apart is not in his own eyes destroying the clock, he is examining the clock"; p. 173). A curriculum developer following Maslow's theory would be more likely to focus on processes of learning rather than the products, objectives, or outcomes of learning.

John Goodlad, author of the highly influential book *A Place Called School* (1984), has been grouped in the process-centered category of key thinkers. Rather than focusing on the outcomes or products of teaching, he promotes understanding of teachers and their work. In his decisive work, he surveyed more than 27,000 individuals who had some association with schools, including students, parents, and teachers from 12 senior high schools, 12 junior high schools, and 13 elementary schools from seven American states. From this study importance is placed on attending to issues of "curricular balance" derived from these identifiable disciplinary areas—"mathematics and science, literature and language, society and social studies, the arts, and the vocations," descriptively coined "the five fingers of human knowledge and organized experience" (p. 286). *A Place Called School* ends with numerous recommendations for improving schools that are wide-ranging and involve many parts of the school infrastructure, including redistribution of teachers and their time, elimination of ability grouping, and development of research and centers.

Finally, Goodlad's big-picture focus on aligning classroom curriculum with school infrastructure, changing questionable learning practices, and including particular elements in educational curricula places him in our process-leaning group. Not product-focused or declarative about *how* curriculum ought to be taught, his concern with teachers' needs (e.g., proposing that the instructional time of teachers be reduced to approximately 15 hours per week, while simultaneously initiating school-based programs of curricular and instructional improvement shared by the entire staff; p. 194) influenced our placement.

Carl Rogers, instrumental in the development of client-centered therapy (psychotherapy), is, for several reasons, included in the process-centered category. Two statements from his most cited work, *On Becoming a Person* (1961), succinctly capture Rogers' views on education:

> It seems to me that anything that can be taught to another is relatively inconsequential, and has little or no significant influence on behavior. ... I have come to feel that the only learning that significantly influences behavior is self-discovered, self-appropriated learning. (p. 276)

These words are rich in process-centric thought and completely (or almost completely) void of outcome/product-centric thought.

Even as a student attending Union Theological Seminary, Rogers was a process-centric thinker committed to learner-centered curriculum:

> A group of us felt that ideas were being fed to us, whereas we wished primarily to explore our own questions and doubts, and find out where they led. We petitioned the administration that we be allowed to set up a seminar for credit, a seminar with no instructor, where the curriculum would be composed of our own questions. (p. 8, emphasis added)

Should the reader have any doubts about Rogers' curricular ideas over the longer haul, these are explicated in conference remarks (that were published in the key work being discussed). In this essay, Rogers outlines his beliefs on education in the areas of testing, evaluation, and degrees:

> We would do away with examinations. They measure only the inconsequential type of learning... we would do away with grades and credits for the same reason. ... We would do away with degrees as a measure of competence partly for the same reason. Another reason is that a degree marks an end or a conclusion of something, and a learner is only interested in the continuing process of learning. (p. 277)

Hybrid Key Thinkers

B. F. Skinner probably falls mainly into the product-leaning camp, even though there are some varying characteristics of his work that might signal otherwise. Skinner is concerned with behavior, of course, and his name has become synonymous with both the theory and methodology of behaviorism. In the defining work, *Science and Human Behavior* (1953), Skinner addresses both behavior and the methods of training, reward, and punishment to encourage or discourage certain behaviors—leading one to conclude that he should be placed in the product-leaning camp. However, not everyone would agree. The key to classification is the "power of magnification" one chooses when examining this model. For example, if one considers behaviorism from 50,000 feet, then one will see only emphasis on a particular behavior (product) and likely conclude that behaviorism is product-leaning in its totality. Conversely, if one "zooms in," such that the often numerous precursor stimuli intended to elicit a behavior can be clearly seen, then the model takes on a much more process-centric focus. Admittedly, the processes associated with the stimuli are typically focused with laser-like efficiency on the goal or object. However, the mere presence of an objective or goal does not necessarily make a theorist product-leaning; even a process-leaning exemplar such as Dewey has objectives in mind for learners, although these may not be codified with the same unyielding precision that a behaviorist might follow.

Another key thinker who crosses the process/product boundary is Edward Thorndike. The decisive work *Animal Intelligence* (1911) details his many experiments on a variety of animals, including chicks, dogs, cats, and fish. Thorndike's work features a section titled "The Mental Life of the Monkeys," which is an exhaustive treatment of the observed learning of his subjects. The laws of behavior he articulated provided a foundation for many of his successors. One of his general laws of behavior, novel at the time even though it seems simplistic today, is "Behavior is predictable" (p. 241). Although Thorndike's focus was on animals, not human beings, it would be faulty to assume that his ideas lack relevance in human learning. In fact, he hypothesizes the process-oriented manner in which human beings learn: "We learn by the gradual selection of the appropriate act or judgment, by its association with the circumstances or situation requiring it, in just the way that the animals do" (p. 284).

PRACTICING TEACHERS AND CURRICULUM

Although we have discretely compartmentalized key thinkers into two "pigeonholes," they might be better viewed as residing along a continuum: Bobbitt might be found at one extreme and Dewey at the other. These two key thinkers have been selected as "anchor points" on this conceptual continuum because they exemplify radically different (and often opposing) beliefs about curriculum (Flinders & Thornton, 2004c). A continuum can be imagined with key thinkers residing at various locations along it, with latitude in a fluid construction for shifting and even changing places depending on the reader and the text being read, as well as the philosophical/ideological changes in the key curriculum thinkers over time.

Notably, at some point on this continuum, a transition occurs from process-leaning to product-leaning key thinkers; in other words, as one conceptually traverses the theorists in the middle ground, a barely perceptible change occurs, during which time the balance shifts. The exact point at which this shift occurs is hard to pinpoint, not unlike the elusive attempt to identify exactly when dusk ends and night begins.

Keeping in mind the process/product continuum, a second theme is briefly presented: Informal observations have shown that many practicing teachers have an affinity for the more process-oriented curriculum theories. By contrast, educational policymakers and other nonsite-based decision makers who are neither responsible for delivering content nor justifying curricular and instructional goals will often have an affinity for the product-oriented end of the continuum.

Teacher Affinity With Process

Having little control over one's use of time at work is a well-known indicator of stress; conversely, many jobs in which the worker has more control and flexibility are the least stressful. Jobs in which individuals must keep their emotions in check while dealing with the public also rank very high in creating anxiety (BPS Press Office, 2005). The duties of many teachers certainly seem to have these attributes; therefore, one might expect the profession of teaching to be stressful. This observation is supported by research, such as that promulgated by the British Psychological Society, which compares the teaching profession to other occupations that share "a lot of face to face contact with a high degree of 'emotional labor'" (BPS Press Office, 2005, para. 1).

From study of process-leaning and product-leaning theories of curriculum, one can infer that process-leaning theory provides teachers with latitude for increased instructional flexibility. In an extreme case, such educators offer "failure-proof" methods. For example, suppose Teacher X is required to teach using a particular teaching process—that is the only requirement. By contrast, suppose that Teacher Y can use any teaching method. However, Teacher Y's students must achieve a certain score on a standardized test, or else Teacher Y will be "punished." In this admittedly extreme situation, Teacher X can be assured of success simply by using the "correct" method (or process)—the state of the students at the conclusion of instruction is not considered. It can easily be seen that Teacher Y, however, can fail in any number of ways resulting from forces beyond Teacher Y's control (e.g., a student's ability to learn in the first place; the difficulty of the curriculum). Because the Teacher Y scenario is more likely to be based on a curriculum advanced by a product-leaning curriculum developer, it does not seem surprising that practicing teachers might have an aversion to the theories and practices of product-leaning key thinkers.

We illustrate the point further by painting another picture of extremes. One might expect that a K–12 public school teacher would resist the most product-oriented curricula, those so demanding that they exemplify what Apple (1986/2004) has coined *intensification*. This curricular territory has symptoms "ranging from being allowed no time at all to even go to the bathroom, have a cup of coffee or relax, to having a total absence of time to keep up with one's field" (p. 188). Such product-oriented curricula as high-stakes standardized testing, together with performance reviews of consequence, generates such a high level of anxiety for many teachers that their own professional development and even creativity, good judgment, and well-being can suffer (Mullen, 2004a).

Teachers or school leaders who have the best interests of students at heart might be naturally attracted to those key thinkers whose theories recognize such fundamental ideas as education focused on the development of children's powers, imaginations, and interests. Such notions were, for Dewey (1929/2004), formed into principles, including "The law for representing and treating material is the law implicit within the child's own nature" (p. 21). This same hypothetical educator might have much less of an affinity for the theories of those key thinkers who espouse views that are goal driven and seemingly lacking a child-centered perspective, as in: "The curriculum of the schools will aim at those objectives that are not sufficiently attained as a result of the general undirected experience" (Bobbitt, 1918/2004, p. 12).

After considering the key thinkers in curriculum, and categorizing them into process-leaning and product-leaning groups, the informally observed affinity shown by teachers for process-leaning theorists is obvious. Generally speaking, capable teachers often favor theorists who place more control and a greater decision-making capacity (and thus more freedom) in their hands.

SUMMARY THOUGHTS

In this chapter we have identified and placed key curriculum thinkers into a product or process category, a seemingly straightforward task that is, in fact, riddled with complexity. Epistemological and methodological overlaps (i.e., gray shades) are apparent in the works of many of the curriculum theorists, making categorization a slippery process indeed. We have undertaken this endeavor with the understanding that readers will probably have other worthwhile constructions to share, as well as sound criticisms. We realize, for example, that many key curriculum theorists have been omitted from our schema and discussion and that, depending on the reader's own philosophical orientation, those selected may or may not spark vigorous disagreement. For this contribution, we have also taken up the issue of product-leaning curriculum as fundamentally nondemocratic through the eyes of some major theorists and practicing teachers.

Although many curriculum theorists, teachers, and leaders would probably agree that a major goal of education is that of improvement of the profession and of student learning in particular, significant variance exists with respect to *how* this issue is thought through. Furthermore, *who* determines *what* those changes should be, as well as *when* and *how* those changes are to be "measured" (if at all) and "administered," are all areas that similarly make for vigorous, ongoing debate. These variances and contentions comprise gaps and even ideological disconnects, as evidenced within the curriculum field. Based on our review of a select number of curriculum theorists, critics of product-leaning orientations take issue with a whole host of interconnected issues that include power and authority, quantity and accountability, consequence and penalty.

Pinar's (e.g., 1978/2004) call for tolerance where varying, if not clashing, perspectives in the curricular field are concerned should probably be heeded. The idea here is that the educational community could really benefit where process- and product-leaning individuals alike proceed more inclusively and with the recognition that these orientations will remain contentious, informing one another and even at times borrowing from the other.

Finally, we hope that this discussion provides support to leaders who must make choices about curriculum for their schools. Central to this choice is the curriculum leader or school's own philosophical orientation toward curriculum as well as the ongoing debate surrounding product- and process-leaning curriculum. Such dynamics and influences need careful consideration as curricular texts and materials, in addition to programs and delivery systems, are selected as well as developed. Part II of this book assists the reader by exploring the underlying tensions between the inner (self-generated) and outer (externally imposed) curriculum. The benefits of integrating these in particular ways to meet the goals of your institution is also discussed.

TABLE 3.1
Key Thinkers in Curriculum Studies

Curriculum Theorist	Educational Purpose	Principles	Content	Philosophical/ Psychological Foundation	Time Frame
Benjamin Bloom	Bloom and his coworkers established a hierarchy of educational objectives, generally referred to as Blooms Taxonomy Cognitive Domain, that attempts to divide cognitive objectives into subdivisions ranging from the simplest to the most complex behavior. The taxonomy provides both a framework for the formulation of educational objectives and a means for formulating evaluation tasks.	Cognitive learning is demonstrated by knowledge recall and intellectual skills. Affective learning is demonstrated by behaviors related to emotions, attitudes, appreciations, and values. Psychomotor learning is demonstrated by physical skills.	The cognitive domain taxonomy has six levels: 1. *Knowledge*—recall, memorize. 2. *Comprehension*—summarize, explain. 3. *Application*—use knowledge in real-life situations. 4. *Analysis*—dissect subject. 5. *Synthesis*—put information back together. 6. *Evaluation*—judge the value of subject matter. Various action verbs were developed for objectives appropriate to each level. Taxonomies for the affective and psychomotor domains were also defined.	Psychological/Cognitive The cognitive taxonomy is predicated on the concept that cognitive operations can be ordered into six increasingly complex levels, with each subsequent level depending upon the student's ability to perform at the preceding level(s).	(1913–1999) 1950s

(Continued)

Curriculum Theorist	Educational Purpose	Principles	Content	Philosophical/ Psychological Foundation	Time Frame
John Franklin Bobbitt	Bobbitt's purpose was to develop a model of education based on efficiency. He viewed curriculum as a science based on systematic activity. A curriculum is a plan for learning that interprets social values based on a vision and consists of one or more structures.	Bobbitt's principles were based on "machine theory," a consequence of the proliferation of science and industry. He stressed the importance of analysis as a component of curriculum construction.	Educators must first determine what is important for students to know. They must then construct curriculum objectives that are specific and measurable. This objective and strategies approach is logical and prescriptive and includes paradigms, models, and sequential strategies.	Technical/Scientific Foundation/Social Efficiency Movement The machine theory is an outflow of science and industry. Larger concepts are broken down into smaller, precise pieces that must all work together to function as a whole.	(1876–1956) 1920s
Jerome Bruner	Bruner examined the structure of a subject and saw education as a process. He developed a model that considered how students learn, as well as the relationships that constructed meaning. He emphasized that knowledge is based on a preceding structural pattern.	Bruner's theory emphasizes that learning, which includes meaningful organization of previous experience, can be transferred to new learning experiences. Bruner rationalized the shift from mastery of essential data to the study of representative data structures.	Transfer of learning occurs when the student has a solid cognitive foundation on which to build new ideas and transfer learning to new situations. Elements are the acquisition of knowledge, the formation of new ideas, and the evaluation of such knowledge. Theory of instruction has four parts: 1. Attitude toward learning. 2. Ways knowledge can be structured so easily learned.	Cognitive/ Constructivist Bruner and his colleagues saw a need to refocus on the structure of information and information reorganization. Bruner's sense of new curricula centered on the belief that knowledge has an internal connectedness. Facts must fit into a meaningful context to be understood.	(1915–) (1950s–1970s)

(Continued)

Curriculum Theorist	Educational Purpose	Principles	Content	Philosophical/ Psychological Foundation	Time Frame
			3. Most effective sequencing to learn material. 4. Nature and pacing of reward and punishment.		
Hollis Caswell	Caswell's aim was to improve the efficiency of instruction. His primary concern was high school curriculum development and evaluation.	Caswell viewed curriculum as a set of guided experiences rather than a set of detailed subject matter. His theory maintains that content, instruction, and learning are inseparable.	Caswell's 7-step method of developing curriculum is as follows: 1. What is curriculum? 2. Why is there need for curriculum revision? 3. What is the function of subject matter? 4. How do we determine educational objectives? 5. How do we organize curriculum? 6. How do we select subject matter? 7. How do we measure the outcomes of instruction?	Behavioral/ Developmental Caswell and his contemporaries held that curriculum development in the high school is an essential component of professional education and must benefit the student.	(1901–1988) (1930s–1940s)
Werrett (W. W.) Charters	Charters developed an approach to curriculum based on the "machine theory," and business, which included systematic activity. He was an early proponent of audiovisual learning and a pioneer in the field of adult education.	Curriculum should be a means to an end. Instruction and learning should be efficient and evaluated based upon the successful completion of specific objectives or individual output.	Objectives are scientific in nature and therefore should be observable and measurable. Assessing the needs of society derives objectives.	Scientific/Behaviorist Charters worked very closely with Bobbitt. The two recommended a behavioral approach to curriculum design.	(1875–1952) 1924

(Continued)

Curriculum Theorist	Educational Purpose	Principles	Content	Philosophical/ Psychological Foundation	Time Frame
		Curriculum is a series of learning experiences.			
James Coleman	Coleman raised the topic of educational equality in *Equality of Educational Opportunity*, also known as the *Coleman Report* (1966).	Schools should serve as equalizers of society. Equality exists only when all students achieve the same outcomes.	Coleman outlined five arenas of inequality: 1. Curriculum. 2. Racial representation. 3. Instruction. 4. Student outcome. 5. Student achievement regardless of background or ability.	Sociological/ Reconstrutionist	(1926–1995) 1960s
	Coleman and his researchers surveyed more than 600,000 students and 4,000 school—one of the largest social science projects ever undertaken.			Reconstructionist	
James B. Conant	Conant's work highlights the importance of curriculum development in American high schools. Conant sought to raise the level of achievement of American students to be competitive globally in the post-Sputnik era by advocating problem-solving methods.	American students need more exposure to science, mathematics, and foreign languages. American high schools must change to include curriculum that challenges students to compete internationally.	Curriculum needs to be upgraded to include more emphasis on science, math, and foreign language; academic subjects take precedence over nonacademic subjects; standards and grades are more rigid; students are challenged to the best of their abilities; and students are grouped according to ability.		(1893–1978) (1950s–1960s)

(Continued)

Curriculum Theorist	Educational Purpose	Principles	Content	Philosophical/ Psychological Foundation	Time Frame
John Dewey	Dewey illustrated the relationship between education and democracy.	Schools are an instrument of democracy. Education enhances democracy. Children are capable of developing experience in all subjects. Scientific inquiry is the most effective method of learning.	Education is a social institution that directly affects society. Society also influences education. Schools are a microcosm where students learn to function in a democratic society.	Progressivism Dewey's ideas stemmed from the Progressive Movement of the early 20th century. Progressivism sought to affect political reform and social change through informed thinking and the acceptance of social values and responsibility.	(1859–1956) (1910–1940s)
Elliot Eisner	Eisner seeks to establish a basis for evaluating school, curriculum, and educational criticism.	Children's realities are holistic and multiple. Curriculum should include consideration of cognitive differences among students.	Differences among students must be recognized. Curriculum should meet the learning needs of all students, and evaluation tools must consider student differences in cognition. Concepts cannot be taught in isolation but rather as relating to personal perception and experience. Eisner developed seven models of thinking: 1. Aesthetic 2. Scientific 3. Interpersonal 4. Intuitive	Progressive/Humanistic	(1933–) 1990s

(Continued)

46

Curriculum Theorist	Educational Purpose	Principles	Content	Philosophical/ Psychologica Foundation	Time Frame
			5. Narrative 6. Formal 7. Spiritual		
Friedrich Froebel	Froebel introduced the concept of kindergarten and stressed natural development in children. He was first to apply educational learning objectives to preschool children.	Learning occurs when the natural impulses of the child are recognized and is based upon the activities and development of the child.	Schools should be organized around the play, interests, and activities of the child. The format is informal and based upon love, trust, and freedom.	Progressive Philosophy of education rests on four principles: 1. Free expression. 2. Creativity. 3. Social participation. 4. Motor expression.	(1782–1852) 1830s & 1840s
John Goodlad	Goodlad questioned the purpose of schools in regard to society and the individual.	Education is a lifelong process. School has a dual responsibility to the social order and the individual.	The purpose of school is to produce people who make the most of life. Education is for growth and meaning of both the individual and society. Curriculum is integrated.	Sociological/Humanistic John Dewey's Progressivism influenced Goodlad.	(1920–) (1960s–1980s)
Robert Havighurst	Havighurst suggested that curriculum should address the personal and social needs of children.	Havighurst emphasized three elements necessary for child development: socialization, the family, and the community. He is ultimately concerned with the "whole child."	Children need social interaction to develop personally and socially; cooperative and independent work are necessary. Lessons are based on meaningful, real-life experiences.	Developmental/ Child-centered Human Growth and Development School (school of thought).	(1900–1991) 1970s

Curriculum Theorist	Educational Purpose	Principles	Content	Philosophical/Psychologica Foundation	Time Frame
Leonard Koos	Koos is credited with founding the junior high and middle school movements and contributed to the development of the junior college.	Young adolescents are a unique segment of students in a distinct developmental stage. Schools should consider and accommodate this.	The purpose of the junior high/middle school is to provide a microcosm of a democratic society and integrate nature with nurture.	Developmental/Reformist	(1881–1974) (1910–1925)
Horace Mann	Mann addresses equality in education and proposes the "common school," which is first established in Massachusetts in 1826.	Education acts as an equalizer for people.	Mann maintained that education had business value, served a democratic society, supported the public welfare, and integrated a diverse society.	Humanistic/Reformist Mann is known as the "Father of American Education."	(1796–1859) 1820s
Abraham Maslow	Education must address human needs and produce "self-actualizing" persons.	There exists a hierarchy of human needs; without each need being met, there can be no learning or human growth.	Six basic needs must be met for children to learn: 1. Survival 2. Safety 3. Love/inclusion 4. Esteem 5. Understanding 6. Self-actualization Maslow also stresses the principles of humanistic psychology, which include learning, self-realization, and individual worth.	Human Relations School of Management	(1908–1970) 1950s

(Continued)

(Continued)

Curriculum Theorist	Educational Purpose	Principles	Content	Philosophical/ Psychological Foundation	Time Frame
Marie Montessori	Montessori proposed curriculum reform, maintaining that curriculum be founded upon the changing needs of a dynamic society.	There are five Montessori principles: 1. Respect for child. 2. Absorbent mind. 3. Sensitive periods. 4. Prepared environment. 5. Self or auto-education.	Montessori advocated the theory of education based upon values, human nature, transmission, society, opportunity, and consensus. Strong emphasis is placed on the early acquisition of language and math skills, individual writing, drawing, and small group instruction and learning activities.	Developmental/ Reformist Montessori stressed children's needs; utilized activities naturally attractive to child; facilitated a human experience for the child; and saw teachers as social engineers.	(1870–1952) 1920s
A.S. Neill	The intent of Neill's ideas was to encourage an existential view of popular education and adopt measures that would encourage an individual student's development.	Education must be humanistic and child centered. Scientific approaches do not take into consideration the "whole child." Four humanistic, child-centered principles are: 1. Allow children to grow emotionally. 2. Give children power over their own lives.	Education is cooperative, not competitive. The teacher facilitates cooperative and independent learning. Freedom, rather than authority, is central to learning.	Progressivism/Humanistic/ Developmental/ Existential Neill's ideas stemmed from existential philosophy applied to education theory, referred to as Neill's Existentialism.	(1883–1973) 1920s & 1930s

(Continued)

49

Curriculum Theorist	Educational Purpose	Principles	Content	Philosophical/ Psychological Foundation	Time Frame
		3. Give children time to develop naturally. 4. Create happier childhood by removing adult fear and coercion.			
Francis Parker	Parker is credited with forming the first "subject areas."	Parker's goals were to move the child to the center of the education process and interconnect subject areas in the curriculum to enhance their meaning for the child.	Parker emphasized such elements of progressive education as group activities, the teaching of science, informal methods of instruction, and the elimination of rigid discipline.	Progressivism Dewey called Parker the Father of Modern Education. Parker studied German Johann Herbart's pedagogy theories.	(1837–1902) (1860s–1880s)
Johann Pestalozzi	Pestalozzi proposed elementary school reform based upon natural child development.	Education should be founded on the natural development of the child, including sensory influences. Pestalozzi believed that teachers should provide a variety of learning experiences for children.	Children learn through sensory activities rather than constructs. The study of common objects facilitates this through experience with everyday things.	Humanistic	(1746–1827) (1790s–1820s)

(Continued)

Curriculum Theorist	Educational Purpose	Principles	Content	Philosophical/ Psychological Foundation	Time Frame
Jean Piaget	Piaget proposed curriculum that is based on cognitive development.	Human development comes in stages. The four models of intelligence are: 1. Sensorimotor period (0–2 years). 2. Preoperational period (2–7 years). 3. Concrete operations period (7–11 years). 4. Formal operations period (11–15 years). These models are distinct but chronologically successive and necessary.	Cognitive development occurs in stages upon a continuum based on previous experiences and knowledge. Mental processes are sequential and include assimilation, accommodation, equilibrium, and environmental experience.	Developmental/ Environmental Cognitive Theory	(1896–1980) (1960s–1970s)
William Pinar	Pinar believes that curriculum needs to be fundamentally reconceptualized in terms of how it functions and might do so in emancipatory ways.	Reconceptualization is an intellectual "movement" formed in reaction to the political stance of the status quo perpetuated by technical rationalists (traditionalists in particular, as well as many conceptual empiricists).	Three types of movements characterize the curriculum field: 1. Traditionalism. 2. Conceptual-empiricism. 3. Reconceptualism.	Reconceptualization/ Political Emancipation	(1947–) 1970s

(Continued)

Curriculum Theorist	Educational Purpose	Principles	Content	Philosophical/ Psychological Foundation	Time Frame
			Although reconceptualists pursue perspectives on curriculum and research that are "politically emancipatory," they aim to increase tolerance for varying perspectives.		
Carl Rogers	Rogers proposed counseling and learning reform based on nondirective and therapeutic learning.	Reality is based upon the perception of the individual. Learning will naturally vary from one child to the next. Fully functioning individuals are characterized as having five attributes: 1. Openness to experience. 2. Existential living (here and now). 3. Orgasmic trusting (do what comes naturally).	Children's perception of reality influences learning. Interpersonal relationships are vital to development. The teacher is a facilitator for self-discovery, providing an environment that includes academic freedom.	Existentialism/Gestalt Psychology	(1902–1987) (1950s–1960s)

(Continued)

(Continued)

Curriculum Theorist	Educational Purpose	Principles	Content	Philosophical/ Psychological Foundation	Time Frame
		4. Experiential freedom (responsibility for choices) 5. Creativity (participate in world).			
Jean Jacques Rousseau	Rousseau shifted the emphasis of education from subject matter to child.	The needs and interests of children must be addressed. Educational objectives should prepare the individual for and promote the public good.	Children learn by experience. The purpose of the teacher is to act as a guide for that child's learning. Children should be taught in the context of their natural environment. Meaningful experiences result in behavioral changes.	Behaviorism/ Existentialism Rousseau and his colleagues believed in the social contract as the means of promoting the general will and the best society.	(1712–1778) 1760s
B.F. Skinner	Skinner introduced the idea of operant conditioning in learning and programmed instruction.	Skinner believed in a process of behavioral shaping. Operant conditioning is learning based on a series of responses and reinforcement.	When an operant response is followed by reinforcement, the operant response strengthens. No specific stimulus causes operant behavior. Learning can be transferred.	Behaviorism	(1904–1990) (1960s–1970s)
Hilda Taba	Taba researched and wrote on the particulars of curriculum development and proposed the concept of a linear curriculum.	Curriculum development principles include:	Students learn and organize based upon a schema. The purpose of education is to fit complex ideas and applications into the schema of the child.	Behaviorism Taba participated in three major curriculum reform movements:	(1902–1967) 1960s

(Continued)

Curriculum Theorist	Educational Purpose	Principles	Content	Philosophical/ Psychological Foundation	Time Frame
				1. Ralph Tyler's 8-year study. 2. Intergroup education (integration of Jews & Christians). 3. The spiral of curriculum development for elementary social studies	
Edward Thorndike	Thorndike conducted experimental testing of the learning process to derive three broad classes of intellectual function: 1. *Abstract intelligence:* • Altitude–difficulty of the task. • Width–variety of tasks that give difficulty. • Area–function of altitude and width. • Speed–number of tasks completed in a given time.	Thorndike maintained that learning is the formation of habits and the connection of habits into a complex structure. The purpose of teaching is to enable the formation of meaningful connections. Thorndike's three major laws of learning are:	Connections are strengthened by positive experiences and weakened by negative experiences. Learning consists of relating new and old experiences. Behavior is influenced by conditions of learning; student abilities can be modified through appropriate stimuli; instructional experiences can be designed and controlled; and, learning must be integrated.	Behaviorism/ Connectionism Thorndike wanted to apply scientific methods to education problems. The ideas he advocated are popularly referred to as Thorndike's Connectionism. Connectionism refers to how learning is the formation of a connection between stimulus and response.	(1874–1949) 1913

(Continued)

Curriculum Theorist	Educational Purpose	Principles	Content	Philosophical/ Psychological Foundation	Time Frame
	2. *Mechanical intelligence*: Ability to visualize relationships between objects. 3. *Social intelligence*: Ability to function in interpersonal situations.	1. *Law of Readiness*— conveyed the structure of the nervous system and the connection or predisposition toward response. 2. *Law of Exercise*— posited that the more a connection between a stimulus and response is reinforced, the stronger it becomes. 3. *Law of Effect*— relates how practice and feedback enhance performance.			

(Continued)

Curriculum Theorist	Educational Purpose	Principles	Content	Philosophical/Psychological Foundation	Time Frame
Alvin Toffler	Toffler alters curriculum into something that considers cultural diversity, equality, and future needs.	Education must take into account the dynamic nature of society and the paramount importance of the future when deciding what to include in the curriculum.	Curriculum should address the diverse needs of a multicultural society. It must consider the accelerated rate of knowledge and technology acquisition. Knowledge should relate to the future.	Reconstructionism/ Futurism Toffler believed that nothing should be included in the curriculum unless it can be justified in the future.	(1928–) 1970s
Ralph Tyler	Tyler was influential in curriculum planning, evaluation, and the relationship between curriculum and instruction.	Curriculum is viewed as a science, a rational process that organizes objectives and the learning experience. Learning is separated into knowledge, skills, and values.	Tyler called for the application of four basic principles in the development of any curricular project: 1. Defining appropriate learning objectives. 2. Establishing useful learning experiences. 3. Organizing learning experiences to have a maximum cumulative effect. 4. Evaluating the curriculum and revising those aspects that did not prove to be effective.	Sociological/ Behaviorist Tyler believed in Dewey's general theory of education.	(1902–1994) 1950s

Note. Adapted from Darlene Bruner, Carol Mullen, and Cameron Spears.

II

Curriculum Leadership Cases
for Schools and Faculties

4

Coping With Transitions as a New Site-Based Administrative Leader

Michael Tabor
Carol A. Mullen
Scott M. Smith

Beginning administrators often characterize their academic preparation as insufficient for dealing with the hard-hitting realities of the job, including the practical knowledge required for success (e.g., Llewellyn, 2004; Mullen & Cairns, 2001; Paquette, 2004). Transitional leaders within their first 3 years on the job in Florida's public schools have confirmed this general observation, commenting, "'My graduate program prepared me well, but then each school specializes in so many different things that there's always a huge learning curve,'" and "'My experience as an AP [assistant principal] prepared me tremendously, but it is still a learning curve once you get into the job'" (Mullen, 2004a, p. 91). Our own administrator-interviewees also, predictably, experienced accelerated learning. In a study of early-career principals, learning curve refers to both the experience of having to quickly learn a new job or role, as well as "the projected knowledge base needed for learning a new set of skills" within the context of an "escalated growth cycle" (Mullen, 2004a, p. 91).

Although 1st-year administrators face a rapid succession of changes in their lives, they can take steps to prepare for the transition, in part by utilizing the tools already available to them. One resource is the administrators and mentors with whom they and others have worked. Such experts have a wealth of information to share about the professional and personal aspects of adjusting to a new educational setting. The changes they once experienced and strategies they used during the transitional phase in their careers could potentially benefit any new administrator. But how many transitioning administrators make good use of the mentors and experts around them? We attempt to demonstrate how aspiring school leaders can accomplish this.

THE SECONDARY ADMINISTRATOR PARTICIPANTS

A good way to understand the changes aspiring and newly practicing leaders face when pursuing an administrative role is to ask questions of individuals in these positions. As teachers striving to become school leaders, in the spring of 2005, we interviewed six secondary administrators located at two public high schools in Florida. Three were White females; two of the males were African-American and one was White. Some were in the throes of transition and others more acclimated: Three were assistant principals, one, a principal, and the remaining two, teachers moving to administration. These administrators ranged in experience from several weeks to 9 years. The reflections of the early career individuals offered us the richest resource, perhaps because entry-level administrators have fresh recall about their recent experiences with transition, as well as empathy for others in similar situations (Mullen, 2004a).

The administrator-participants were asked questions based on both professional and personal changes resulting from their transition into administration. Within the professional frame of administration, we inquired about why they decided to become curriculum leaders and asked about increased workload, time management, organizational management, and, of course, barriers encountered. As the interviews progressed and issues surfaced, we invited each administrator to elaborate on the situation he or she raised. We aimed to identify the most significant concerns of these leaders with regard to becoming an administrator and to reveal sources of apprehension. Concerning their personal lives, we also explored the impact on family, and, finally, we examined the learned behaviors new administrators are expected to embody and exhibit.

PROFESSIONAL ADMINISTRATOR CHANGES

Each school leader was first asked why he or she decided to move from teaching into administration. They all responded that an administrative role would provide them with the opportunity to better care for students, and for a greater number of them. All six agreed that students are and continue to be an important part of the job. In fact, this was a recurring theme throughout the interviews. Essentially, they believed that the farther one climbs up the administration ladder, the more impact one can have on student populations. "You should never lose the personal touch you have with the children," declared one principal. Another added, "It is important to never forget why you became a teacher, and the love and feeling you get when you see a student achieve some sort of success."

School principals are in a position to positively affect student success by helping teachers become the best they can be. If administrators want students to improve academically, then they must allow teachers to do the same (Robbins & Alvy, 2004). Aspiring leaders must maintain this understanding and caring for students as they move into administration even though, ironically, the "higher" they advance, the less direct contact they have with students. Principals are responsible for overseeing many more students than a classroom teacher and attending to a higher volume of mandated paperwork. All of our respondents struggled with the paradox of having less personal contact with the very population they were committed to help succeed. As a strategy for maintaining contact with students as individuals, one interviewee agreed to coach the wrestling team. His desire for positive and connecting relationships with students remained constant as an administrator.

One way new administrative leaders have contact with student populations is acting as a liaison between them and their teachers. To become the school's liaison, our interviewees informed us, administrators must change their approach toward disciplining students and overly empathizing with teachers. In most schools, teachers are responsible for notifying the assistant principal or dean of a student's misbehavior. The dean then talks with the student and assigns an appropriate course of action. This leader also evaluates both sides of the story, not only acting as a liaison between the teacher and student but also listening with an open mind to both parties, which can prove challenging. But, as a mediator, an administrator must be able to appropriately diagnose any problem and then generate solutions. As veteran principals Schumaker and Sommers (2001) advise, administrators should create an overall strategy for resolving the issue while maintaining faith that it will be handled. Finally, they must possess the belief that their actions can empower those directly involved, as well as the whole school.

Beginning administrators must also learn about the culture of the new school and the community in which they are going to work. It is their responsibility to maintain or create a healthy school culture. As one beginning administrator shared, "If I had the last 8 months to do over again, I'd spend more time learning about the school's history and working harder to build trust and rapport" (Mullen, 2004a, p. 92). Bolman and Deal (1997) also encourage beginning leaders to become familiar with their new culture by studying its history and participating in its rituals and ceremonies. In Mullen's (2004a) study of beginning leaders, this population "tacitly under-stood culture as a collection of practices for which school leadership is responsible. Consequently, cultural training was associated with skills build-ing in areas ranging from attending parent–principal conferences to inter-acting with students with varying disabilities" (p. 93).

Endeavoring to create a healthy school culture, administrators must set high academic and overall performance expectations for the teachers and students in their care. A primary task for the new administrator involves helping the school make the transition from one leader or leadership team to another, and from the past to present and future. This elusive challenge involves building meaning and commitment, creating symbols that convey core values, and helping others achieve the shared vision of the school (Bolman & Deal, 1993). Cultural adaptation not only involves the experience of the beginning school administrator in the new setting, then, but also the experience of a group as it adapts to or develops the expected ways of thinking and behaving. Hoyle (1995) believes that "great leaders have a knack for inventing their own future" by imagining what they want to accomplish before taking action and, importantly, by "model[ing] ways to create the future rather than suffer its con-sequences" (p. 18). Cultural lenses change depending on a host of factors, including one's curriculum leadership role and the perspective this takes. The administrators we talked to explained that classroom teachers have a different frame of reference than administrators. Understandably, teachers are mainly concerned with what occurs within the parameters of their own room, focused on their own students' academic progress, as well as safety and well-being. The bell schedule frames teachers' sense of time, we were told. For the administra-tor, the jurisdiction of their work is school-wide, and the responsibilities, com-prehensive. When practitioners journey into administration, they soon realize that they are legally and morally responsible for the school in its entirety. At first, the transitional leader will see only parts of the whole, but over time, more and more of the big picture will be revealed or, more than likely, inferred. As the administrators emphasized, even though the leaders' purpose and vision differ from the teachers', they must never lose sight of the fact that all share in the business of reaching kids.

Another issue recognized by our interviewees is that new administrators never completely grasp the extent to which their time will be absorbed by extra work. Worth noting and monitoring, the time spent on the job can create personal difficulty, a problem that we address shortly. These secondary-level leaders found it necessary to complete tasks they had no idea they would be doing. In high school settings, leaders attend sporting events, club banquets, community meetings, and more. Besides showing leadership at extracurricular events and participating in new school community initiatives, administrators must keep an eye on what is happening behind the scenes. They do not passively assume a leadership role at events but rather ensure, through participation in the planning or delegation of responsibilities, that these will run smoothly.

Take, for instance, the planning of a student pep rally. The administrator must ensure that everything goes according to plan—the itinerary will need to be kept on track even though adjustments to the original plan are commonplace. Importantly, all students attending the event must be escorted into the area safely and quickly, and their safety during and after the event must be accounted for in the preparation.

The larger concern with student safety has redefined the traditional administrative role of school overseer. Other early-career school leaders have also shared that school safety program management is an important area of their work (Mullen, 2004a). The safety principle (5.3) appearing in the Educational Leadership Constituent Council (ELCC) standards for school leaders, for example, increases the expectation for quality of leadership in schools and quality of preparation for aspiring leaders (National Policy Board for Educational Administration, 2002).

The administrator-interviewees also enumerated various other, often unforeseen, tasks that increase the daily workload. Whether it is staff development, counseling students about their personal problems, breaking up the occasional fight, or just dealing with paperwork, their workload compounds from the time they were teachers. As one summarized, "The amount of work you have dramatically increases as you move up." According to a nationwide study, administrators spend on average 62 hours per week at their schools (George, 2001). This basic observation corresponds with an Australian study, which found that administrators spend more than 50 hours a week working (Cranston, Tromans, & Reugebrink, 2002). In order to deal with the new and increased demands placed on them, new administrators must quickly develop strategies for coping with the pressures that threaten their well-being.

One major change that our participants noted is the issue of time itself and how it seems to dissolve like smoke, without rhyme or reason. From the moment they walk onto the school grounds until late at night sometimes, these six administrators must continually "stay on their toes" just to survive. "Sometimes my days involve running around putting out fires," one assistant principal explained, using a cliché widely known in educational leadership circles. He referred to having to constantly disarm student fights, remove misbehaving students from classes, and schedule conferences with parents to discuss problems with their child, just to name a few. Gone are the days of relative "luxury," taking refuge in one's office all day doing paperwork, making phone calls, and working on the computer.

The increased workload is overwhelming for some, a by-product of the learning curve syndrome. As new administrators become acclimated to the job, many invest time and energy similar to that of beginning teachers. One key to dealing with the workload demands is efficient time management and organizational skills. With the increased workload, beginning curriculum leaders spend more time learning than teaching and attending to new, not familiar, tasks. Even if they happen to have the requisite skills, some days they simply have no control: "It's tough to stay on schedule when you don't dictate your own schedule," one interviewee shared. Another concurred, "It's imperative that new administrators become effective in the way they use their time."

Even though you cannot dictate what happens during your day, it is nonetheless vital to actively plan. A calendar or date book is essential for keeping track of appointments, due dates, and even people's names and roles (Schumaker & Sommers, 2001). A simple day planner or palm pilot will save you the embarrassment of a failing memory—always record the vital information and estimate the time spent on major duties. Planners can be divided into sections for major tasks so that you can "organize and execute around priorities" (Covey, 1989, p. 149). Good time management is a learned process, and even a person with poor managerial skills can become better organized by reading handbooks, observing best practices, and experimenting with different practices.

Another way to overcome many of the difficulties that transitional leaders encounter in their first few days, months, and years is to find a mentor. In this context, a mentor is another administrator that guides, teaches, and coaches them. A mentor can help develop the skills and knowledge necessary to succeed and be promoted. Bolman and Deal (1993) tell the story of a new principal who turned to a seasoned administrator from another school for mentoring; through a series of coffee breaks they tackled complex issues, such as the lack of acceptance experienced by the newcomer within his own school, and developed solutions. (In this case, the solution centered around holding an "exorcism," an event honoring the former principal that allowed the faculty the opportunity to release their emotion in a constructive manner.) Paquette (2004), an aspiring principal who conducted interviews with two beginning administrators, learned that mentoring can be accomplished in different ways. Like Bolman and Deal (1993), she recommends that new administrators be paired with an experienced principal from another school who will serve as a mentor, not an evaluator.

Successful mentoring programs for new principals are underway throughout the United States. In a California school district, one such program creates a context for veteran administrators to work "with six 1st-year principals, all of whom experience regular phone contact, site visits, and job shadowing" (Paquette, 2004, p. 114). Such team-based mentoring processes reduce isolation, increase self-efficacy, promote professionalism, and deepen reflective capacity (Mullen, 2004a). Paquette (2004) concludes that "experience and advice from a mentor/coach" can fill new administrators "with the confidence and cultural knowledge needed to perform their jobs successfully" (p. 116).

Becoming part of a leadership team within an organization requires social, organizational, political, and cultural skills. New leaders will only experience progress in these requisite areas if they are proficient at balancing their professional and personal lives. As we discover, the most stressful aspect of being a leader can come *before* one even gets to the office.

PERSONAL CHANGES FOR ADMINISTRATORS

An intensive level of commitment and responsibility quickly materializes for school leaders, even though as teachers they devoted a great deal of time and energy to their careers. The new obligations often come as a surprise to administrators and their family. Uncovering some of the realities of the principalship, our interviews with the six administrators produced unique as well as shared experiences. One consistency across testimonies focused on the difficulty of managing one's time. The two assistant principals spend 55 hours to 80 hours each week at their respective school sites. These longer work hours are self-imposed—one of the new administrators did not know how many hours per week she was actually required to work. However, she explained that an implicit expectation exists that one will work long hours every day. Not surprisingly, these new workloads intensified the level of stress in the administrators' relationships with their spouses and children, an issue that aspiring leaders should prepare for by talking with their families and undertaking careful planning.

An experienced administrator reported that her greater dependency on day-care support required adjustment. During the 3 years she taught, she was able to pick her child up at 3:00 p.m., 5 days a week. In contrast, both parent and child were at the whim of a demanding new schedule. All the administrators lamented having less contact with their children—they felt that they were losing touch with knowing them as people. This shared realization led them to develop a new emotional approach to parenting, one that centered on cherishing the precious time they had with their children, as opposed to upsetting easily and worrying about the small stuff. A pivotal moment occurred for one of the new principals when her 3-year-old son asked at bedtime, "Do you love those kids at school more than us?" By the end of the next week, she had reduced her time at work by 10 hours. This moment, one that many busy parents experience in some form, changed her perspective on what she valued and how she spent her time.

Two of the six participants shared that they had experienced a relationship change with their spouses. The special set of circumstances surrounding one of these new administrators made her example particularly noteworthy. Not only did this individual have an opposite work schedule from her husband's, she was also pregnant and her husband was preparing to leave for active military duty. The compounding issues were having a devastating effect on the marriage. The administrator regretted having to learn about her husband's life activities by way of cell phone or through their children. On the weekends, she and her husband would find themselves in a whirl attending to the domestic domain of shopping, cooking, and so forth. Despite this contact, she concluded, "I feel as if I'm stranger in my own house, and the situation is about to get worse."

Besides balancing the new demands placed on one's family life, beginning administrators also have to develop and apply leadership qualities or capacities. When asked about the personal skills required to manage the job, one administrator cautioned that leaders must learn to speak carefully in order to avoid getting into sticky situations: "The impact of your words as a leader are more powerful than you might realize." He also underscored that "new leaders must learn to support all administrative decisions whether they agree with them or not." This approach to leadership is a foreign notion to most classroom teachers, one that requires pause for reflection. Teachers who disagree with the position taken by school or district leaders have been known to occasionally spread negative rumors: "Teachers tend to gossip. The administrators who want to stay at the school for a long time do not gossip." Another way of looking at this situation is to turn the critical lens back onto the administrator—it might be that the need to maintain the status quo and to not "rock the boat" even when it should be is deserving of critique.

Confidentiality is a definite key to survival and success. Some information is inherently litigious, such as sexual harassment, and, if shared, could have a negative impact on the people with whom they work (Daresh, 2004). Administrators also cannot share teachers' evaluations with other teachers, but keeping issues confidential can be stressful for the administrators. In Florida, the Sunshine Law or Public Records Law (Chapter 286 of the Florida Statutes; Office of the Attorney General of Florida, 2005) allows all school records, including teacher evaluations, to be accessed by its citizens.

Administrators must make every conceivable effort to keep school matters from becoming targets of gossip (and media coverage) and to communicate the positives.

We asked our interviewees if they found it necessary to alter their personality in light of their promotion, especially with regard to the way they communicate with teachers. If they responded in the affirmative, we then asked for an instance when speaking or acting without consideration caused them undue anxiety. One assistant principal shared his role in having had a social studies instructor inadvertently transferred from the school. The teacher had acted inappropriately toward another teacher, an incident that the assistant principal absentmindedly mentioned to his administrative colleague. However, the principal, on learning about the encounter between the two teachers, permanently removed the social studies teacher from this school. A rumor quickly spread that this teacher had gotten into a physical confrontation, worsening the situation that should have remained confidential in the first place. As the new administrator put it, "a private conversation got turned into a firing because I didn't know when to keep my mouth shut." Interpersonal dynamics among the key players involved became unnecessarily complicated, as trust was lost. The lesson is that beginning administrators must watch what they say to colleagues, even more so than when they were teachers—always conduct yourself professionally or else what you say or do could come back to "haunt" you.

Beginning administrators not only have to look at themselves though a powerful new lens but also understand that others are looking at them differently. "School personnel will have put you under the microscope," a male noted. This is not to imply, once again, that new administrators should shut themselves in their offices; instead, they should spend time in all of the classrooms in their building, providing instructional support and morale for teachers. As Gerke (2004) explains, getting into the classroom can help personalize the image of administration while maintaining a professional demeanor (see chap. 10 for ideas on administrator walk-throughs). This action should help to create a caring environment that will, in turn, strengthen the school's climate. It also lets the staff and students know that the administrator cares about learning across the campus and the professionals who keep it going.

What can new leaders do to better manage the various changes and challenges they face? One way is to stay grounded and take some "me" time. This will help them stay motivated while rejuvenating their career (Umphrey, 2004). Another way is to avoid negative collegial circles full of innuendo and rumor. Additionally, they should become a collaboratively oriented curriculum leader, asking for input and applying it when possible, even if the feedback seems counterintuitive. This can be a challenge for many new administrators who are cautious about appearing as though they cannot handle a situation. To achieve the collaboratively oriented status as leader, it is essential to step out of one's comfort zone and ask for help if needed. Remember, administrators have a large pool of people from which to obtain information and feedback and thus do not have to complete every task alone; in fact, one should learn the delicate art of delegation. Lastly, administrators should stay balanced and centered. It is best not to try to be everything to everyone; conversely, do not end up being nothing to nobody.

As we have learned, there must be some kind of balance between the priorities of office and home. In the short term, as our interviewees have suggested, it seems inevitable that long hours will be spent at the school at the beginning of administrative careers. But our principals also indicated that long-term benefits result from developing a routine, managing one's time, and establishing a doable workload. There is light, then, at the end of the "overload tunnel." Efficiency is key to effective time management: It is not how much time one spends at work but how that time is utilized that matters. Reflection is also a powerful tool that can help to relieve stress. Administrators should take the time to think and write about their experiences and even keep a personal transition journal. As Mullen (2004a) writes, this strategy is a problem-solving tool that can prove educational and revealing, if not cathartic. In the end, remember what the administrators we interviewed said is most important: family. Keep pictures of loved ones in your office and periodically update them. They can be a reminder that "enough is enough for today," as one administrator put it.

FINAL THOUGHTS

As we have discovered, most of the curriculum leaders we interviewed found that the greatest change from teacher to administrator was the loss of time, both professionally and personally. The new role in the school also created a need for better time management, new levels of commitment, and self-vigilance. Despite these hardships, not one of the secondary administrators lost sight as to the reason he or she moved into administration—the opportunity to improve the quality of many more students' lives, education, and well-being.

Anyone who commits to the administration journey will see tremendous changes around themselves and from within. Ever hear of the trickle-down effect? The more accomplished one becomes as a leader, the greater will improvements appear within individuals, across groups, and relative to the overall school climate. The conflict between one's professional and personal life may never be completely resolved, but the goals are to exercise vigilance, maintain perspective, and to always remember one's core values.

PRACTICAL, REFLECTIVE ACTIVITIES

- Ask the new school leaders you know how much time and effort they apply to each of the following domains of their work: instructional supervision, school organization, student services, community relations, and school management. Alternatively, you can conduct an action study with beginning administrators in order to find out how much weight they place on these areas, as well as the types of duties performed within each category. (For information about these five leadership domains and the tasks associated with each, consult Mullen, 2004a.)
- List the major personal and professional challenges of your own job. Ask the beginning or experienced administrators you know to do the same. Compare the lists. What overlaps and gaps are apparent? To what extent are they similar or different? What does this tell you about life in administration?
- Shadow a school leader for a specified period (e.g., 2 hours). Discuss with this individual the struggles regarding curriculum. Focus on how this administrator creates a learning environment and gathers information from others. Is a collaboratively and democratically oriented approach to curriculum leadership being used? If so, in what ways? Cite specific examples.

5

Information Literacy Development for Students and Equitable Access

Carol A. Mullen
Robert M. Jordan

Information literacy has moved beyond developing facility with the traditional set of encyclopedias, the dictionary, the card catalog to the Internet, online databases, and networked classrooms. Although these recent media innovations have brought a wealth of information to students, instruction on the effective use of these resources has not been as strong as it could be (Lance, 1994). In an increasingly media-dominated culture, it is imperative for all students to possess information literacy and to have equal access to technology. Schools with high concentrations of minorities and low-income populations represent pressing social justice concerns: "Among these are the pivotal problems of adequate technology training for students, teachers, and parents and the equitable distribution of resources to poor students and schools" (Mullen, Kealy, & Sullivan, 2004; see also Hendershot, 2001; Wiburg, 2003). As a former 8th-grade language arts teacher, Robert Jordan developed a strong professional relationship with the media specialist whom he admired for being proactive as a teacher of research and media skills. She encouraged high traffic in the media center and assisted all classroom teachers requiring use of its resources, including her personal, up-to-date knowledge base.

Robert observed firsthand the difficulties that middle school students, particularly those who were academically low-performing, experienced when attempting assignments dependent on basic research skills. Robert always found that despite the wealth of information available to his students at school and home through both the Internet and traditional sources, it was hard for them to apply it to academic work. Writing library passes for students to check out novels was a straightforward activity, but sending students to the media center to conduct research often led to fruitless searches and unsupervised meandering. Taking the whole class to the center was a solution, he found, but having to assist simultaneously more than 30 students proved overwhelming. These realizations motivated us to investigate the research skills unit taught at the featured Florida middle school and to read the current information on literacy and equity, collaborating on the design of this project and interpreting the results.

It seems obvious that effective math teachers would not give their class problems to tackle without instruction and practice, and expect proficiency. The same principle holds true for the learning of research skills. School leaders who facilitate the partnering of media center staff with classroom teachers, parents, and other relevant stakeholders create a pathway to information literacy for all students. The faculty and staff in this school implemented just such a program. Demonstrating that "team effort increases individual achievements" (Smith, 1995, p. 48), the media specialist and language arts teacher at this location have shown that collaborating on research skills instruction can enhance students' information literacy.

INFORMATION LITERACY DEFINITIONS AND FRAMEWORKS

Information literacy has been defined as "a set of abilities requiring individuals to recognize when information is needed and have the ability to locate, evaluate, and use effectively the needed information" (American Library Association, 1989, p. 1). Importantly, according to Farmer (2001), research skills training goes beyond merely locating sources to synthesis-level thinking. Specifically, Eisenberg and Johnson (1996) have identified six major skills needed for informational literacy: task definition, information seeking strategies, location and access, use of information, synthesis, and evaluation.

In this rubric, the student progresses from passive learner to active user and evaluator of information, well beyond traditional uses of library and media centers.

Research skills training is compensatory, and so it targets students in regular-level language arts classes. In Robert's experience, students in these classes, which generally have a significantly higher minority and disenfranchised population, are less likely to possess the research skills needed to succeed in high school. Additionally, these students have tested below the 35th percentile on the high-stakes, norm-referenced reading test given with the Florida Comprehensive Assessment Test (FCAT). Studies have shown that at schools where information literacy is taught, more students visit the media center, resulting in higher test scores (Lance, 1994). With the FCAT school-grade emphasis on increasing the scores of the lower quartile, targeting this group makes sense for both the students and the school. Moreover, as Lankshear and Knobel (2004) describe, although information literacy involves skills development it is also a process of sociocultural learning. Media libraries, as one such context, are interactive forums wherein students are initiated into particular academic discourses, affirming their interests and development. Literacy is not simply a basic skill, then, but rather a complex way of thinking and being that is informed by one's environmental as well as social and moral contexts.

Information-literate students know how to use traditional (e.g., dictionary) and alternative (e.g., Internet) sources, and for both basic and critical purposes. More importantly, they also have learned how to encode and decode messages, and "make judgments about the worth and validity of the message itself" (Kealy, 2004, p. 288; see also Carter, 2004; Lankshear & Knobel, 2004). Visually literate people have the capacity to "receive visual information, comprehend its intentions then respond visually" (Carter, 2004, p. 291). As media scholar Kealy further explains, "verbally literate" people can tell when someone is manipulating language or when "a writer is trying to trick them with doubletalk" (p. 288). Similarly, he asserts, media literate people can tell when graphics visually distort information, attempting deceit. Interestingly, you can learn about the "lie factor" by imagining the chart Kealy describes that shows a company's 50% increase in sales from one year to the next:

> [A] straightforward way to show this is with a bar chart that uses, say, a 2-inch bar to indicate the first year and a 3-inch bar to represent the second year. But suppose instead, that the display uses two side-by-side images of dollar bills: one that is 2 inches high and the other 3 inches high. Because the bars in this case are dollar bills with a standard proportion, the taller one is also much wider. As a result, the

difference in the overall sizes of the two rectangles formed gives the illusion that the increase was not 50% but 125%. (p. 288)

Critical literacy involves asking questions about who controls ideas and information (Kincheloe & Weil, 2004), as in the case of media production. Being able to access and receive information is a vital part of a democracy; a powerful group cannot control media or people will become passive listeners (Kealy, 2004). A Marxian perspective on this issue is that media are a means of production used to maintain the power of the ruling class. When working classes lack access to media—especially mass media—they are robbed of the opportunity to generate alternatives to the values and reality imposed on them. By contrast, when people have the chance to express themselves through the media, they become contributors to a more culturally diverse society. As Kealy (2004) concludes, society greatly benefits from having information literate citizens who "make critical judgments about the information contained in newspapers, and on radio, television, and the web" (p. 291). Carter (2004) concurs, adding that critically literate students and teachers engage in "discovery and inquiry" as curious individuals who question and "test the limitations" of their own assumptions, lives, and worlds (p. 296).

As we know from the introductory chapters, goal-oriented curriculum leaders do not just stick with routine tasks; instead, they endeavor to provide quality learning experiences for all students. In fact, as Glatthorn (2000) argues, the most successful school teams facilitate learning programs that are both "vigorous" and "relevant." Information literacy—specifically the critical function it provides in turning passive learners into active knowledge-seekers—plays a serious role in helping schools meet this important aim of curriculum leadership. Literacy leaders understand, then, that curriculum work involves making difficult decisions and that it is political.

Once primarily the charge of library media specialists, curriculum leaders in the school community have become responsible for the modeling and teaching of research skills to all students. Schools where the media specialist plays the dual role of information literacy facilitator and teacher trainer report higher reading test scores and academic achievement (Lance, 2001). Lance's four-state study found that student performance on reading tests is improved at schools where information literacy is taught, regardless of the type of student population and other variables, such as educational background of parents, family income, neighborhood status, and so forth.

Successful curriculum leaders do not believe that "the classroom is the only place where all learning takes place," as this "defies logic" (p. 54).

Schumaker and Sommers (2001) elaborate that such individuals turn their sites into good schools by using "all the resources on and off the campus to provide a practical, real-life learning environment" (p. 54). Curriculum and leadership form a powerful whole when different types of curriculum leaders across the school collaborate to promote the development of students as information literate, lifelong learners.

It is imperative that curriculum (instructional) leaders support informational literacy development by "manag[ing] the educational production function" of their job. Among the relevant duties involved, they should commit to "promoting quality instruction," "allocating and protecting instructional time," "coordinating the curriculum," and "monitoring student progress" (Murphy, 2004, p. 27; see also Mullen, 2004a). Within this teaching–learning context, effective leaders work with others to frame and communicate these goals to adult educators within their community. They specifically "work to ensure that instructional support services are coordinated both among themselves and with the regular program" (Murphy, 2004, p. 31), a practice that fosters high academic expectations for student learning.

Highly effective principals help teachers improve their craft by using as motivational forces the commitments and coalitions—what Sergiovanni (2005) terms promises and communities of practice—of their faculty to implement new literacy programs or improve existing ones. Their own follow-through by supporting such activities and, where appropriate, participating in the planning and evaluating with their staff is essential. They must provide "active instructional leadership" and school-wide goals that emphasize student achievement within the context of a professional learning community (Murphy, 2004; see also Blasé & Blasé, 2004). One way to move beyond traditional instruction programs is for faculty to create interdisciplinary learning teams that organize curriculum using themes (Mullen with Kohan, 2002; Schumaker & Sommers, 2001). Through this school-wide process, the teaching/learning culture within media centers also changes. By collaborating with their colleagues, teachers no longer work in isolation or with library media specialists only.

TEACHING RESEARCH SKILLS TO STUDENTS

Before turning to the Florida middle school we studied and its Student Research Skills Development Program (SRSDP), we turn to another successful example of information literacy. At the Florida State University School (FSUS), a K–12 public laboratory school, the library media specialists encourage collaboration with the teachers and report feeling supported by their school director for this work. Franklin (1999), one of the librarians, has worked jointly on stimulating ideas to support students' research efforts. With teachers, she has developed lesson plans, one of which introduced classes to Electric Library, a new computer resource at the time. Benefiting from the fact that children find television programs exciting, she "used a scan converter to show the computer monitor enlarged on a television screen" (p. 107). The leadership team treated one student group to computer-generated photographs of giant squid integrated with information about these creatures. Franklin relayed that

> The students loved learning that although Giant Squid have never been captured, that their tentacles, measuring more than 26 feet, have washed up on beaches. Their mouths dropped open when I explained that the eyes of a Giant Squid ... are as "large as dinner plates." (p. 107)

The library/teacher team followed through by having the students research other "'unsolved mysteries' such as the Loch Ness Monster and Bigfoot" (p. 107).

Most of the research ideas ventured at this site were big hits, whereas others required modification. In one such case, when students were asked to locate information about various professional careers, the team leaders failed to realize that

> the students would have difficulty reading "between the lines" to grasp certain concepts about job performance, working environment, and skills development. The students wanted to be able to instantly find the information we requested. We, on the other hand, wanted them to search for subtleties embedded within several paragraphs. This was a lesson that probably needed more explanation about, and demonstration of, our expectations for such discovery learning. (p. 107)

At the school site we investigated, a research skills unit (SRSDP) is in use specifically for language arts classes that report to the library media center for assistance. Curriculum leaders (teachers and librarians) use a pretest known as the Library and Reference Skills Test to obtain base scores denoting students' current knowledge about reference materials and their applications. The same test is disseminated at the end of the unit for comparison. The first part of the assessment requires students to match a particular type of resource (almanac, thesaurus, Cybercat) with the function it supports. For the second half, they supply short statements about a variety of skills presumably taught during the unit. The questions, all open-ended, prompt students to demonstrate whether they understand the various resources and their purposes and functions. Questions such as, "What types of information will you find in an almanac?" "What would a Cybercat keyword search on France list?" and "What does the last book in a set of encyclopedias contain?" all help to determine a student's level of research knowledge.

Prior knowledge of and facility with research skills is determined within the center. For this purpose, the following activity is used. After the pretests are completed, each student is given a note card with a question pertaining to sources in the media center. The student then tapes it on one of the large papers posted on the wall designating various resources in the media center. For example, a question asking, "Where would you find information on the average rainfall in Morocco?" might appear on the almanac paper. After all students place their cards on what they think is the correct source, the media specialist and the 7th-grade language arts teacher go over the responses. Incorrect placements become sources of group discussion; whenever consensus is achieved, the card is placed on the proper source. This serves as the first learning activity of the research skills unit. Students become involved in thinking about the many available resources and their varied purposes and functions. With results in hand, teachers end up with a picture of a class' strengths and weaknesses, areas they and others can address in the research skills unit.

The media specialist continues the unit by giving each class a general overview of the organization of the center. By walking around the room (a large, open space), the student patrons become exposed to the location of various sections of the library media center: fiction, nonfiction, research materials, periodicals, computers, and more. A computer projector then guides them through a variety of activities that deal with different aspects of the library and its resources.

Cybercat is this school's electronic card catalog. After being shown how to log into the catalog, the students are guided, via the media specialist's examples, on conducting author, title, and subject searches. Question sheets test students' abilities to undertake these searches. They are also asked to identify various sources in the school's media center on particular subjects and the number of holdings of a given title.

Resources instruction via the Gale Virtual Reference Library (see http://www.gale.com/free_resources/bhm) familiarizes the classes with the library's online database, a key component of information literacy. These middle school students use Gale for accessing articles on a variety of subjects covering diverse topics of interest (e.g., Saddam Hussein, Mad Cow disease, FCAT). After recording the title and author of the article, students take enough notes to formulate a paragraph outlining the main idea and pertinent facts of the article they have selected.

The program continues with an activity known as Using the Library. Starting with the electronic card catalog, students are guided through the basic format of the resource cataloging system (author, title, publisher, call number, etc.). Questions on a typical entry are answered to ascertain familiarity with the indexing system. Hands-on experience is then achieved with a library scavenger hunt. Specific questions dealing with the location of resources, ordering of the shelves, navigating through an almanac, and origin of quotes requires that students know where and how to find information and use it.

Online encyclopedia skills are taught through the school's access to World Book. After being instructed on how to log into this resource, students are given several subjects to research (e.g., cell phones, sports team, Frederick Douglas). They respond to specific questions requiring evaluation of the information found. By prompting the students to synthesize and evaluate the facts from the encyclopedia entries, they demonstrate that they not only know where to find information but also can construct meaning based on what is read.

The many days of instruction culminate with a repeat of the Library and Reference Skills Test. Comparison of the pre- and posttest scores should show a substantial gain in knowledge (recorded in percentages). Of the 52 students participating in the research skills unit at this site who took the pre- and posttests, an average gain of 69.86% was recorded. This reflects steady improvement for library users, from the 48.71% average gain in 2003 to 60.2% the following year. Possible explanations for this positive change, and within such a short time period, point to the synergy that Franklin (1999) and Mullen and Lick (1999) say teacher collaboration and experimentation generates. At this school, the media specialist and language arts teacher have, through experience, found which examples and teaching techniques tend to work best for the research skills unit, following through with implementation in the media center. Like most endeavors, seeing how your students react to the curriculum, and learning what works well and what does not, will change the way you approach the same material the following year.

NEW RESEARCH SKILLS STUDENT SURVEY: RESULTS

After completing the research skills program, an ethnically diverse group of 52 students was administered the New Research Skills Student Survey that Robert designed; it was completed on hard copy in the students' language arts classes. What were the learners' perceptions of their newly acquired skills, we wondered. The first question dealt with the availability of resources in the home; students indicated that television is the primary source of information (45%) to which they are exposed. Computers (41%), dictionaries (41%), the Internet (35%), and books (35%) ranked somewhat lower, whereas specific sources such as encyclopedias (13%), thesauri (12%), and atlases (12%) were available in fewer homes.

These results suggest that materials traditionally found in a school's media library are typically not prevalent outside of that setting, a finding that fits with empirical studies of equity and access (e.g., Hendershot, 2001; Wiburg, 2003). When asked who provided assistance with research, students' most common responses were parents/guardians (75%), teachers (72%), friends (58%), and media specialists (49%). Most of these students visited the school's media center at least once monthly, and the majority sought assistance at that time. When asked if the research skills classes helped them develop the requisite skills, only one student replied in the negative—a notable testament from an age group that is often stingy with praise for educational activities. Most students felt confident that they had learned the research skills taught, and a small number believed that they still needed to work on certain areas. This perception of success falls somewhat short of matching the 69.5% average on the posttest, but when taken in consideration with the 69.8% average gain from the pretest, it makes sense. Although what would amount to a D+ test score does not immediately sound impressive, the gain from the pretest scores is actually quite an accomplishment.

It is this perception of success on the part of the students that was the most remarkable result from their survey comments. Most students felt that a significant change had occurred in both their abilities to conduct research and the methods they used. Typically, they would have immediately headed for the Internet on arrival at the media center, expending energy and time in dead-end searches. Now, the newly educated students entered the media library with their research topic in mind and with a purpose, consulting the most appropriate sources for their interests and needs. Written affirmations to this effect included, "Without having these research skills, I would be helpless when I do projects," "I'm more advanced now in looking for the things I need," and "The research program helped me learn about some of the other resources to use instead of the old ways." These comments suggest that the participating students changed the way they conducted research and the strategies they used for doing so; as developing researchers, they also became more confident and effective in approaching informational tasks.

TEACHER PERCEPTION OF STUDENT RESEARCH SKILLS SURVEY: RESULTS

The Teacher Perception of Student Research Skills Survey results contrasted with the students' responses. Robert distributed this instrument to the science, math, and geography teachers, those who had taught the students in the language arts classes and participated in the research skills training; the language arts teacher also served as a survey respondent. Although the only teacher participating in the media center training was the 7th-grade language arts teacher, Robert wanted to determine the type of research projects assigned by the other subject area teachers, as well as the frequency with which they took their classes to the media center or sent individual students.

The main goal of the teacher surveys, though, was to determine the program's success in terms of student performance on research projects. Of these four core subject teachers, all except the math educator indicated having seen improvements in their students' research skills. The teachers typically commented that students "know how to write a research paper and bibliography," "need less help," "can find useful Web sites," and "know how to use other forms of research on the computer such as Gale/World Book, not just the Internet." The math teacher escorted her students to the media center once monthly to "check out books only," adding that they are not required to use research in their assignments.

As the language arts, science, and geography teachers frequently brought their classes to the media center *and* assigned research projects, they seemed more cognizant of the changes in their students' research skills. Specific research skills they observed include "finding information about individual countries," "learning how to write a research paper and bibliography," and "knowing where to find information in the media center." When asked if this unit had made their job more manageable, the language arts teacher wrote, "Yes, I have found that students seek out reference material instead of complaining they don't know where to look." The science and geography teachers noted that they also had more time for helping individual students since most no longer required assistance finding relevant materials.

On a scale of 1 to 10, the core teachers as a group rated the research skills program's effectiveness as 7.5. They thought that the students still needed help with "reading for specific facts," "how to take notes," and "summarizing pertinent information." Overall, though, they applauded the improvement that was discernible in their students' ability to conduct research on their own, while accessing the sources most likely to contain the relevant information.

MEDIA CENTER STAFF SURVEY: RESULTS

The Media Center Staff Survey that Robert also designed asked questions similar to the teacher survey about the program's effectiveness and specific skills learned. According to the survey results, an average of 400 of the school's 1,416 students visited this media center daily. This particular school's population at the time was 47% White, 24% Black, 17% Hispanic, 6% Asian/Pacific Islander, .5% Native American, and 4.5% other. When prompted, the media specialist provided information about her patrons' racial composition, in addition to patterns of center use she had observed on the part of minority and lower achieving students:

> Lunch is a good time to see the type of students who enter on their own. The Black students come in at that time. I think this is because many do not have Internet access at home, abundant reference materials, or parents who will take them to the public library and provide for their research needs. Once here they surf on the web and also do word processing and print reports. They use books but prefer the computer. Of course, when classes are scheduled, you get a cross-section of all the kids, but when they come on passes, the minorities and lower achieving students visit more frequently.

The media specialist and the center's secretary also witnessed improvement in the research skills of frequent users. Importantly, the students' level of independence seemed to increase as their abilities improved: "These patrons learn which type of reference book will be best to use for a specific topic." The media specialist noticed that students in general overly rely on the World Wide Web for information. They benefit from realizing that the use of specific databases provided by the district, such as Gale and World Book, actually help them "find items much quicker than the WWW." These staff felt relieved when students who had completed the research skill training asked them questions. Nonparticipants seemed unskilled in comparison.

   These professionals gave the research skills program an effectiveness rating of 7.5. The media specialist characterized the participating students as better at "choosing appropriate reference tools" that were "best to use for a specific topic." Although she also noted that these students were more independent and made greater cognitive gains, she felt the results could be more dramatic if the students had "done a better job of listening." The media secretary concurred that a number of students "did not pay attention to instructors and so asked for help on finding information," although now "most know how to look up materials on their own." A listening skills component should probably be integrated into this unit to further improve its effectiveness.

Given the posttest and survey results from three participating groups, the research skills training offered at this site should be continued. By emphasizing the "process of learning rather than the dissemination of information" (Farmer, 2003, p. 36), a media specialist/classroom teacher collaborative can positively affect students' learning curves. This school program has provided the very opportunity that researchers stress children need if they are to experience academic success in an information-rich environment (Donham, Bishop, Collier Kuhlthau, & Oberg, 2001).

The primary barrier to further gains at this point may be participation by all core-subject teachers. Although mathematics does not ordinarily involve research projects, veteran principals Schumaker and Sommers (2001) assure that integrating all subjects through unifying themes provides a challenging but highly promising vehicle for student learning. Establishing training for all teachers with regard to information literacy and its promotion within a media center, for example, could encourage involvement by those reluctant to leave their classroom. Some of these teachers benefit from being supported in making fundamental changes to stymied routines and curricula.

A major supporter of or hurdle to any media center's full utilization is the school's administrative team. The principal's role as curriculum leader in promoting "faculty/librarian interaction" (p. 4) is, in a word, crucial (Hartzell, 2002). This school's principal eliminated one of the media secretary positions, though. Previously, the media specialist, who had two assistants, had greater latitude for collaborating with teachers and working directly with individual students. Additionally, the one employed secretary was assigned duties in other areas of the school, a situation that threatened to undermine the positive impact of the media center on student achievement. Due to student overcrowding at the school and removal of many portable classrooms, "floating" classes were often held in the media center, further limiting the accessibility of resources and staff. Additional uses of this center, such as an inclement weather shelter and place for staff meetings and trainings, further reduced the opportunities students had for conducting research and learning the relevant skills.

Because "designing a master schedule is one of the most important tasks an administrator can advance" (Mullen, 2004a, p. 139), it seems wise for curriculum leaders to devise schedules that protect the mission of their learning units. In contrast with the nonproductive leadership exhibited along these lines at the middle school, the FSUS collaborative overcame hardship when advised by the Southern Association of Colleges and Schools (SACS) to build a new library media facility on the premises. As Franklin (1999) reflects, it made good sense that SACS identified this as a necessary area for school improvement, as "the existing library at the time was small, cramped, and unable to accommodate more than a single class at a time" (p. 109). Instead of putting this new requirement on the back burner or ignoring it altogether, the school's director engineered its expedited construction. This story no doubt serves as an educational lesson to any practicing or aspiring school leader.

A FINAL WORD

Taken as a whole, the literacy gains for these middle school students draws attention to the value of school programs that enable the development of students' research skills, together with equitable access to resources and accommodations for all learners. The research skills unit collaborative that exists at the school is giving students the knowledge and empowerment they need to make the most of the media center's resources. When properly implemented, just such a collaborative instructional unit can reap benefits for both students and staff, but the guiding hand of the literacy (curriculum) leader is necessary. The potential for better prepared, independent-thinking students with higher reading scores and improved self-efficacy, in addition to collaboratively-oriented teacher researchers should make this kind of program attractive to all school leaders. A dedicated staff and an administrative team willing to lend full support have been known to bring about many desirable changes across the curriculum.

PRACTICAL, REFLECTIVE ACTIVITIES

- Formally or informally, investigate the media library center at your school or another and find out about any research skills (possibly programs) that are being taught and by whom. What skills are students learning and to what effect?
- Compare the racial composition of the student users at a media library center to the school's demographics. With this information in hand, you can ascertain the patterns of use by minority or low-performing students in particular and extend opportunities centered on resources and assistance when needed.

- Develop an instrument for distribution to students and/or teachers at a school of your choice. You can use or adapt the items on the surveys for students, teachers, or media staff paraphrased in this chapter, with acknowledgment of this source.
- Read the available literature on information and media literacy and talk to media specialists and scholars. With your new knowledge and insight, you can pilot your own research skills unit or improve an existing one.

6

Inclusion and School Preparedness to Educate Students With Disabilities

Kristy L. Cantu
Carol A. Mullen

DEFINITIONS AND FRAMEWORKS OF INCLUSION

One of the most controversial issues still facing education today involves the extent to which children with disabilities should be included in general education classrooms (e.g., Mullen, 2001; Werts, Wolery, & Snyder, 1996). Inclusion, defined by the federal government and specifically the U.S. Department of Education (1999), refers to the instruction of all students, with and without disabilities, in the general education classroom (see http://www.ed.gov). Inclusion is rooted in the premise that all individuals with disabilities have a right to be included in naturally occurring settings and curricular activities with their peers, siblings, and friends (Erwin, 1993; Mullen, 2001). If implemented successfully, it involves more than reconfiguring special education services—highly effective curriculum leaders analyze and change the entire organizational structure of their schools to become more inclusive (Murphy, 2004).

In its "purest" form, inclusion requires teachers and administrators to shift what retired principal Oleson (2005) refers to as *mental images of schooling*. By so doing, they redefine their role as educator, examining anew every aspect of teaching from classroom management to curriculum delivery methods (Heflin & Bullock, 1999). However, "institutional conformity" (Jackson, 1990/2004) makes it difficult for many curriculum administrative leaders and teachers to leave their place of comfort only to face the unknown, characterized by risk, uncertainty, and creativity, as well as potential failure. But with the gaining momentum of the inclusion movement, this is exactly what needs to happen.

Recent studies that examine the role of administrative support in the efficacy of inclusion programs report that it is fundamental to the institution (Cook, Semmel, & Gerber, 1999). Because the general education classroom services more students with disabilities, over the past few years a dramatic decrease has occurred in the number of self-contained and pull-out special education programs at public schools (Erwin, 1993; Kavale & Forness, 2000). The changing legislation and its constitutional grounds, as well as ethical considerations, have propelled the inclusion initiative forward (Baker, Wang, & Wallberg, 1994; Kavale & Forness, 2000). A shift in service delivery is especially evident in elementary schools, where the number of students with disabilities being educated in self-contained classrooms is greater.

Before the early 19th century, educational services were simply not available to people with disabilities (Southwest Educational Development Laboratory [SEDL], 1995). Residential institutions slowly began accommodating those with hearing, visual, mental, or emotional impairments (SEDL, 1995). But it was not until the 1950s and 1960s that parents of children with disabilities began seeking access to public schools, which culminated in a civil rights movement for those with special needs and their advocates. The Education for All Handicapped Children Act of 1975, or PL 94–142, resulted from parental pressure on the educational system (SEDL, 1995). This mandate declared that all children have a right to a free and appropriate education in the "least restrictive environment." It had a direct impact on the number of self-contained classrooms and resource rooms that were in place, in that they increased. The rise in specialized classrooms continued until 1986, when the Regular Education Initiative was introduced (D'Alonzo, Giordano, & Vanleeuwen, 1997).

The Regular Education Initiative jump-started the inclusion movement by calling for greater efforts to be applied to educating students with mild or moderate disabilities in general education classrooms (D'Alonzo et al., 1997). In 1991, the updating of PL 94–142 introduced the well-known Individuals with Disabilities Education Act (IDEA; Hammel, 2004). IDEA was recently reauthorized in July 2005. Since its inception, public education has gradually moved toward adopting a more inclusive environment to accommodate the learning needs of all students in the regular education classroom. Although federal law does not mandate full inclusion, its practice is influenced by state commissioners of education who interpret educational trends, school district administrators who apply state regulations, and general and special educators who implement programs within their schools (Shade & Stewart, 2001).

As with any change in legislation, positive as well as negative aspects surface when it is put into practice. The provisions of IDEA allow children with disabilities to be educated in the "least restrictive environment," usually translating into their day-long instruction within the general education classroom (Henning & Mitchell, 2002). However, just physically being present in the general education classroom is not inclusion per se. As Adler (1982/2004) observes, "Equality of educational opportunity is not, in fact, provided if it means no more than taking all the children into the public schools for the same number of hours, days, and years" (p. 160). If, once in a public school, students are categorically divided, however subtle or unintended, into who will succeed in life and who will not, then democracy will have failed—we will have achieved only the same *quantity* of public schooling, not the same *quality* (Adler, 1982/2004; Kincheloe & Weil, 2004; Mullen with Kohan, 2002; Oakes, Selvin, Karoly, & Guiton, 1992).

The degree of inclusion mandated within schools depends on the child's individual education plan (IEP). Curriculum leaders are legally required to carefully examine each student's needs and abilities. As an experienced teacher of the emotionally handicapped who works in Florida, I believe that it is unreasonable to integrate every student with a disability in the regular education classroom, just as it is unreasonable to exclude every child with a disability from the regular education classroom. Consequently, the extent to which inclusion exists from one school to another will and should vary.

AREAS OF HIGH NEED WITHIN ELEMENTARY SCHOOLS

What IDEA does not take into consideration is that the person who is primarily responsible for educating students with disabilities in the general education classroom is the general education teacher. Unlike special educators, who have had training and experience working with special needs students, the general educator is typically ill-prepared to handle such a challenge (Henning & Mitchell, 2002). Martínez (2003) has clarified that "the success of the inclusive movement thrives largely as a function of general educators' willingness to work with pupils who have disabilities" (p. 473). Paradoxically, general educators .... have frequently expressed that they feel inadequately prepared to teach children with disabilities who are in their inclusive classes. In particular, general education teachers report that they are unable or unwilling to adapt their teaching to meet the needs of individual students. (Martínez, 2003, p. 473)

Relevant literature and analysis of the results of our survey, which was distributed to 30 general educators, confirmed that the readiness of these instructors to facilitate learning in the inclusion classroom needs attention. Common themes emerged, underscoring five interrelated areas of high need: administrative support, teacher collaboration, staff development, differentiated instruction, and ongoing assessment

Administrative Support

If educators are to continue placing students with disabilities in the general education classroom, it is imperative that curriculum leaders work with their staff to enhance teachers' preparation and guide their use of effective curriculum strategies. Administrative support is key to the success of inclusion. In fact, one major study examining 32 inclusive school sites (in 5 states and 1 Canadian province) found that the extent of administrative support and vision was the most powerful predictor of general educators' attitudes toward inclusion (Villa & Thousand, 2003). As administrators who are policy leaders, principals influence reform implementation decisions, reinforce high academic standards, control resource allocations, and exert a supervisory role relative to school personnel (Cook et al., 1999; Mullen, 2004a; Murphy, 2004).

Before school leaders plunge headfirst into major restructuring efforts involving curriculum and programs, they must address certain areas of reform. Among these, six are considered critical to the overall success of inclusion: articulating a clear vision, allocating the necessary resources, offering staff development and training, monitoring and evaluating personnel, providing ongoing coaching to inclusion teachers, and, importantly, creating a school context that supports change (SEDL, 1995).

Teacher Collaboration

Collaboration has long been a buzzword in education. Collaborative teaching is a service delivery model in which teachers leave their separate environments to work as teams with colleagues from different disciplines (Fennick & Liddy, 2001; Mullen with Kohan, 2002). This form of interaction is critical to the success of the inclusion model. In order to meet the varied needs of students with disabilities, special educators adapt curricular materials and activities; they even make changes in classroom environments that are not routinely planned for by general educators (Fennick & Liddy, 2001).

Although a controversial figure in the curriculum field, human behaviorist Ralph Tyler (1949/2004) declared that "education is a process of changing behavior patterns of people" (p. 53). Integrating students with disabilities in general education classes means exactly this—that classroom teachers will need to overcome working in isolation. As Austin (2001) confirms, teachers alone do not possess the necessary skills or training to effectively reach all learning needs. Effective administrators know that teachers who are willing to work together need time for formal meetings where they can plan together, a learning strategy that requires sensitivity and resources.

For years, teachers and other school resource personnel have been encouraged to seek ways to help better educate students by gathering as a team (e.g., Buell, Hallam, & Gamel-McCormick, 1999) and making public their promises that all will endeavor to uphold (Sergiovanni, 2005). However, once the school bell rings, teachers typically shut their doors for the day, closing out colleagues. As far as I am concerned, this work culture has prevailed to such an extent that teachers often feel uncomfortable working collaboratively with others in spite of their natural inclination.

Inclusion especially presents a challenge to the educational philosophy of many curriculum leaders who have been educated in the old ways of delivering instruction, such as presenting the same material the same way to all students regardless of their learning style. This concept digresses from the traditional instructional role, as well as from the ingrained image of "classroom." In years past, teachers have taught the same lesson to the entire class, usually in a lecture format accompanied by a written test at the end of each unit. This style has not yet become outmoded, even though it is particularly challenging for America's elementary students who, like our society as a whole, are much more diverse today (Villa & Thousand, 2003).

Nonetheless, teachers who plan together transform their separate special education and general education domains into new roles and responsibilities. This change promotes cohesiveness by involving shared management for a large number of students, only some of whom have disabilities (Fennick & Liddy, 2001). In order for inclusive education to work well, it is essential that educators function as capable team members (Villa & Thousand, 2003) and that administrators support their goals and planning (Murphy, 2004). The collaborative teaching model is ideal not only because it serves students with disabilities but also because it addresses the learning needs of entire groups by allowing teachers to jointly examine each child's abilities and challenges.

Staff Development

Significant staff development can address misconceptions on the parts of teachers and administrators alike (Reick & Wadsworth, 2000). In addition, fears associated with inclusion can be openly aired. As Buell and colleagues (1999) explain, many general educators are understandably apprehensive about absorbing students with disabilities in their classrooms. In addition, they can form negative impressions based on hearsay. Offering a viable staff development program is one way to bridge the gap between general and special educators, helping to ensure success for students with disabilities entering the regular classroom.

The most common form of staff development focuses on the "typical" child, rarely touching on students with special needs. Interviews with students in inclusive classrooms and their cooperating teachers within New Jersey and Pennsylvania schools indicated that a critical component of staff development programs features alternative curricular strategies in the classroom (Kamens, Loprete, & Slostad, 2003). This also holds true for preservice teacher preparation. Aspiring teachers and leaders alike could greatly benefit from hands-on opportunities aimed at modifying curriculum, including activities and materials related to the different and specific needs of student groups.

Many teachers have expressed the concern that although staff development workshops are appropriate for introducing topics, they fail to create and sustain change (Gottesman, 2000; Reick & Wadsworth, 2000). In response, administrators and staff developers must provide ongoing professional development to all personnel in an inclusive setting (Beninghof, 1996). Rather than the traditional, one-time, single-day programs, teachers need ongoing in-classroom follow-up support to apply information to specific situations and children (Gottesman, 2000; Kamens et al., 2003).

General educators' experience with inclusive classrooms varies greatly, and so approaches to staff development must match each teacher's stage of readiness. As Beninghof (1996) argues, there is no "one-size fits all" formula for inclusion—success will come from tailoring each inclusive situation to the needs and experiences of the teachers involved.

The Concerns-Based Adoption Model (CBAM) is a useful conceptual framework for recognizing seven stages of readiness general teachers experience when preparing for inclusion (Loucks-Horsley, 1995)—awareness, informational, personal, management, consequence, collaboration, and refocusing. For example, in the awareness stage (lowest level), the teacher has little concern or involvement with the innovation. In contrast, at the refocusing stage (highest level), the educator is aware of possible benefits of the innovation and can generate alternatives. Perhaps this model can be tested within schools and districts as a strategy for encouraging professional staff development.

Without the necessary training, teachers can unintentionally worsen a child's academic standing (Heflin & Bullock, 1999), a reality that has implications for entire school communities and school improvement efforts nationwide. As O'Shea and O'Shea (1998) caution, although initial staff development opportunities are somewhat helpful, long-term in-servicing, with continuous monitoring of progress, is what supports the success of inclusion.

Differentiated Instruction

When students with disabilities are included in the mix of the general education classroom, finding time for teachers to collaborate is one issue and learning how to accommodate the range of learning needs is another. In my experience, these skills are difficult to master, partly because, as Lipskey and Gartner (1996) reinforce, the increased number of pupils with disabilities in general education classrooms places new demands on the general educators. In the traditional retrofit model, general educators determine both content and instructional strategies without taking into consideration the special characteristics of actual learners (Villa & Thousand, 2003). Only if a mismatch occurred between what a student could do and what he or she was being asked to do would educators entertain making an adjustment. Obviously, because there is such a diversity of learning styles in most classrooms, this mode of instruction would not benefit students in an inclusion setting. Although teachers may not need to adjust instruction for every student, the mindset of the teacher should be focused on how to deliver instruction so that each child has the opportunity to effectively absorb what is being taught.

Differentiated instruction is not a new concept in education, but it has been reinvigorated due to the rapid increase in inclusive classrooms within school districts (Tomlinson, Brighton, & Hertberg, 2003). Differentiated instruction allows educators to understand students individually and with respect to their personal learning styles before assigning curriculum content, processes, and products that lead to the delivery of instruction (Villa & Thousand, 2003).

In a survey that general educators from three New Jersey school districts filled out, 92% indicated lacking knowledge of how to differentiate instruction (Hammel, 2004). Of particular concern to general educators is the ability to adapt the curriculum to meet the needs of students with disabilities, especially in the upper elementary grades (Daane, Beime-Smith, & Latham, 2000). In most teacher preparation programs, the general education major does not receive much training on making accommodations or modifications to instruction; instead, they are taught methods that address the learning needs of the average student (Mullen, 2001). The classroom make-up consists of much more than the average student though—there are those with identified learning problems, highly advanced learners, students whose first language is not English, and those with diverse economic and cultural backgrounds (Tomlinson et al., 2003). With more preservice training in differentiating instruction, the ambivalence felt toward inclusion among general educators could dissipate (Daane et al., 2000; Mullen, 2001).

The rapid increase in academic diversity within and across student populations has prompted further awareness. More accountability for student learning is placed squarely on teachers' shoulders, largely because of the federally mandated NCLB Act of 2001 (U.S. Department of Education, 2002). The nation's public schools are scrutinized and graded, with greater weight distributed to certain subgroups, including students with disabilities. Now more than ever, general educators feel pressured to ensure that every one of their students makes the expected academic gains, which means that more time must be spent on individualizing instruction. However, researchers continue to argue that general education teachers, and especially preservice teachers, may lack adequate preparation for making the necessary "educational modifications" involving students with disabilities (Martínez, 2003). In Hootstein's (1998) investigation, most (90%) of the high school teachers surveyed in a New Jersey district reported that addressing academic differences was important but that they, once again, lacked the time and resources to effectively differentiate instruction.

Half of the middle school teachers who responded to a nationwide survey revealed that the primary instructional strategy they used was the overhead projector (Moon, Tomlinson, & Callahan, 1995). The overhead projector is used to instruct an entire class by writing notes that all can see or by displaying worksheets and correct answers. Use of this equipment as a primary instructional tool goes against the intent of differentiated learning and even lessons learned about effective teaching practice. Differentiated learning addresses individual learning styles mainly through a variety of instructional delivery methods that reach all modalities of learning, such as visual, auditory, tactile, and kinesthetic. Many teachers, whether they realize it or not, tend to teach more to the visual learner. Although use of the overhead projector may be an appropriate instructional method for some learners, it is certainly not for all. Most general educators believe that they address individuals' learning needs when only minor and occasional classroom modifications at best are being made (Tomlinson et al., 2003). If general educators are to succeed at inclusion, they and their colleagues must reassess their classrooms in the context of the bigger picture of curriculum regarding what needs to be taught and how. Differentiating instruction involves more than simply changing a single method of teaching—it necessitates closely examining all aspects of curriculum and instruction.

One way to combat the misconceptions teachers have about differentiating instruction is by providing a clear definition and model of the scope of effective differentiation (Villa & Thousand, 2003). For teachers who feel inept at differentiating instruction, alternative strategies are available for reaching all students but many lack the confidence to effectively use them (Daane et al., 2000). A typical request of general educators is to have a working model in place that highlights ways to adapt their curriculum (Hoover & Patton, 2004). Downing and Eichinger (2003) explain that general educators can become better prepared to teach in an inclusion setting when shown such strategies as cooperative learning, hands-on learning, and instruction that benefit from, for example, the theory of multiple intelligences (see also Schirduan & Case, 2004). However, some researchers claim that even if teachers were to use these strategies, they would most likely resort to the more familiar lecturing, reading, giving directions, and whole-group discussion as primary delivery methods, which oftentimes does not accommodate for including students with mild to moderate disabilities (e.g., Downing & Eichinger, 2003; Hoover & Patton, 2004). Working with special educators can further assist general educators in learning how to differentiate instruction and accommodate numerous learning styles. Teachers and support staff who function as collaborating professionals will enhance the delivery of instruction in the classroom and provide a more meaningful and rich learning environment for all students.

Ongoing Assessment

How do general educators know when their differentiated instruction is meaningful and effective? Frequent, ongoing assessments must be implemented to concretely determine whether a regular student, not just one with disabilities, is making learning gains. Eleven of 47 experts in the field of disabilities—consulted because they had authored works on useful practices for inclusive settings—reported that performance-based, authentic, and in-context assessments were essential for measuring the academic gains of those with disabilities in the general education classroom (Jackson, Ryndak, & Billingsley, 2000). These three types of assessment are intended to honor students' personal progress rather than compare it to the norm, as well as provide meaningful feedback that assists with further instruction. Recurrent assessment allows both the special and general educator to see exactly which concepts students have grasped and where they may still be struggling.

In a survey of staff members at several elementary schools in Pennsylvania, 84% reported that assessment was taking place but they were unaware of the intervals at which they should do it (O'Shea & O'Shea, 1998). Once again, teachers identify time as a primary barrier to making assessments more relevant for students. General educators reported resorting to publisher-supplied assessments for evaluating student knowledge (O'Shea, 1999). When asked through O'Shea's (1999) survey whether they, in fact, modify class assessments, create simplified study guides for tests or quizzes, or assess content in shorter increments, 83% of the general educators responded that they occasionally did, and not consistently. (We do not know from this study how many teachers completed the survey, only that Scruggs and Mastropieri [1996] had conducted a review of studies whereby 11,000 general educators were surveyed.) Similarly, in a survey circulated in New Jersey, 88 elementary teachers were asked what percentage of all tests used in the general education classroom were teacher-made, to which they reported an average of 28% (Waldron & McLesky, 1998).

As many know, paper-and-pencil tests may not be the most beneficial way for students to exhibit understanding of a content area. Yet 13 out of 15 inclusion teachers interviewed in North Dakota acknowledged that they primarily used this to assess content knowledge (Olson, Chalmers, & Hoover, 1997). When asked about other forms of assessment, 12 reported being familiar with portfolio and oral assessment in particular but lacked a sufficient grasp to use them consistently. If teachers can be supported in rethinking their approach to individual and group assessment, they should be able to better serve those who are struggling and advance those who are excelling.

Teaming with the special educator and coplanning for assessment will help the general educator learn the necessary tools needed to prepare appropriate assessments given more frequently (Kamens et al., 2003). General educators must learn these skills, such as retyping assessments to include more white space and rewording certain types of questions, assessing after skills have been taught instead of waiting until the end of a unit, and using accommodations (e.g., word banks) on assessments when deemed appropriate. Most times, the special educator only spends a portion of his or her day in the regular classroom. Students with disabilities require academic accommodations throughout the day, not just when the special educator is present.

GENERAL EDUCATOR SURVEY AND RESULTS

In 2005, I distributed an instrument I designed to 30 general educators employed in 6 different elementary schools in Florida. In elementary schools, general educators are highly influential figures, as they instruct students in all academic areas, and their students do not typically change classes at all. The average number of teaching years for our participants was 17, none having taught less than 3. I selected this population of teachers to complete the survey as a strategy for identifying how prepared they were for working full-time with students with disabilities.

The survey had two parts, one an interval scale and the other, open-ended questions. The first part asked teachers to answer prompts listed in a Likert scale format ranging from a score of 5 (strongly agree) to 1 (strongly disagree), with moderate options in between. Addressed on this instrument were the five major educational issues we have highlighted with regard to inclusion (administrative support, teacher collaboration, staff development, differentiated instruction, and ongoing assessment). Specific items were included within each of the survey's categories. Teachers were asked to determine the degree of administrative support for inclusion relative to their grade level and to rate (using the Likert scale) whether they had had adequate time to plan with their special education peers. As another example, respondents indicated whether they had received sufficient staff development for enabling them to work with children with special needs.

Notably, 62% of the participants indicated that they were not given adequate planning time with the special educators at their location. Written explanations attributed this problem to the lack of common planning time in the school day, the overwhelming demand of paperwork, and poor administrative support for implementing the necessary changes to support inclusion. Concerning instructional planning time wherein general educators develop their weekly lesson plans (which can be done alone), all respondents reported that the time provided was insufficient.

Respondents were provided a list of instructional strategies and asked to indicate which they used and for what percentage of time in the course of a week. The instructional strategies were listed as follows: overhead projector, whole-group instruction, small-group instruction, modified assessments, extra "white space" between problems, study guides, color-coded assignments, word banks, bold lettering, and visual and auditory formats for giving directions and providing examples. For the time allocation, the teachers calculated their effort as a percentage and recorded that number on the survey. Of the responses received, 75% of the participants specified personal use of the overhead projector an average of 70% of the time weekly. Twenty-five percent reported using study guides for assessments more than 80% of the time, also weekly.

Open-ended questions invited participants to describe ways they used differentiated instruction in their classrooms. All respondents identified small-group instruction for addressing specific areas of deficit. In addition, 20%

applied Howard Gardner's multiple intelligences and/or Benjamin Bloom's taxonomy to differentiate among learners. Gardner's theory is based on multiple intelligences (e.g., linguistic); teachers who apply it teach to a student's area of strength. For example, if a student has strong linguistic skills, written assignments might appeal to this type of learner—the teacher would teach to the student in a way that enhances that strength. Regarding Bloom's taxonomy, teachers reported having applied different levels of questioning, from simple recall to analysis and evaluation, so that all students could engage in a lesson at their ability level. Bloom's theory allow for differentiation using a hierarchy of questioning. One's advanced students may be at the synthesis and evaluation level whereas others are only at the application level. Adaptation using Bloom's theory determines a student's level of difficulty with a skill, as well as the extent to which students should explore a particular concept in order to make gains.

Finally, another survey question inquired about support for staff development. Surprisingly, 50% of the participants reported having adequate staff development to work with children with special needs. Almost all of the research we reviewed indicated that very few teachers felt the professional development provided to them was adequate (e.g., Reick & Wadsworth, 2000). A discrepancy appears to exists between the results of the survey and the studies reviewed: The instrument was only distributed to schools with higher socioeconomic levels in which curriculum leaders have the resources to provide for staff development. After analyzing the results of the open-ended question on differentiated instruction, it was evident that the respondents had only a minimal idea of what it takes to differentiate instruction. Like most general educators I have spoken with, those completing my survey expressed overwhelm at the prospect of changing their instructional delivery. My experience is that most teachers are willing to try differentiated instruction but quickly revert to their established teaching habits once they realize how difficult it is.

PARTING WORDS

With recent changes in U.S. legislation, the expectation for school leaders to adopt inclusive education is high. In order for successful implementation to occur, though, administrators, teachers, related service staff, parents, and students must put their faith in full inclusion (Monahan, Marino, & Miller, 1996). Supportive partners in the learning enterprise recognize that when it comes to problem solving in special education, a curricular leadership team can accomplish more than any individual (e.g., O'Shea, 1999). If all learners in the inclusive classroom are to be reached, it is imperative that general and special educators collaborate for the greater good. Inclusion is not something that will go away 5 years from now, owing to the provisions of the IDEA and its 2005 reauthorization, in addition to the NCLB federal mandate. So that inclusion can work for all teachers and students, site-based curriculum leaders must be initiating. Inclusion does not involve a modest change in the school–community environment—it promotes the "buy in" of its stakeholders and a positive outlook. Full support of administration and other stakeholder groups can go a long way toward making it possible for general educators to help children with special needs thrive academically and socially.

PRACTICAL, REFLECTIVE ACTIVITIES

- Write a brief essay on your philosophy of education with regard to inclusion, the general education classroom, and students with disabilities. Uncover your own biases and feelings as you write, perhaps by remembering salient schooling experiences.
- List 5 to 10 specific ways in which administrative curricular leaders can assist general education teachers in accomplishing inclusion.
- Locate several informative Web sites and/or guidebooks and identify practical tools that general educators can use. Assemble your own toolkit of curricular ideas and strategies. You can record your findings in written form and even develop teaching materials.
- Collaborate with a colleague and experiment with the curricular activities you find most compelling. Keep a journal of your experiences and any breakthrough ideas. Report your results to an educational group.

7

Nurturing School Culture and Collaborative Curriculum as Campus Leader

Kayla English
James Osborn
Carol A. Mullen

ELEMENTARY SCHOOL AND ESE CENTER HISTORIES

The elementary school we studied in rural west central Florida prides itself in nurturing the confidence of students who intellectually challenge themselves. Traditionally a migrant family school, it has been subject to a high mobility rate. However, with the combined efforts of the school, government, and social organizations, in addition to employment stability, the mobility rate has decreased. Consequently, most students now remain for the entire year. The school implemented a mandatory uniform policy 3 years ago and continues to maintain an emphasis on technology infusion at the classroom level. Most of its classes have approximately 25 students, in keeping with the benefits received from Title I funding and other migrant funding sources.

This elementary school is unique in that an Exceptional Student Education (ESE) center serving trainable mentally handicapped (TMH) students (ages 3–22) shares its campus. Many of the students come from low socioeconomic backgrounds or group homes. The focus of the curriculum is community-based involvement, daily life skills training, functional academics, and vocational-skills training. This school's mission is to develop contributing members of society by facilitating students' ability to attain the highest level of skills and self-sufficiency.

Both schools are located on a single campus and share a principal, a media center, a multipurpose room, and student nutrition services. However, they operate on two different bell schedules with a separate elementary assistant principal and ESE site administrator. Title I funds are also used to provide support personnel at both sites, namely a social worker, school psychologist, and technology specialist.

ELEMENTARY AND ESE COLLABORATION:
PAST AND PRESENT

In the past, the administrators of these two schools endeavored to integrate their separate curriculums. Partnership development between ESE classrooms and general education classrooms was accomplished by implementing reading buddies, collaborative art projects, and shared classroom situations. The teacher of deaf and blind students worked collaboratively with elementary teachers for more than 15 years and developed numerous inclusion activities, such as a grant for art materials that allowed the entire third grade to work with ESE students bimonthly on tactile art projects. Other examples of integration included simulations for the regular elementary students to better appreciate the exceptionalities of the ESE center students (e.g., being blindfolded and wearing earplugs). While blindfolded, students moved around, getting a drink of water, hanging up their coats, and selecting different candies from a bowl. These activities took place without the knowledge or encouragement of the administration.

Throughout the last two administrations, the elementary principals were unaware that the ESE teacher and her students were participating in integrated activities with the elementary campus. During this time, the teacher's students, all first through fifth graders, were more age appropriate for inclusion in the elementary classrooms. Her leadership in the development of integrated curriculum activities allowed for many years of successful opportunities for students. Also at this time, the two schools operated on the same bell schedule, better facilitating teacher collaboration and curriculum integration.

Currently, however, the schools experience very little teacher collaboration. One notable exception involves a 3rd-grade class reading to an ESE primary class (ages 7–9 striving toward 1st-grade benchmarks). Also, two age-appropriate students from the deaf and blind class participate in selected activities (e.g., physical education, music, and classroom center time) with elementary students. The staff at these two campuses generally gather twice a year, once at preplanning and then again at the annual banquet. It is our desire to find effective ways to reshape the culture of these schools. A major goal involves finding productive ways to help strengthen professional relationships, which can benefit both the general education and exceptional education student populations.

Learning about human differences and similarities is one of the many benefits of integrated school curriculum (see chap. 7). In addition to awareness, students learn how to relate to and interact with students with severe disabilities. Regular education students who have interacted with disabled students are generally more positive and accepting, display less fear, and demonstrate more understanding of the person with disabilities (Stainback & Stainback, 1985). Some educators express concern that the integration of students with disabilities in the regular education classroom would have negative effects on grades and test scores. However, researchers have found that this problem does not occur, neither for academic nor behavioral achievement (e.g., Villa & Thousand, 2005). In fact, integration has allowed for achievement that is more satisfying for both the general education students and exceptional education students, in addition to enhancing self-esteem (Villa & Thousand, 2005). We noticed that the interaction among the regular elementary students and ESE students at this site was tightly structured and that it followed a weekly time schedule. This allowed the teachers to monitor student behavior and reorganize groups as needed to maximize learning opportunities for the learners involved.

Researchers such as Moore (1998) have found no significant differences for the exceptional education student (those served as TMH) in the integrated school environment; however, changes are apparent in his or her academics, behavior, and social interactions. Teachers at the site reported more socially appropriate behaviors from the ESE students after 7 weeks of interaction. However, academic changes were less noticeable, although the researchers believe the interactions had a positive impact on the ESE students' academic progress. Of course, it is expected that curriculum content and the quality of that content for students with disabilities integrated into general education environments will differ. Changes are evident in the level at which students with disabilities are engaged, the type of activities in which they are immersed, and their level of participation. Also, the social interactions initiated by a student with disabilities are more frequent and more appropriate when these learners are integrated into the general education classroom (Moore, 1998).

SCHOOL CULTURE DESCRIBED

As we began exploring this topic, it became evident that the school culture of these two sites was a key issue. Barth (2002) espouses that instructional leaders must become aware of a school's particular culture before initiating any changes. Culture is defined as "the underground stream of norms, values, beliefs, traditions, and rituals that have built up over time as people work together, solve problems, and confront challenges" (Peterson & Deal, 1998, p. 28; see also Lind, 2003; Mullen 2004a). School culture, although often overlooked, is one of the most important aspects of creating high-performing schools. Peterson and Deal (1998) clarify that "culture influences everything that goes on in schools: how staff dress, what they talk about, their willingness to change, the practice of instruction, and the emphasis given student and faculty learning" (p. 28).

Ponticell (2005) argues that you can change a culture by adding a new layer to its mores, but you cannot create an entirely new culture. One crucial step involves making the new values of the culture more desirable than the existing ones. Peterson and Deal (1998) suggest that school (curriculum) leaders reshape culture by first understanding the school's history and current culture. Leaders must also reveal and convey the core values of the culture, then identify the aspects that are healthy or toxic. As a final step, the positive elements of the culture must be reinforced. Curriculum leaders shape culture using approaches that range from what individuals communicate, recognize, and celebrate to institutional mission and shared focus. Specifically, proactive school leaders demonstrate facility by

> communicat[ing] core values in what they say and do. They honor and recognize those who have worked to serve the students and the purpose of the school. They observe rituals and traditions to support the school's heart and soul. They recognize heroes and heroines and the work these exemplars accomplish. They eloquently speak of the deeper mission of the school. They celebrate the accomplishments of the staff, the students and the community. They preserve the focus on students by recounting stories of success and achievement. (Peterson & Deal, 1998, p. 30)

The beliefs, norms, and assumptions that guide a school are at the heart of its culture (Bolman & Deal, 1997; Lind, 2003; Mullen, 2004a; Peterson & Deal, 1998). If we hope to lead in the integration of curriculum for exceptional education and regular education students, then we must be sensitive to the culture and norms of the school and to what may need changing.

ADMINISTRATOR INTERVIEW RESULTS

Within the school context we studied, the leader must model collaboration as a core value to foster teamwork in both school cultures. We first believed these schools to have two very different cultures; however, after interviewing the principal (see Table 7.1) of the elementary school and site administrator of the ESE center, we found these cultures, although separate and distinct, to

TABLE 7.1
Administrator School Culture Interview

Principal Demographics

Length of time spent at site _____
Total schools served in as an administrator _____
Grade level of schools served in as an administrator _____

General Questions

1. How would you describe your school's culture?
2. What do you perceive your role to be concerning the school's culture?
3. Why do you think teachers stay at your school?
4. Why do you think teachers leave your school?

Targeted Questions

1. In what ways do you demonstrate that you value your teachers' ideas?
2. How do you empower your teachers to make professional judgments?
3. What structures are in place at your school to encourage teachers to work collaboratively?
4. Does the flow of giving and receiving assistance occur naturally among your faculty?
5. To what do you attribute this occurrence, for the better or worse?
6. How strongly do you feel that the school's mission drives daily operations? Provide examples.
7. In your opinion, what drives the decisions and policies of your school?
8. What are some of the beliefs, norms, and assumptions that guide behavior at your site?
9. Do you ever use stories to motivate, humor, comfort, reassure, or even alarm faculty and staff? What might be the purpose or educational value associated with this use?
10. What processes are used in your building for addressing and resolving problems, and for making crucial decisions?
11. In what ways do you foster open and honest interaction among your staff?
12. How do you approach the unique relationship between the elementary school and the ESE Center on your campus? Is it celebrated? If so, how?

Note. From James Osborn and Kayla English. Adapted from Lind's (2003) School Culture Survey and the Effective Teams' (2005b) Team Health Check.

be fundamentally similar. Nonetheless, as is revealed in this chapter, numerous fine-grained distinctions are evident in these leaders' styles and approaches to shaping school culture.

Concerning their administrative profiles, the elementary principal, a 60-year old White female from a middle-class background, has been the leader of this school for 10 years and in administration for 20. Previously, this leader was at an elementary site serving a higher socioeconomic population. She is personable with her staff and willing to listen whenever a teacher needs to discuss problems. Daily school business is handled professionally, and she appears to be aware of her personal biases and to monitor these to the extent possible when making decisions that are in the best interest of the school. The site administrator has been at the ESE center for 6 years, since interning at this site as a college student. She is also a White female, in this case 46 years old, and an engaging, open, energetic, and fun-loving leader. She believes that the best of life lies ahead, and this positive attitude is reflected in her leadership style.

When describing the school culture, both administrators used a family metaphor, referring to an atmosphere that promotes staff collegiality and emphasizes the best interests of children. As leaders, they felt that by giving teachers the opportunity to make professional decisions and serving as "sounding boards," they empowered staff to take ownership in developing the school's culture. By taking an active part in school committees and orchestrating extracurricular programs (e.g., science club, fall festival, Spanish heritage, walk-a-thon), staff knowingly fostered the school's culture. Importantly, they shared the belief that all students can learn.

These leaders also valued celebrating successes, no matter how small. The use of stories was relayed as being indispensable in motivating and celebrating staff as well as students, in addition to serving as a vehicle for active listening and disclosure about motives. The principal commented, "Projecting the idea that I listen to all sides of the story is important. I'd rather hear the truth than have my faculty put up a facade." Likewise, the site administrator said, "I'm always available to my staff and feel compelled to offer the 'why' behind the decisions I make." When asked about problem-solving and decision making, both administrators underscored the importance of staff involvement and disseminating information to appropriate persons. Each touted the benefits of an "open-door policy." Being on different bell schedules was identified as the largest obstacle for shared activities between the two sites. When asked to describe a perfect world, both administrators spoke of more interaction, improved curriculum integration, and better personal relationships.

When describing their administrative roles in reshaping culture, however, the two site-based leaders revealed differences. The principal viewed her role as "a facilitator in developing the culture of our school and the direction of our curricular issues." However, the site administrator portrayed hers as more of a cheerleader for her staff: "I view myself in the parental role where I acknowledge attained curricular targets and best practices. I also serve as a buffer between my staff and the downtown offices."

Both administrators expressed value for the staff at their respective schools, wanting them to feel supported in their professional judgments. Their illustrations, however, differed: The principal described her leadership style as listening to her staff's ideas and then encouraging teachers to experiment with them. She provided needed resources (e.g., professional literature, educational learning tools, and other additional supplies) and worked with them to develop teacher teams: "If teachers have the supporting research, then they are free to go ahead with their plan and know that they will be supported."

Overall, the principal showed a greater inclination for focusing on teacher development in the area of designing individual class plans, contrasting with the site administrator, whose focus was at the systems level with respect to teacher values, characterizing this as a general staff support system. The site administrator also thought that allowing the faculty to plan the proceeding year's homerooms, student groups, and schedules promotes buy-in. Because the center is home to only 15 teachers, the site administrator saw her staff as coparticipants in deciding the direction of the ESE school, a collaborative strategy that benefitted its culture and, presumably, democratic governance.

When asked what drove their decisions and policies, these administrators had varying priorities. The principal explained that she first adhered to the district's policies, and then used team leaders to help make decisions where latitude was given within the district directives. The site administrator, however, cited student safety as the controlling factor in making decisions. Because of the special population of the center's children, the site administrator explained that creating policies governing the loading and unloading of the busses, teacher facilitation of classes, de-escalation of behavior issues, and student health issues (e.g., seizures) had to be addressed before the academic curriculum could function as planned. This leader summed up, "When the environment is safe, then curriculum just flows."

The elementary principal underscored the beliefs that all students can learn, that high expectations for student performance is essential, and that all students can become lifelong learners. On the other hand, the site administrator attributed the staff's attitude of "what you see is what you get"—the tendency to share what they feel is important without retribution—and the friendly atmosphere of the ESE center as its drivers. It appears that the elementary school concentrated more on academics, whereas the center was more behaviorally focused. These different foci are understandable—they can be attributed to the responsiveness of the curriculum leaders to the particular schooling context in which they worked, determined largely by the nature and needs of the children.

TEACHER SURVEY RESULTS

To further investigate the school culture of the elementary school and the ESE center, as well as to verify the claims of the administrators, we conducted a survey. We designed this instrument (see Table 7.2) and distributed it to teachers serving as 2005 summer school instructors at the school elementary and ESE center.

Teachers at the elementary site had been teaching an average of 21 years, 13 at this particular school. The ESE center's educators averaged 19 years of teaching experience, 15 at this location.

The results of this survey (see Table 7.3) suggest that these two facilities shared many of the same perceptions about their school cultures. Both teacher groups reinforced that their administrative leaders valued and acted on the ideas of staff. Examples given by the elementary teachers included study groups, team meetings, the elementary writing program, and support of new program implementation. The ESE center teachers gave one-on-one consultations in which colleagues coached, assisted, mentored, and encouraged one another. Teachers indicated that they were included in the decisions concerning student group placements, which in turn fostered awareness of individual student's curricular needs.

The teacher respondents at both sites also reported that the leadership trusted their professional judgment, citing, as examples, promotion and retention of students, report cards, and referrals. Only one staff member complained that although teachers' judgment was valued, the decisions made were sometimes contrary to teacher input. Another common characteristic of the two cultures entailed teachers working together cooperatively in groups in such contexts as study groups, grade-level teams, continuous progress houses, and biweekly meetings. One teacher commented that faculty were able to work cooperatively, and more efficiently and effectively, when the master schedule allowed for mutual planning time and classroom collaboration.

They agreed that the leadership provided them with assistance, as needed, in such areas as establishing support for mentors, peer teachers, substitutes, and paperwork and planning. However, two individuals felt that it was the same teachers repeatedly offering the help and that another was only willing to offer support if her instruction were not interrupted. In general, the teachers noted that colleagues who wanted to learn and develop were open to assistance and that the help being extended to them by their leaders was offered in a positive, not punitive, manner.

The importance of the mission of these schools was evident in the awareness of the vision that existed among staff, as well as the schools' values as

TABLE 7.2
School Culture Survey of Teachers' Perceptions

Background Questions:
How many years have you taught at this school? _____
How many years have you taught in your career? _____

Instructions:
A. Please complete the following statements:
I like working at this school because _____.
I'd like working at this school better if _____.

B. Circle the number on the Likert scale that accurately describes or reflects your school. Any statement that you're uncertain of or have not directly experienced should be marked with a No Response "NR." If you have examples to support your answer, please list them directly underneath each statement.

1. School leaders value teachers' ideas.

5	4	3	2	1	X
Strongly Agree	Agree	Somewhat agree	Disagree	Strongly disagree	NR

Examples:_____

2. Teachers are encouraged to dialogue and plan for collaboration between the elementary school and the ESE center.

5	4	3	2	1	X
Strongly Agree	Agree	Somewhat agree	Disagree	Strongly disagree	NR

Examples:_____

3. School leaders trust the professional judgments of teachers.

5	4	3	2	1	X
Strongly Agree	Agree	Somewhat agree	Disagree	Strongly disagree	NR

Examples:_____

4. School leaders facilitate teachers working together.

5	4	3	2	1	X
Strongly Agree	Agree	Somewhat agree	Disagree	Strongly disagree	NR

Examples:_____

5. Teachers work cooperatively in groups.

5	4	3	2	1	X
Strongly Agree	Agree	Somewhat agree	Disagree	Strongly disagree	NR

Examples:_____

6. Teachers are open to offering assistance whenever needed.

5	4	3	2	1	X
Strongly Agree	Agree	Somewhat agree	Disagree	Strongly disagree	NR

Examples:_____

(Continued)

TABLE 7.2
(Continued)

7. Teachers are open to accepting assistance when offered.

5	4	3	2	1	X
Strongly Agree	Agree	Somewhat agree	Disagree	Strongly disagree	NR

Examples:_____

8. Teachers are aware of the importance of the school's mission.

5	4	3	2	1	X
Strongly Agree	Agree	Somewhat agree	Disagree	Strongly disagree	NR

Examples:_____

9. Our school's values are reflected in the decisions and policies of the school.

5	4	3	2	1	X
Strongly Agree	Agree	Somewhat agree	Disagree	Strongly disagree	NR

Examples:_____

10. Unwritten expectations exist for the staff at my school.

5	4	3	2	1	X
Strongly Agree	Agree	Somewhat agree	Disagree	Strongly disagree	NR

Examples:_____

11. The interesting occurrences of our school are made into stories that have the power to motivate, humor, comfort, reassure, alarm, hurt, or disappoint our faculty and staff.

5	4	3	2	1	X
Strongly Agree	Agree	Somewhat agree	Disagree	Strongly disagree	NR

Examples:_____

12. The school leader's actions are exemplary of our school's mission and purpose.

5	4	3	2	1	X
Strongly Agree	Agree	Somewhat agree	Disagree	Strongly disagree	NR

Examples:_____

13. Teachers understand what their roles are and where these overlap with other teachers.

5	4	3	2	1	X
Strongly Agree	Agree	Somewhat agree	Disagree	Strongly disagree	NR

Examples:_____

14. Our school has an efficient process to solve problems and make decisions.

5	4	3	2	1	X
Strongly Agree	Agree	Somewhat agree	Disagree	Strongly disagree	NR

Examples:_____

(Continued)

TABLE 7.2
(Continued)

---

15. Teachers and staff feel their ideas and input are listened to by the rest of the faculty.

5	4	3	2	1	X
Strongly Agree	Agree	Somewhat agree	Disagree	Strongly disagree	NR

Examples:_____

16. Differences and conflicts are resolved openly and constructively.

5	4	3	2	1	X
Strongly Agree	Agree	Somewhat agree	Disagree	Strongly disagree	NR

Examples:_____

17. Interactions between staff are open and honest.

5	4	3	2	1	X
Strongly Agree	Agree	Somewhat agree	Disagree	Strongly disagree	NR

Examples:_____

Note. From James Osborn and Kayla English. Adapted from Lind's (2003) School Culture Survey and the Effective Teams' (2005b) Team Health Check.

reflected in the decisions and policies. However, although both teacher groups agreed that unwritten expectations existed for staff, concrete examples were not provided, a potentially unresolved issue.

When addressing the use of (or by-product of) anecdotes for motivating, comforting, and reassuring, or even alarming, hurting or disappointing, the faculty all seemed to think that their leaders' storytelling always met positive ends. It came to our attention during the distribution of the survey that the question involving the use of stories was unclear to many, leading to a high percent of faculty choosing "no response" (NR). Individuals completed the survey without verbal directions, and many teachers questioned this item after returning their survey. Those that responded with NR understood the statement to mean that the stories their administrators shared encompassed all attributes expressed earlier (e.g., motivate, humor, reassure, or alarm). Because the question was unclear, no one chose to describe the way his or her administration utilized anecdotes when developing school culture.

Importantly, all of the teacher respondents reported that their school leader's actions were consistent with the mission and purpose of the school. As summed up by the ESE faculty, "Both leaders work hard to help our school to fulfill our mission statement and reach our goals." Reflecting on why the ESE faculty referred to both leaders, we realized that they had a more advantageous position to view the principal and site administrator's commitment

TABLE 7.3
Elementary School and ESE Center Survey Results

	Strongly Agree	Agree	Somewhat Agree	Disagree	Strongly Disagree	No Response
1. School leaders value teachers' ideas and input.	42% 33%	58% 42%	25%			
2. Teachers are encouraged to collaborate by dialoguing and planning between the two sites.		33% 25%	42% 8%	25% 17%	25%	25%
3. School leaders trust teachers' professional judgments.	33% 17%	42% 50%	25% 33%			
4. School leaders facilitate teachers working together.	42% 42%	58% 42%	8%	8%		
5. Teachers work cooperatively in groups.	55% 17%	36% 66%	9% 17%			
6. Teachers are open to offering assistance whenever needed.	55% 58%	27% 17%	18% 25%			
7. Teachers are open to accepting assistance when offered.	36% 33%	45% 50%	18% 17%			
8. Teachers are aware of the importance of the school's mission.	36% 17%	55% 50%	9% 25%			8%
9. Our school's values are reflected in the decisions and policies of the school.	27% 33%	64% 42%	9% 17%			8%
10. Unwritten expectations exist for staff at my site.	18% 25%	64% 58%	9% 17%		9%	
11. School events turn into stories with the power to motivate, humor, comfort, reassure, or alarm staff.	9% 33%	45% 25%	9% 25%			36% 17%

TABLE 7.3
(Continued)

	Strongly Agree	Agree	Somewhat Agree	Disagree	Strongly Disagree	No Response
12. The leader's actions are exemplary of our school's mission and purpose.	*36%* 42%	*55%* 25%	*9%* 8%			25%
13. Teachers understand what their roles are and where these overlap with their colleagues.	*25%* 8%	*75%* 58%	16%	8%		
14. Our school has an efficient process for decision-making and for resolving problems.	*17%*	*42%* 42%	*25%* 17%	*8%* 17%	8%	*8%* 8%
15. Staff feel that faculty listen to their ideas and input.	*17%* 8%	*35%* 16%	33%	*8%*	8%	
16. Conflicts at the school are resolved openly as well as constructively.	*17%*	*50%* 17%	*17%* 25%	33%	*8%* 8%	*8%* 8%
17. Interactions between and among staff are open and honest.	*25%*	*33%* 17%	*33%* 17%	50%		*8%* 8%

Note. Legend: Elementary School (***italicized/bold*** font); ESE Center (regular font).
From James Osborn and Kayla English. Adapted from Lind's (2003) School Culture
Survey and the Effective Teams' (2005b) Team Health Check.

to the vision and mission. In contrast, the majority of regular education
teachers was found to be unaware of the efficacy of the site administrator's
leadership due to the uniqueness of the shared campus experience.

Regarding other findings, it became clear that varying perceptions existed of these schools' cultures with respect to problem solving and decision making. Overall, the elementary teachers seemed to have a greater sense of their roles and where these overlapped with fellow teachers' than did the ESE teachers. The elementary staff concurred that the school had an efficient process for solving problems and making decisions, while the ESE center did not have solid agreement. Based on the interviews with the two administrators, this outcome proved contrary to our expectation. The ESE center site administrator indicated that she took problems directly to the staff and allowed them to construct solutions, a process that sounds effective, if not democratic. However, the results indicate that staff held an opposing view.

The elementary faculty were united in the faculty governance they experienced. On the question of teachers' ideas being heard by the rest of the faculty and school principal, they felt supported, indicating that they were free to agree or disagree at staff meetings. Most of the ESE teachers also felt their suggestions were well received by other staff and the site administrator.

Concerning the open and constructive resolution of differences and conflicts, the majority of the elementary faculty was in agreement with this assessment. The one elementary respondent that strongly disagreed indicated that many decisions were made privately, with other staff members questioning the resolution. The ESE center staff indicated a breakdown in consensus, with over one third of the respondents specifying the existence of interpersonal problems between teachers and staff. When reflecting on staff interactions, the majority of elementary staff portrayed these as open and honest, while the ESE center indicated 50% agreement. Two elementary respondents suggested that although interactions were open and honest, they were not necessarily constructive and tactful. Another ESE faculty member characterized the interactions among the staff at the ESE center as open and honest only at times. Another offered staff gossip as a reason for believing that interactions at this particular site were not positive and healthy.

Faculty at both sites agreed that their leaders attempted to facilitate teachers working together. But when asked about being encouraged to dialogue and plan for collaboration between the two facilities, many responded that these operated as separate schools, with only a few teachers making the effort to work with others across the campus. The general spirit was that more should be done to encourage a stronger connection between the two sites.

SUPPORT LESSONS ON TEAMWORK

According to Barth (2002), collegiality in the form of collaborative team building is one of the healthy cultural norms necessary for reshaping an unhealthy school culture. Educational leaders who possess group- and systems-learning skills will be in a position to demonstrate collaboration, described as the "development of high-performing work teams and learning communities" (Mullen, 2004a, p. 152). Based on our survey results, we feel that a focus on strengthening the collegiality between staff at different but shared campuses would foster collaboration within and across sites.

Metaphorically speaking, teachers and administrators alike can learn invaluable leadership lessons from observing how geese fly, by creating a sense of community, staying in formation, practicing turn-taking, experiencing empowerment, and supporting colleagues in difficult times ("Effective teams," 2005a):

Community.	As each goose flaps its wings, an "uplift" is created for the birds that follow behind. Flying in a V formation, the whole flock adds 71% greater flying range than if the birds flew alone. Lesson: People who share a common direction and sense of community can reach their destination more quickly and easily because they are traveling on the thrust of one another.
Formation.	When a goose falls out of formation, it suddenly feels the drag and resistance of flying alone. It quickly moves back into formation to take advantage of the lifting power of the bird immediately in front of it. Lesson: If we have as much sense as a goose, we stay in formation with those headed where we want to go. We are willing to accept their help and extend ours to others.
Turn-Taking.	When the lead goose tires, it rotates back into the formation, and another goose flies to the point position. Lesson: It pays to take turns doing the hard tasks and sharing leadership. As with geese, people are interdependent on one another's skills, capabilities, and unique gifts, talents, and resources.
Empowerment.	The geese flying in formation honk to encourage those up front to keep their speed. Lesson: We need to make sure we honk. In groups where there is encouragement, the production is much greater.
Support.	When a goose gets sick or wounded, two geese immediately drop out of formation and protect it. They stick by until it dies or is ready to fly again, launching out with another formation or catching up with the flock. Lesson: We must stand by one another in difficult times, as well as when we are strong.

TEAM-BUILDING COMPONENTS

Basics of Team Building

Curriculum leaders are being called on to create an environment that fosters team building and collaboration as "second nature." Heathfield (2005) proposes that "in a teamwork environment, people understand and believe that thinking, planning, decisions, and actions are better when done cooperatively" (p. 2). As a core value, expected and demonstrated by the organization, teamwork cannot be limited to an activity performed at an annual retreat—it must be practiced daily. In order to create a team-oriented culture, leaders must "form teams to solve real work issues and to improve real work processes" (Heathfield, 2005, p. 3). They should also "provide training in systematic methods so the team expends its energy on the project not on figuring out how to work together to approach it" (Heathfield, 2005, p. 3). Three domains—fun, movement, and risk—lay the foundation for successful team building (Mullen & Graves, 2000). As Heck (2005) further describes,

> A great team-building activity is fun. … It engages the imagination. Every great experiential team-building activity/program I've ever seen gets people moving, up and out of their seat, interacting with the space around them in a new or different way. There must be a degree of risk or challenge involved in the activity. This could mean falling backward into the arms of the group, or it could mean sharing a thought or feeling. … You want to set things up so people have opportunities to step outside their "comfort zones." A skillful leader is able to create a supportive and nurturing environment that encourages risk taking. (pp. 4–6)

Another essential element in team building involves "hold[ing] department meetings to review projects and progress, to obtain broad input, and to coordinate shared work processes" (Heathfield, 2005, p. 3). Interpersonal problems are not always the product of people's personalities, as uncertainty about the steps required in achieving a particular goal breeds discomfort. Heathfield (2005) also recommends "building fun and shared occasions into the organization's agenda" (p. 3) through such means as holding pot-lucks, treating staff to sporting and other events, sponsoring dinners, and going hiking or to amusement parks. Icebreakers, team-building exercises at meetings, and voluntary activities are additional ideas. Another involves the often forgotten ritual of publicly celebrating group successes.

Strategies for Team Building

A team-building activity that we think could benefit faculty rapport between the elementary school and the ESE center is "diversity tangrams" (Anderson, Cavert, Cain, & Heck, 2005). For this, faculty teams of four to six are provided with a tangram puzzle: "Tangrams have seven pieces that include five triangles (two small, one medium, and two large), a square, and a parallelogram. The pieces can be combined to form many different figures" (Thornton & Lowe-Parrino, n.d., p. 41). Each team creates various shapes and then learns about the creations of other groups. A meaningful discussion can ensue based on these (or other) questions:

- What shapes or patterns do we all have in common?
- What shapes or patterns can each group uniquely make?
- Is it important that all groups are the same? (Anderson et al., 2005, p. 39)

Each of the four puzzle variations has seven pieces in common. How they are assembled and the form they ultimately take differs depending on the arrangement of the pieces (e.g., a roman numeral I, a rocket, and an arrow). Facilitators can guide groups to understand the parallelism implied—that is, that some "pieces" of different organizational units or schools will be similar, others dissimilar. However, in the end, what matters is that all of the pieces fit together to create a "shape," as in a shared vision or common goals. This activity allows units or schools to engage in creative and kinesthetic problem solving, exploring such issues as diversity, cultural sensitivity, inclusion, good choices, and clear communication (Anderson et al., 2005). As with tangrams, the two schools we studied share many cultural aspects, but when their "pieces" are put together, they appear different.

FINAL THOUGHTS

The tangram activity, like the geese illustration, is about learning to move as a single unit while team members create shapes and patterns that are unique to who they are. The metaphor of the geese, when applied to our survey results, suggests that two strong, independent flocks exist in an otherwise shared space. Singular V formations committed to curricular collaboration can go a long way toward improving the culture of schools. Leaders must model and expect staff collaboration if it is to be upheld as a core value and appreciated as an integral part of one's culture. Teamwork and team building naturally follow as activities to be incorporated into daily routines, giving support to a school's diversity and its cultural, as well as procedural, norms.

The certainty of knowing that one's colleagues are available in times of need allows for positive synergy to develop, leading to creative problem solving and exploration of new strategies. Leadership within and across the school sites should be shared, interdependent, and collaborative, not top-down, autocratic, or distant. Moreover, encouragement and celebration of successes are necessary components for fostering effective, self-perpetuating team building among faculty. The training of teams on methods for enabling collaboration to work smoothly facilitates the ability of individuals to focus on an issue or task rather than on learning how to work together.

In the unique situation involving the two sites, each school operates on a separate bell schedule that, although clearly a hindrance to their collaboration, does not have to be an obstacle. Within each of these sites, a feeling of family and home permeates the culture; however, we learned that modifications are nonetheless required if this emotional base is to be nurtured between the campuses. Collaboration and inclusion must be the expected norm. Programs that are already in place, although few, should be publicly celebrated along with people who endeavor to collaborate on curriculum and create an inclusive environment. If these two strategies are established as core values, the school's schedules will reflect and facilitate their reality, and if well planned and supported in their developments, sites like this could serve as models for collaborative initiation on shared campuses and those potentially joined.

PRACTICAL, REFLECTIVE ACTIVITIES

- Develop a portrait of a school or administrator's effectiveness in building school culture. Conduct action research by adapting the interview and survey protocols provided here (with the proper acknowledgment). Or, use other sources to generate perceptions, such as existing school climate surveys and documented communication with parents and community members. Share the results with curricular leaders to support organizational improvement.
- "Try some of the classic trust-building activities for groups, such as blindfolding in pairs and rope entanglement, or try more adventuresome team-building activities, such as wilderness trekking, mountaineering, or rock climbing" (Mullen, 2004a, p. 158).
- "Collect your favorite quotes about team building or another topic and share them with your school. Use the sources of inspiration as an icebreaker at beginning-of-the-year events and school and faculty meetings. Build the quotes into your revised mission statement" (Mullen, 2004a, p. 158).
- "Do a self-assessment inventory exercise, either with administrative staff, and discuss the results. Arrive at a shared understanding of one another's strengths and areas of responsibility, and develop teams that support these deeper, more explicit processes" (Mullen, 2004a, p. 158; chap. 7 of the 2004 book provides examples of inventory surveys).

8

Countering Interruptions of Teaching With Curricular Leadership

Janice L. Hutinger
Carol A. Mullen

The following story was compiled from actual events that Janice Hutinger, an upper elementary teacher, experienced in her classroom one day in the spring of 2004.

Just as I begin introducing the day's schedule to my class, the phone rings. Gesturing for the students to remain quiet, I work my way through a sea of desks to my telephone. The secretary wants to know if I will talk to a frantic parent. Assuming it must be urgent, I agree and thank the students for their patience while the call is transferred. Explaining he has again forgotten to give his son—my student—his medicine for attention problems, Elliot's father expresses concern that the day may not go well for him.

After discussing several options, I hang up and return to the front of the room. Although quiet, the students have begun drawing or working on assignments. A familiar ripping sound alerts me that Elliot has begun tearing the corners of his paper, a behavior he displays when fretful that he will be without his medicine. Glancing at the clock and sensing the pending anxiety I often feel from my class and myself this year, I find I am now 7 minutes behind schedule—phonics instruction should have already gotten underway. Before I have time to resume speaking, Elliot falls and hits his head on the desk behind him, causing his chair to scrape Mary.

While attending to both students and hushing the now amused audience, the phone rings again. This time, the occupational therapist would like to reschedule Sandi's therapy and, due to the restrictions on her time at this site, she would like to see Sandi immediately. Considering this student's urgent need for occupational therapy, I agree to the schedule change. Returning to Elliot and Mary, I decide to send them to the clinic to have their injuries addressed. With three students now missing my introduction, a segment designed to share important information, I reluctantly continue, knowing I will need to inform the others on their return.

Now almost 15 minutes behind, I quickly readjust the schedule: They will skip the daily phonics review and phonemic practice and go directly to small-group reading. Finally gaining their full attention, I begin my daily introduction. The students, disappointed with the cancellation of a musical activity, are promised it for the next day. Once back on track with reading groups, my students have finally settled into their familiar routine. Once again, the phone rings.

CRITIQUING INTERRUPTIONS AND DISTRACTIONS

I (Janice) developed interest in actively investigating interruptions and distractions soon after having transferred in 2003 to a different elementary school. Located in west-central Florida, my new school served a primarily middle-class population, with 20% of students receiving free or reduced lunch. The school had consistently received an "A" rating according to Florida's school-grading system, and it met all standards for yearly progress according to the NCLB Act of 2001 (NCLB; U.S. Department of Education, 2002). Like many teachers, I enjoyed the stable, close-knit environment supported by the long-term administration, but one cautionary flag was evident as I began my new assignment—my classroom was connected to a center pod, that is, four or more classrooms linked to a larger common room containing sinks and bathrooms.

During my 20 years as a classroom teacher, only 4 of my classrooms had been connected to other classrooms or pods, and I found that interruptions and distractions from the proximity to neighboring classes frequently hindered students' concentration and academic progress. The learning environment of the classroom had proven so crucial to the academic and social gains of my students that I had even decided at the previous site to remain in a portable rather than return to a pod configuration. It is not surprising, then, that I feared that my new assignment would present significant challenges for combating interruptions.

My class was part of a team called the Explorers that contained 3rd- to 5th-grade students. A neighboring team, the All-Stars, occupied by the same grades, shared the pod. Between the two teams, there were 11 teachers, 3 paraprofessionals, and approximately 250 students. Five classrooms connected directly to the pod, and the remaining ones were portables. Classes routinely used the pod for personal needs, small-group instruction, whole-team assemblies, and routes for entering and exiting their rooms.

During the second week of school, I was surprised by the frequency of interruptions that occurred during instructional time. In addition to a continual stream of distractions from the pod, one afternoon I received not fewer than five phone calls from school personnel, halted a lesson to discipline unattended students in the pod, assisted a teacher with computer difficulties, and abandoned a second lesson due to an unexpected fire drill. I knew that if the frequency of interruptions was interfering with my day, causing mounting frustration, other teachers and their classes must be similarly affected.

IMPACT ON STUDENT LEARNING

Researchers from many fields have analyzed the effects of interruptions on task completion. Business leaders, for example, have relied on research to investigate how interruptions affect worker production in offices and factories (Speier, Valacich, & Vessey, 1997). Bailey, Konstan, and Carlis (2000), using reading comprehension and data analysis tasks, found that subjects took between 5% and 40% longer to complete tasks when interrupted compared with a noninterrupted task, suggesting that it is financially beneficial to minimize interruptions and hence workers' anxiety levels.

When interruptions or distractions occur in classrooms, students automatically shift their attention to the interfering factor (e.g., outside noise, students talking), often not remembering what the teacher or peers have been saying (Bruning, Schraw, Norby, & Ronning, 2004). Bailey and colleagues (2000) found that individuals who were engaged in a first task and interrupted to perform a second perceived the original task as more difficult. Even during independent seat-work, interruptions and distractions have consequences: Like other workers, students have to redirect their attention and backtrack through previous thought processes to regain organization and move on to the next step (Altmann & Trafton, 2004). For students and teachers alike, the continual effect of interruptions not only reduces adequate time for tasks but also produces anxiety and frustration (Kovalik, 1994).

A distracting environment may compel students to rush to complete tasks and guess answers before logically thinking through a problem, and a decreased level of comprehension leads to lower achievement (Gettinger, 1989; Kovalik, 1994). If educators want to improve learning, they must be conscious of the influence interruptions and distraction can have on students' ability to process information and consequently provide an environment that allows student attention to be channeled only toward learning (Bruning et al., 2004)

CURRICULUM LEADER INITIATIVE-TAKING

During the third week of school, I noticed that my class was leaving for lunch by way of the pod at the same time a newly scheduled intensive remediation reading group was being held there. Although my class was quiet and orderly, 25 students filing past a distractible group of 8-year-olds could only be considered disruptive. Although not a direct path, I vowed to use the outside door when leaving for lunch, a minor sacrifice that helped reduce the distraction that my own class caused.

My awareness now heightened, I observed unattended students, teachers on break, or groups of volunteers engaged in animated conversation close to my classroom door. Classes lined up for drinks and bathrooms after lunch or recess seemed indifferent to the need for silence.

Taking the risk of sharing my observations with the six teachers on my team, I was surprised at their reactions: indifference to the concerns raised, hesitation about confronting an unpopular topic, and perhaps defensiveness to the perceived implication they had not been appropriately conducting their classes. One teacher responded that the situation I was describing was merely the typical behavior allowed in pods and that if it got too noisy I could simply shut my door. Another teacher felt that children should not always have to be quiet; however, she did concede that if a problem existed, the teacher or paraprofessional teaching the lesson was responsible for asking noisy students to settle down. A third commented that her class had a right to use the pod just as much as any other, implying that her students should be able to make noise freely. Joan, a teacher with 28 years experience, but new to the team, did not comment.

Through this team discussion, I learned more about cultural norms in schools, which act as a strong driving force: The teachers had resisted any alterations in their individual and team's behavioral pattern. First, the veteran teachers, original Explorers team members, did not want to change their students' pattern of pod use. They felt the school's "A" grade from the state, combined with meeting Adequate Yearly Progress (AYP) and strong approval from parent surveys, was proof that the students were thriving academically, even with frequent interruptions. Second, all six teachers believed they managed their classes effectively, and so the issue was pointless. Third, they did not feel responsible for "policing" the noise level of the pod (shared by the Explorers and All-Stars teams), a comment I found troubling, as participants in the intensive reading groups were often their own students. The new teachers to the team, Joan and I, were expected to quietly adjust to the culture's unwritten codes that the veteran teachers had largely established.

Deciding on Strategic Plans

During the following weeks in 2004, although no initiative had been taken to decrease classroom interruptions, the teachers on the Explorers team began sharing their own experiences and frustrations. It was obvious that my initial set of queries, although first met with resistance, had stimulated the teachers to reflect on their own situations and beliefs, leading to their willingness to openly discuss them. I noticed that my teammates did not share my perception of an interruption or distraction, but I was interested in learning more about their thoughts so discussions could be productive, solution-seeking experiences rather than complaint sessions. As researcher, my focus was threefold: (1) to allow teachers the opportunity to evaluate their own viewpoints concerning interruptions and distractions; (2) to explore the impact of teachers' decisions on the learning environment of all students, especially those in the pod; and (3) to identify possible strategies for confronting daily interruptions and distractions.

Undertaking the Investigation

In an effort to encourage the needed school-wide changes I felt were critical to the learning environment, I decided to focus on what types of interruptions and distractions affect teachers and students during the instructional time of their day. I collected site-based data via an anonymous teacher survey that we (Hutinger and Mullen) codesigned (see Tables 8.1 and 8.2),

TEACHER SURVEY: FACTORS THAT INTERFERE WITH INSTRUCTION

Each of the six teacher participants from the Explorers team was given a cover letter and survey that contained 15 daily documentation sheets. The teachers were asked to fill out one documentation sheet each school day for 15

TABLE 8.1

Letter Accompanying Teacher Survey "Factors That Interfere With Instruction"

Instructions for Teacher Participants

Please respond to these two questions:

1. What factors interfere with a teacher's ability to complete planned lessons?
2. What specific academic activities are partially taught, postponed, or altogether abandoned due to interfering factors?

Next, please complete the following chart with respect to your daily lesson plans. The researchers assume that you have a predetermined plan for the reported day as well as expected outcomes for each lesson.

A crucial component of this survey is the activity or anticipated instruction that was affected. Be very specific when describing your instructional example. (E.g., "reading group" would be too vague. A more specific example would be "phonemic instruction in rhyme.")

---

days during a 3-week period. This time span was chosen to allow data concerning interruptions to be accumulated over time and to help prevent any diminishing of the teachers' commitment to complete all the documentation sheets during the collection period.

Through our analysis, we hoped that the survey data would reveal the nature of interruptions that occurred in the classrooms, as well as identify interruptions or distractions that happened regularly. The teachers at this school or any other could then use the results to develop a plan to eliminate or reduce the effects of interruptions on classroom instruction.

In letter format, participants were asked these two questions:

1. What factors do you think interfere with a teacher's ability to complete planned lessons?
2. What specific academic activities are partially taught, postponed, or even abandoned due to factors that interfere with instruction?

The introductory letter also read, "Please complete the chart based on your daily lesson plans. It is assumed that you have a predetermined plan for the reported day, as well as expected outcomes for each lesson." It was also noted that "a crucial component of this survey is the activity or anticipated instruction that was affected." Participants were asked to be "very specific when describing the material." The example of "reading group" was too vague, we

TABLE 8.2
Factors That Interrupt Teacher Instruction

Interrupting Factors	Teacher Response (Total)
Factors Related to School Management	
Telephone calls	5
Intercom messages	6
Fire drill	6
Inclimate weather	2
Hurricane preparation	6
Student Council Elections	1
Watching an addition class	2
Administrative meeting	2
Factors Specfic to Technical Needs	
Printer not working	2
Copy machine dysfunction	3
Technology specialist fixing Equipment	1
Workers fixing sliding panels	2
Factors Related to Student Needs	
Bathroom/drinks	2
Student(s) leaving class	6
Student(s) arriving late	2
Sick or injured student	2
Arrival of new student	4
Student's violent behavior	4
Student's disruptive behavior	2
Contacting parent	2
Accommodations for visually impaired student	1
Factors Specific to Personnel	
Volunteers	5
College intern	3
Classroom teacher	6
Reading specialist	2
Behavior specialist	1
English Speakers of Other Languages (ESOL) teacher	1
Factors Related to Teacher Responsibilities	
Diagnostic assessments	4
Entering names in computer	1
Complete paperwork	6
Individualized testing of students	3
Completing progress reports	2
Extended conference	2

TABLE 8.2
(Continued)

Interrupting Factors	Teacher Response (Total)
Factors Specific to Pod Classrooms (four teachers)	
Students passing through	4
Students using bathroom	4
Teachers talking	4
Parent/teacher conference	4
Other classrooms	4
Parent with toddler	4
Student with volatile behavior	4
Factors Related to Portable Classrooms (two teachers)	
Lengthy bathroom breaks	2
Extreme weather conditions evacuation	2
Students playing outside	2
Workers	1
Work vehicle entering and exiting	1

Note. From Janice Hutinger and Carol Mullen.

indicated; better examples of specific instruction (e.g., "phonemic instruction in rhyme") were thus sought.

Survey Results

Of the 90 documentation sheets distributed, 56 were returned by 6 teachers, 36 in written form; 20 were handled orally, with teachers providing verbal statements that I recorded. (Twelve surveys were not returned due to the unexpected cancellation of school.) The teacher participants provided 45 interrupting factors (see Table 8.2), and we grouped the responses into categories designating the origin of the interrupting factor or location of the teacher's classroom. Examples of factors relating to school management included telephone calls, intercom messages, fire drills, and watching an additional class. Technical needs included "printer not working," "technology specialist fixing equipment," and "workers fixing sliding panels." Factors involving student needs were "late arriving or early release students," "disruptive student behavior," and "phoning parents." Teacher duties included "diagnostic assessments," "completing paperwork," "individual student testing," and "extended conference."

Responses to planned activity included a variety of examples from the academic areas. Teachers completing the instrument in the 1st week of the survey period recorded specific activities, such as "teaching story elements," "writing a paragraph," "teaching decimals," and "examples of chemical changes." During the 2nd and 3rd weeks, teachers rarely included specifics and simply referred to the activity as reading, writing, math, or science.

The specific material/activity gave the teachers an opportunity to explain what they had not been able to accomplish due to a particular interruption. Some entries were specific to the subject affected. Examples included "students were not given measuring instruction," "did not finish vocabulary introduction," and "did not give our practice sheet for story elements." Other entries were stated in more general terms such as "less time to read," "behind in all subject areas," and "gave alternative worksheet."

The last column prompted the teachers to approximate the number of minutes lost due to the interruption or distraction. Individual interruption entries cited by teachers ranged from 3 to 60 minutes. For example, one entry listed 3 minutes lost due to a phone call, 10 minutes because of a screaming student, and 30 minutes due to unscheduled student evaluations. The total number of minutes cited by teachers for one day ranged from 3 to 105. Fifteen of the surveys did not record any minutes.

Interruptions Differ With Classroom Location

As data from the surveys were analyzed, it became apparent that the actual location of a teacher's classroom impacted the results. Three of the teachers had classrooms connected to the pod, two were in portable classrooms, and one held her classes in a corner of the pod, partitioned by 4-foot bookshelves. The five teachers in classrooms connected to the pod or in portables identified telephone calls as the most frequent interruption. The teacher in the pod without access to a phone did not list this item as interruptive, which reinforces this observation. Another major distinction was the difference between the classrooms connected to the pod and those in portables. Only the two teachers in the portables listed bathroom/drinks as an interruption, and neither specified noise from the pod, which was noted by the other four.

Student Evaluations as Interruptions

Four out of six teachers indicated that student testing was a major interruption to their instruction. The reference was to district-mandated assessments that require each student to be individually evaluated in five areas of reading. Testing for each student took from 30 to 40 minutes. Teachers listed reading, math, and writing as subjects not taught due to the standardized testing and assessment.

TEACHER INTERVIEWS: IMPACT OF
INTERRUPTIONS ON INSTRUCTION

Impact on Instructional Time

During the personal interviews, teachers were asked "How do interruptions during instructional time impact you and your students?" This open-ended question was designed to allow the teachers latitude in expressing their thoughts and feelings. Interviews were conducted individually in a private room and were documented with note-taking.

Teachers felt that the chief obstacle pertaining to the delivery of the long-range, scheduled instruction was the increase in the number of reading evaluations for students. The district had required additional individual assessment during the 1st month that limited time for instruction, and on a daily basis. All interviewees reported that the extra assessments took valuable time away from teaching, which may have amplified the negative reaction they had to anything perceived as interrupting the already compressed instructional timeframe. These teachers were not only concerned with daily instruction but also how the cumulative loss of time would put them behind on scheduled theme rotations and completing the required math and science curriculum.

Audrey, a 3rd-grade teacher with 10 years of experience, was especially sensitive to any added interruptions. Many of her students required special services, and she frequently received telephone calls requesting that she give additional information to colleagues or establish evaluation or observation schedules with specialists or administration. Exasperated, she shared,

> One of my biggest distractions is that when I get called during class, I'm expected to stop everything I'm doing and immediately handle other people's needs. If the office calls asking for documentation or for a paper I have on a child, I need to stop, find it, and send it to them right then and there. All these things add up to lost time—wasted time.

Paperwork as Interruptions

All the teachers characterized paperwork as an interruption. My initial thought on reading the survey data was that they had misunderstood my written directions. Examples of their responses were "writing individual education plans (IEP)," "finishing progress reports," "typing up student observations," "filling out paperwork for office," and "writing lesson plans." I was seeking traditional examples of an interruption (i.e., phone call, loud children) but not paperwork, which I assumed was a routine teacher responsibility. As

I asked more questions, I found they were adamant that paperwork was a major interruption. In fact, any other interruptions or distractions paled in comparison. These teachers were literally using hours of instructional time on a weekly basis to do paperwork. Joan, a 4th-grade teacher with 28 years experience, felt she was justified in finishing any paperwork during her instructional periods if it could not be completed during her planning period. Audrey stated that she did not get paid to spend time after school filling out required forms for students, so the administration would have to understand if she used worksheets or films to keep students busy while she completed paperwork. These two teachers were not willing to entertain the alternative—attending to the paperwork on their own time.

Donna, a resource reading teacher who held small-group lessons in the pod, was required to keep detailed records on all the students. A new district requirement meant she had to track students' reading skills (e.g., phonemic awareness, fluency, comprehension) daily instead of weekly. She was assigned to teach specific reading skills to 30 students a day, feeling as though her entire lesson was interrupted by constant note-taking:

> Paperwork is probably the biggest thing that distracts me every day. With each interruption, I'm stopped and lose one more kid each time. The kids have to be constantly engaged or they're gone [loss of interest and attention]. At the end of the day I will feel as though they're all gone and that I'm losing it too.

Bev, a 5th-grade teacher with 20 years experience, indicated that phone calls, repairing broken equipment, and helping individual teachers, although still considered interruptions, were a typical part of the day. Her greatest concern was her students' inability to concentrate due to outside noise. Bev's portable classroom was grouped with five additional portable classrooms. Classes walking past or going out for breaks often made noise that proved distracting. Although she had expressed her concern to the administration, she did not notice any change in noise level. She also felt strongly that additional testing had impacted the time she had for direct instruction, so she was especially sensitive about students leaving her portable classroom to go to the bathroom while she was teaching. No matter how many bathroom breaks she would permit, it seemed that there was always someone else to accommodate just as she was starting a lesson. Going to the bathroom was never a quick trip: Including the walk to the building and waiting in line, students could be gone as long as 10 minutes, with the effect that lessons either had to be delayed or sections missed or retaught. Frustrated, Bev exclaimed, "Out here in a portable, if I had a dime for every time my lessons got interrupted by a student needing to go to the bathroom, I'd be a very rich woman."

When I asked Joan what interruption or distraction most affected her class, I presumed knowing how she would respond. Joan's class was a district model for inclusion of students with autism. Teachers, parents, and administrators from several districts would frequently visit to observe how the curriculum and schedules of students with autism were designed to accommodate their special needs. I was aware that Joan had a student with autism who presented many challenges. The student's behavior was even listed as an interruption by nearby teachers. Joan had been responsible for several students with autism in the past and so was accustomed to adjusting schedules and preparing for interruptions, but her response surprised me:

> The biggest distraction for me occurs when adults walk into my room, whether it is to use it as a shortcut or to enter and observe a student. They sit in the back of the room and talk the entire time. I know people think it has to be the behavior of my student with autism that's the problem but it's not—it's those who observe him.

Terri, a 5th-grade teacher who had previously spent 15 years as a business manager, felt her need for organization and efficient scheduling often conflicted with the hectic, unpredictable life in an elementary school. She felt her worth as a teacher was measured by her ability to meet the daily instructional goals she had set for her students. She asserted,

> One of my biggest distractions is the amount of anxiety I personally feel. There seems to be just too much for one person to handle and, in the end, there's not enough of me left over for the students. Today, for example, during math I wrote an anecdotal [observation and documentation of behavior for 30 minutes] on a disruptive student, taught the math lesson to the class, but never got to my gifted students or those with academic improvement plans that needed additional help.

Similarly, Debbie, the team leader and 12-year veteran teacher who had recently received her National Board Certification (NBC), shared:

> One of my biggest distractions in a day is my constant worry that I'm not teaching my kids everything they need. The phones and the memos and the paperwork are constantly distracting me. My biggest concern is that I'm not doing what I'm here to do, and that's to teach the kids. There are so many distractions every day that I just start to lose the kids. If it's not one thing it's another—from a parent calling about having forgotten a child's lunch money to sending a child to the office to filling out paperwork for interns. It is everything but teaching the kids that gets in your way. Debbie's thoughts shed light on how the experience of distraction can be internalized for teachers, to the point of never feeling completely focused on students' needs.

OBSERVING TEACHERS DURING SCHOOL HOURS

Observations of teachers during scheduled school hours involved situations in which I was an observer or engaged in informal conversations with the six participants. By watching the teachers' actions and participating in their discussions, I was able to understand why particular interruptions and distractions were being identified over others. During the conversations about this topic, I limited my participation to probing questions.

Interruptions Versus Personal Decisions

On the survey, the teachers had all recorded paperwork as an interruption. Although there were frequent conversations at the school concerning the amount of paperwork that needed to be completed, Donna, Terri, and Debbie could be seen most mornings during scheduled planning time having coffee in the pod and discussing personal issues, typically for 15 minutes. One might wonder how teachers who vehemently complain about not having enough time to complete paperwork and who staunchly defend their use of instructional time to complete it have time for coffee breaks. Perhaps the underlying point is that these teachers are mentally exhausted and welcome each other's sympathetic ears. It may not be intentional neglect of duty or mismanagement of time that accounts for this but rather the strengthening of the support system required to sustain a cohesive team relationship.

From our data analysis, it was evident that all the teachers had identified outside influences and district paperwork requirements as interruptions of instructional time but not personal activities. One morning while I was teaching, Bev flew into my room. She was desperately searching for a telephone book to call her loan agent. She had left her students doing seatwork and needed to get the loan application completed by noon. On another occasion, during lunch break, Audrey shared she was delighted she had just finished her paper for her graduate class: That morning she had replaced all her planned lessons with seat-work in order to complete her assignment. I asked Audrey if her personal activities could be considered interruptions, but Donna chimed in, "If I change something, then I call it rearranging my schedule. It's not an interruption."

I noted that five of the six teachers occasionally addressed personal issues during scheduled instruction. I also saw these same teachers staying after school working on specific tasks for their classrooms that equaled or surpassed the time they had spent on personal issues, a point Audrey stated when I asked how they felt about using the instruction time. I sensed the culture of the school supported this behavior. The administration recognized there were many outside demands placed on the faculty: To help teachers balance their personal and professional lives, the administrators verbally supported the behavior and even set up early release time in exchange for additional school commitments, as long as the academic needs of the students were being met.

TEACHER READINESS FOR PERSONAL AND TEAM CHANGE

After I interviewed Terri one afternoon, Audrey and Bev joined in. They began discussing some of the ways the team could reduce interruptions. Terri admitted she did not want to be interrupted but had not considered it intrusive if she called Bev with a quick question. I asked them if they thought all telephone calls were interruptions. Bev said it all depended on who it was—if it were a team member or someone she knew well, then she would not mind. Audrey pointed out that because a phone call was a phone call, it is still a distraction. Choosing her words carefully, she explained, "I never seem to be able to complete a lesson. I don't want to be rude to other teachers who need my help, but I need to teach!"

I observed that the teachers on the Explorers team had developed a support network that utilized the strengths of its members for resolving issues and responding to questions. Unfortunately, a downfall to this arrangement is the familiarity and friendship they felt, which conflicted with the need for undisturbed instructional time. I asked if they would be as inclined to call a teacher from another team or drop in to pick up something. All of them agreed they would wait until the teacher had a break, or before or after school. Those who had previously taught in self-contained classrooms thought they had been disturbed less often, although they also felt more isolated from their colleagues.

Actions That Reduce Interruptions

Sensing the Explorers was beginning to seriously reflect on the ways it could reduce or eliminate classroom interruptions, I openly shared the study data with the team. As the teachers became more aware of the interruptions and distractions active within their own spaces and on a daily basis, their frustration level increased. Debbie, the team leader, called a formal meeting to discuss what could be done. With the awareness they were gaining through informal discussions, the Explorers team seemed ready to attempt a major change. To assist in guiding the discussion, I asked them to focus on two important questions during the meeting: "How can the effects of interruptions be minimized?" and "How can interruptions be reduced?" After the Explorers team meeting, Terri and Debbie met with the All-Stars teachers to share the same questions and to gather their observations and concerns regarding pod use.

Every teacher from the two teams who was housed near the pod cited numerous interruptions caused by students or other classes. These findings, along with some of our observations, were brought to a meeting of the two teams. After presenting the information that had been gathered, the teachers discussed their feelings and brainstormed possible solutions. Several teachers from the All-Stars team did not agree that specific guidelines were needed, feeling that it was their prerogative to decide how their students would behave in the pod.

The thoughts of the All-Stars teachers were reminiscent of the first meetings held with the Explorers team. Several All-Stars teachers proved extremely resistant to using their outside doors to reduce possible interruptions to those in the pod, thinking that the students in the intensive reading group or nearby classes would just have to "learn" to ignore them or anyone else using the pod. Debbie, who had once declared that students needed to learn to ignore distractions, now cited several reasons they could not be expected to focus when being constantly interrupted. Terri explained that because the team had been frequently discussing distractions and spending time examining the survey data, she was now aware of the many ways she had been interrupting her teammates in addition to how loud she could be in the classroom. Others laughed as they joked with Terri about having to close their doors when she started lecturing.

Terri and Debbie's honesty was a critical factor in influencing the All-Stars team's decision to agree to implement changes in the way the pod was used. It became apparent to all the teachers that, regardless of past procedures, the goal was to ensure an appropriate learning environment for the small groups and reduce interruptions to classrooms. With altered perspectives, both teams agreed to meet again and develop guidelines for shared use of the pod, including the types of traffic patterns that could be expected during the day.

During the next meeting, the Explorers and All-Stars teams collaborated to design several workable solutions. They agreed on a new furniture and supply arrangement that allowed for greater privacy for small groups, a schedule indicating when classes could enter through the pod versus their outside doors, increased monitoring during the use of bathrooms, and guidelines for noise levels of classrooms located off the pod or those using the pod for group activities. By the following week Bev, Terri, and Donna were amazed at how quiet the pod had become; although not all the distractions had been alleviated, there was noticeable improvement. Consequently, they noticed that their classes had become more focused and that they were already providing higher quality instruction.

FINAL REFLECTIONS

Our original goal when designing this project was to give a voice to a particular group of teachers on the topic of interruptions and disruptions, with the intention of improving the teaching–learning environment. Like many other professionals, the teachers at this school endured countless interruptions and disruptions daily yet still managed on the whole to provide students with an exceptional education. At the same time, these professionals, often unintentionally, created or allowed their students to interrupt in ways that affected their teammates and their classes. We also noted that although the teachers all voiced commitment to their students' education, their actions indicated that personal needs occasionally dictated their instructional time.

We hoped that the data would reveal the amount of time and potential learning that was being lost, but the lines of delineation between what was and was not an interruption or distraction began fading. Personal perceptions of what constituted an interruption did not necessarily align. In fact, when the data collection was over, although there were many similar listings (e.g., phone calls, outside noises, paperwork), the Explorers team consistently agreed on only a handful of items as absolute interruptions. While reflecting on the intricacies of interruptions, it dawned on us that interruption is in the eye of the beholder. Teachers' perceptions revealed personal preferences and situational circumstances leading to inconsistent consensus, as in "If the kids are working in small groups and the phone rings, it's not an interruption, but if I'm lecturing, then it is."

An unintended result of this project was the effect it had on the teachers who participated. As their awareness grew, they began to reflect on the circumstances surrounding interruptions and distractions. Because the team naturally spent so much time together, the issue of interruptions frequently arose. Through their own dedication to improve their craft and the education of their students, this change effort naturally gained momentum. The totality of the experience transformed not only the initiator but allowed others to find a shared voice, not just to express their individual problems, and to turn problems into solutions.

PRACTICAL, REFLECTIVE ACTIVITIES

- Reflect on the teacher statement, "It is everything but teaching the kids that gets in your way." Do you agree with this position? Why or why not?
- Make a list of all of the interruptions and distractions in your own workplace and then compare your list to "Factors that Interrupt Teacher Instruction" (Table 8.2). What similarities and differences are apparent between these two lists? Explain the results and speculate on any major gaps.
- Create a grade-level or schoolwide guide that identifies interruptions and distractions at your site. Talk with teachers, administrators, and students to identify salient interruptions and distractions (use Table 8.2 as a reference). Alternatively, collaborate with a team and devise the guide together, following up with action steps and collective promises. Carry out this exercise informally or formally as an action-based case study (see chap. 17 for a list of action research steps).
- Observe your students or a classroom during an instructional period. Look for hidden factors in the classroom that may be distracting the students. It may be a mechanical type of problem such as a buzzing overhead light or an uncomfortable room temperature. Additionally, ask the students what interrupts or distracts them from learning and discuss how the class can work together to alleviate any concerns. Share the results with fellow teachers or your administration.

9

Reflective Analysis of National Board-Certified Teacher Mentoring Programs

Jennifer E. Varholy
Carol A. Mullen

In 2004, I, a middle school language arts teacher, received my National Board Certification (NBC). The long and rigorous application process had stretched out over 2 years. During this journey, I transformed into a much stronger educator, an improved classroom-based reflective practitioner, and a better scholarly and practical writer. Along with the granting of the certification, I was allocated a monetary reward from Florida's state legislators. Initially, I was given a bonus check of $4,000, which was to arrive every December for the 10-year life of the certificate. The financial benefits did not end there, however; I was given the opportunity to earn an additional $4,000 annually in exchange for mentoring teachers, whether first-year or more experienced, and for assisting National Board candidates with the application process. These funds would be distributed to me each June, assuming that 91 hours (equivalent to 12 days) of mentoring were logged.

As a new National Board teacher, I worked with multiple teachers at my school and within the district. For instance, during the 2004–2005 school year, I coached two teachers, both new to the profession. I met with them on a weekly basis, assisting with developing lesson plans, projects, and grading rubrics, as well as identifying suitable classroom management techniques. I also assisted a fellow teacher who was pursuing a master's degree by helping him develop his portfolio (a collection of coursework assignments and reflective writing that documented his professional growth) and by aiding in creating a unit on building students' science vocabulary.

Throughout this process, I felt empowered, but I was also quite frustrated. Many of my peers needed assistance yet chose not to act on my advice. They would approach me for help but then return to their classrooms only to resume the same old habits, often revolving around ineffective teaching strategies.

In addition, I did not have the opportunity to develop curriculum at my school to the extent I desired. My department head, a more seasoned veteran, told me she did not require my assistance with the language arts curriculum calendars, a system my school had adopted to ensure that all language arts teachers were teaching the same content in the same order simultaneously. Consequently, I was unable to lend my expertise.

At the same time, the administration team at my school proved supportive throughout the process of my development as a National Board-certified curriculum leader. Principals should strive to provide such an environment that encourages teachers to examine and reflect on their teaching and school practice, adopt specific behaviors to facilitate reflective practice, and make it possible for teachers to implement ideas and programs that result from reflective practice (Perie & Baker, 1997).

NATIONAL BOARD FOR PROFESSIONAL TEACHING STANDARDS

Concerning the national policy context, *A Nation Prepared: Teachers for the 21st Century*, issued by the Carnegie Task Force on Teaching as a Profession (1986), encourages placing classroom teachers at the center of educational reform efforts focused on student learning and achievement. This report emphasizes the importance of creating new leadership roles for teachers that acknowledge the centrality of classroom teaching and extend educators' decision-making power school-wide.

This same influential report calls for the establishment of the National Board for Professional Teaching Standards, or NBPTS. This decision-making body would be responsible for defining and monitoring excellence in teaching. Since the inception of NBPTS in 1987, this group of accomplished educators has grown dramatically—more than 40,000 teachers in the United States have now earned certification in a variety of subject areas and grade levels.

What is NBPTS, exactly? Many Americans—many teachers, for that matter—do not know the basics regarding this organization, its purpose, and functions. To clarify, this board's mission is "to advance the quality of teaching and learning" by

- Maintaining high and rigorous standards for what accomplished teachers should know and be able to do;
- Providing a national voluntary system certifying teachers who meet these standards; and
- Advocating related education reforms to integrate NBC in American education and to capitalize on the expertise of National Board Certified teachers. (Steeves & Browne, 2000, p. ix)

NBPTS (2002), in a report titled "What Teachers Should Know and Be Able to Do," outlines five core propositions or beliefs that the organization holds about accomplished teacher practices:

1. Teachers are committed to students and their learning.
2. Teachers know the subjects they teach and how to teach those subjects to students.
3. Teachers are responsible for managing and monitoring student learning.
4. Teachers think systematically about their practice and learn from experience.
5. Teachers are members of learning communities. (pp. 3–4)

Furthermore, NBPTS, as a teacher-based organization, promises to:

- Reshape the public's perception of teaching, leading to a better appreciation of the demands on, and requirements for, accomplished practitioners;
- Enhance teachers' self-esteem, working environment, and compensation;
- Create more professional and educationally rewarding relationships among teachers and between teachers and administrators; and
- Restore public confidence in the schools. (pp. 2–3)

When examining these core propositions and beliefs, several patterns emerge. One concerns the integration of "professional relationships" with "financial compensation," a curriculum leadership trend that informs this chapter's focus.

Before proceeding, we wish to openly acknowledge the lively debate that surrounds such professional standards for teaching excellence and their underlying values. Some educational researchers argue that the national teaching commissions, including NBPTS, have generated policy for standardizing teacher proficiency. These policies and standards essentially reduce exemplary teaching to teacher qualification and student achievement on standardized tests (e.g., Mullen & Farinas, 2003). Thomas and Schubert

(2001) believe that the professional standards promote the "bureaucratization of teaching" while also skewing the nation's ability to even recognize a quality teacher. Teaching commissions, they believe, fail to value democratic vision or the capacity to "challenge social assumptions about what is worth knowing" (p. 230).

THE NATIONAL BOARD'S MENTORING "PUSH"

In one of its key documents, NBPTS (2004b) frequently uses the terms *mentoring* and *coaching*, forcing readers to see the National Board process as intertwined with these educational processes. NBPTS states that schools should aim to achieve three goals, centered on "treat[ing] each child as an individual, embrac[ing] student learning as the highest value, and foster[ing] distinguished teaching by drawing fully on the accumulated wisdom of the faculty" (p. 5). A position this report takes is that although exemplary teachers do work in America's schools, "it is rare that such teachers are recognized for their accomplishments or asked to share their expertise with others" (p. 7). In my experience as a seasoned 8th-grade educator, veteran teachers are rarely called on to perform leadership roles at their school sites, whether related to professional development, teacher mentoring, or curriculum development. The National Board literature reinforces this viewpoint, explaining that mentors are underutilized at most schools: "The incentive structure in schools fails to promote the spread of … knowledge and expertise of the most accomplished teachers among fellow faculty members" (NBPTS, 2004b, p. 7).

However, as NBC increases in popularity among teachers around the country, so too do roles for mentors. NBPTS (2004b) claims that "with many initial candidates for NBC coming from the current teaching force, there should emerge a new and burgeoning market for preparing teachers for the National Board's assessments" (p. 8). I agree that this teacher preparation market could quickly develop, as more and more teachers at my school and within my district inquire about NBC every year. The year that I applied, one other teacher and I were pursuing certification—the first to do so at that site. Since then, seven teachers have attempted certification, with four more initiating the process in 2005. And in my district, interest in NBC has also grown: In 2004–2005, 21 informational meetings about the National Board process were held, with more than 35 informational meetings offered the following year.

But mentoring extends beyond assisting NBC candidates. National Board teachers can agree to work with teachers outside the certification process. For me, this has largely been the case. Although I did mentor three certification candidates during the 2004 mentoring cycle, I coached seven teachers at my own site, focusing on daily lesson planning and classroom management. NBPTS encourages this network of extended mentoring:

> Peers will seek out accomplished teachers noted for their expertise. Novice teachers will request constructive criticism to improve their practice. … Expert practitioners will become a valued commodity and acquire the respect and admiration they deserve from colleagues and researchers alike. (pp. 9–10)

Given this expectation for curriculum leadership at their schools and the opportunity to coach teachers at other schools, mentors can serve in a multitude of roles. They might be asked to assist new teachers in developing lessons and managing classrooms or help struggling teachers find new ways to assess student learning. Or they might be utilized as a proofreader of applicants' entries for certification application. The functions, roles, and tasks for productive and willing National Board mentors are, it seems, plentiful within any school community.

The NBPTS (2004b) document also provides real-world examples of how National Board-certified educators could assist teachers. One "involves a middle school math teacher who could be called on to diagnose student misunderstanding in mathematics" (p. 11) classrooms all over her school. By having the opportunity to review student work from peer teachers' classrooms, this National Board teacher could assist others school-wide or in her unit, or even in a department from a different school, "work[ing] with her fellow teachers in formulating a solution to each case" (p. 11). Another illustration spotlights an elementary teacher and "science expert" who together coach preservice and beginning educators needing practice with scientific concepts in classroom contexts. The teacher mentor could model lessons for teachers and students alike while working with the novice teacher on skills such as lesson planning, implementing, and evaluating, as well as developing interactive units for students. Once the new teacher feels confident in her science skills, the mentor could take on the role of a peer coach, observing the new teacher and providing valuable feedback (Gottesman, 2000; Mullen, 2005c).

A CLOSER LOOK AT MENTORING

As we know, mentoring did not begin as a concept or practice with the inception of NBPTS. In fact, educational researchers have long underscored the value of teachers working together to collectively identify and solve problems (e.g., Mullen, 2004a, 2005c; Portner, 2005). McCann and Radford (1993) expound on this value of mentoring as applied to the school context: "Teachers are their own most valued resource in the teaching profession. Teachers not only need to be acknowledged for their talents, skills, and abilities, but also must be allowed and encouraged to share these valuable resources with colleagues" (p. 43). Gottesman (2000) concurs:

> One avenue of improving the quality of teachers is to provide a culture in which teachers are expected to interact with each other to discuss their vocation. …Teachers need the opportunity to have conversations with other teachers regarding teaching and learning. (p. 29)

However, in many districts across America, these types of teaching/learning discussions occur only at district-mandated in-service workshops or, at best, voluntary university classes. Researchers agree, though, that mentoring should be an ongoing aspect of life in our schools; moreover, this process should be accommodated as a natural part of professional development and teacher scheduling. Teacher-to-teacher mentoring can greatly benefit all parties involved, from the mentor to the protégé to the school system. Rees (2003) writes that protégé teachers gain by developing "professional competence through a cycle of observation/assessment/practice/assessment" (p. 2), which allows for continuous improvement and ongoing feedback.

Mentoring, imagined as a cyclical process, as depicted in Figure 9.1. It begins with an observation. One teacher might be called on to act as a coach to a struggling teacher. In this way, the teacher observer could focus on elements of curriculum. Questions to investigate might include study of whether all students in the room exhibit understanding of the concepts being taught and whether they are all on task during the lesson. After observation, the coach and classroom teacher could engage in reflection and, when and if appropriate, assessment, wherein they would speak openly about what was observed and experienced (Gottesman, 2000). A discussion of strengths and weaknesses could occur, and the teacher being coached would be encouraged to reflect aloud on his practice and without the usual blame and praise that many teachers expect. Next, the practice phase would commence, and the teacher would implement strategies discussed with the coach to improve his or her teaching methods. Finally, another assessment phase would lead both teachers to reflect on the outcomes experienced through mentoring and curriculum implementation, possibly experimentation. Here, the observer serves in a nonjudgmental, helping capacity while remaining focused on the practice and improvement of a colleague.

Seasoned teachers can also gain from the mentoring process, finding worthwhile their engagement of novice or struggling teachers in their school, district, and state (Mullen, 2005c). Huling (2001) reinforces the idea that experienced teachers thrive on "the opportunity to pass on their expertise [and to create] an environment conducive to lifelong [learning]" (p. 2). Moir and Bloom (2003) corroborate this position, writing that such educators become invigorated professionally as they make a difference in another's life,

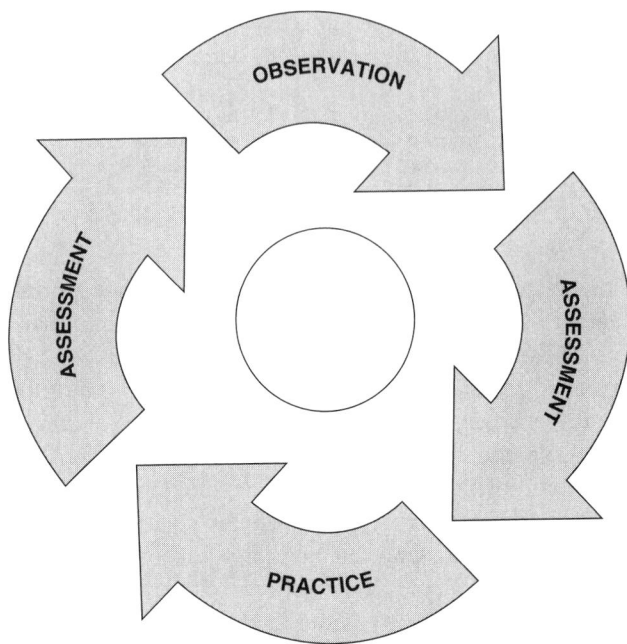

FIG. 9.1.   A teacher mentor–protégé mentoring cycle.

simultaneously growing in their school-based leadership roles. As one critical effect, teachers are more likely to stay in the profession for a lifetime rather than move out of the classroom or exit teaching altogether (Lind, 2003; Moir & Bloom, 2003).

Huling (2001) identifies seven substantial benefits associated with teacher mentoring programs:

1. Professional competency—"The quality of teaching by mentors improves."
2. Reflective practice—Teachers think about "their own beliefs about teaching, students, learning, and teaching as a career."
3. Renewal—"Mentors [are] reenergized and often strengthen their commitment to the teaching profession."
4. Psychological benefits—Mentoring "enhances mentors' self-esteem … empowers experienced teachers and gives them a greater sense of significance in their world."
5. Collaboration—"Continued contact with mentees provides some of [the] richest collegial interactions."

6. Contributions to teacher leadership—There are opportunities to participate in "structured professional development including training and experience in classroom observation and coaching skills."
7. Mentoring combined with inquiry—"Lead mentors … participate in university research projects or teacher research." (pp. 2–5)

A few years ago, when I began advanced study at the University of South Florida, I expected to become a principal. But now that I have attained my NBC and, importantly, fulfilled the vital role of mentor, I feel less drawn to the "front office." Instead, I am enjoying being continually challenged and feeling validated within and beyond my own classroom. My testimony supports Tell's (1999) finding that teachers often respond more positively to one another than to an administrator, and without opportunities to exercise leadership, many of the most effective teachers feel forced into administration.

In examining mentoring as a concept, it is also important to respond to the question, "What makes a good mentor?" Along with many other researchers, Rowley (1999) addresses this topic, pinpointing six essential qualities of a "good mentor":

1. The good mentor is committed to the role of mentoring.
2. The good mentor is accepting of the [mentee].
3. The good mentor is skilled at providing instructional support.
4. The good mentor is effective in different interpersonal contexts.
5. The good mentor is a model of a continuous learner.
6. The good mentor communicates hope and optimism. (pp. 20–22)

NBC teacher mentors could benefit from giving close consideration to this list by reflecting on the extent to which they fulfill each of these qualities in the attempt to promote effective mentoring.

NATIONAL BOARDS AND THE MENTORING LINK

As previously illustrated, educators' successful completion of the National Board process can enhance accomplished teaching practices and, hence, teacher-based mentorship. The board, in its encouragement of mentoring programs and strategies, provides a manual that assists potential teacher mentors (referred to as *facilitators* in most NBC reports) through the process of "recruiting" and "assisting" mentee teachers (candidates, according to the NBC literature). Steeves and Browne (2000), board affiliates (and former assessors of the application entries) organized this text into three sections: precandidacy, candidacy, and postcandidacy. In precandidacy, mentors access ideas for holding informational meetings, recruit candidates to apply for certification, and initiate the mentoring process. Regarding candidacy, mentors are informed about the following 10 areas of the National Board application process:

- General
- Getting started
- Standards
- Portfolio
- Videotaping
- Reflective practice
- Written commentary
- Developing a student case study
- Finishing the portfolio
- Assessment center (pp. 19–23)

Each area proves crucial, Steeves and Browne (2000) assert, for teacher protégés. In order to achieve success as certification candidates, they will need the guidance of accomplished, experienced teachers.

These chapters also include sample entries for mentors to review. Those unfamiliar with a certain subject can study a model entry. Steeves and Browne (2000) encourage mentors to assist candidates from outside their own subject area—sound advice. As a mentor from 2004–2005, I read and reviewed entries for a middle school special education teacher and a secondary math teacher even though my discipline is language arts. By stepping out of my "curriculum box," I could objectively react to the writings of these teachers, look openly and honestly at their strategies, and not get bogged down with details.

Postcandidacy deals with how to recognize and even celebrate the accomplishments of teacher mentees once their application process is completed. This phase, say Steeves and Browne (2000), is the one most likely to be overlooked by mentors, as well as school and district leaders. By asking reflective questions of mentees, such as "What did I learn from the NBPTS assessment process and the support I received?" (p. 164), applicants can come full circle with the National Board process, becoming mentors once certified.

My experience of NBC process closely follows Steeves and Browne's (2000) procedural outline. I began in September of 2002, attending an informational meeting after my principal indicated that I was a good choice for candidacy. After deciding that I could handle the additional workload, I submitted my application and $200—my district paid the rest of the fee. I then waited for a response. In October I received the application materials, as well as directions for each section of the form.

Because I was pursuing certification in early adolescence English/language arts, there were four entries to complete. The first required that students' growth in reading and writing be assessed. The second and third entries involved videotaping and analyzing my classes, one in small group setting and the other, a whole-group lesson. The final entry, common to all areas of certification, concerned documentation of my professional development and commitment to staying in contact with students, parents, and the community. My school administration proved supportive during this process, allowing 2 days off for preparation of the entries, in addition to class coverage for my peers who videotaped my teaching. Having completed the entries 5 months later (in March 2003), I mailed my package to the National Board headquarters. The process culminated 4 weeks later with an assessment whereby I was asked 6 questions, 2 about my knowledge of the language arts, 2 about my capacity to teach language arts, and 2 about my ability to assess students' development in language arts.

Throughout this reflective learning process, the mentoring component proved key. I worked primarily with a National Board-certified teacher from my district. This individual diligently reviewed my portfolio entries and videotapes and guided the development of my reflective writing. I worked closely with another teacher from my school too, someone also immersed in the application process. Luckily, we were both were pursuing the same certification, so we commiserated daily about the National Board process.

However, when November 2003 arrived and I logged on to receive my scores, I found out that I had missed attaining my certification by a mere 7 points. I was devastated and disheartened. I began to regret having devoted the time and energy to pursuing certification. The other teacher at my school had received her certification, and neither that educator nor my mentor could understand how I had fallen short of the board's expectations.

I contemplated quitting candidacy altogether, but I knew that would mean having to repay $2,000 (the part of my application fee covered by the district), so I thought it best to stick with the plan. In January 2004, I videotaped another whole-group lesson, wrote my reflective teaching entry, and mailed the package. I was relieved to learn months later (in November) that I had earned my certification. Again, my school leaders proved encouraging— posting my name on the school's marquee, presenting me with flowers and balloons, and recognizing me at the next faculty meeting.

In hindsight, this process proved positive, overall. However, it was emotionally draining, I admit, and I still do not understand why or how I had missed the mark the first time. Unfortunately, scoring rubrics were not provided before I applied. When I did not pass one section, the rubric was finally revealed, and I was dismayed that the National Board withheld this information from me the first time around. Worse than that, I saw that other teachers in my district had achieved certification with apparent ease, seemingly because they were good writers and not necessarily excellent teachers. For all of these reasons, I look at the certification process with a skeptical eye. As Mullen and Farinas (2003) explain, although teacher qualification in such forms as certification may be indicators of quality teaching, they are not synonymous with it. Qualified teachers are not necessarily educators of quality, meaning that "teacher qualification" cannot automatically substitute for "quality teaching."

HOW STATES COMPARE AS MENTORING-BASED CERTIFICATION SPONSORS

On the National Board Web site, a chart, "State Policies and/or Appropriations Providing NBC Incentives & Supports" (see http://www.nbpts.org/about/images/stateincen_sup.table.pdf), lists data from all 50 states for the benefit of potential candidates and National Board-certified teachers regarding

- How states defray application costs
- How states provide mentoring and assistance for candidates
- How states reward mentors who assist others in the NBC process

Current as of May 2005, 24 states do not provide any information about mentoring programs associated with the pursuit of NBC. Fourteen states, however, offer information regarding mentoring but none concerning financial benefits related to this function. Some (12), though, extend mentoring assistance to candidates, indicating that mentors are financially compensated in some way. A variety of nation-wide mentoring opportunities and benefits are noted, although clear trends have yet to emerge.

In Florida, our own home state, the Dale Hickam Excellent Teaching Program Act legislation, signed in 1998 by the state senate and House of Representatives (see http://www.firn.edu/doe/etp/legislation.html) has increased the appropriation in 2005 to $67.7 million. This covers 90% of the individual applicant's certification fee, provides teachers who achieve NBC with a 10% salary increase for the life of the certificate, with an additional 10% to those who agree, in writing, to provide the equivalent of 12 work days of mentoring and related services to public schools. Beneficiaries of this mentoring are teachers within the state who do not hold NBC. Financially speaking, Florida's teachers are among the highest monetary reward recipients in the nation. Only Tennessee boasts higher bonuses for National Board-certified teachers; however, its bonus is not contingent on the logging of mentoring hours (see "State and Local Incentives;" http://www.nbpts.org/about/state-info.cfm?state=Tennessee). (As will be revealed, our teacher mentor–participants criticized this logging practice as monotonous and even questionable.)

After examining the data for the different states, the question arose, "Are there more National Board-certified teachers working in states that pay monetarily for mentoring?" As an educator, I might be more inclined to assist another teacher through what many, including myself, experience as a tedious but rewarding NBC process if financial gain could be expected. To answer this question, consult the chart "NBCTs by State" (see http://www.nbpts.org/nbct/nbctdir_bystate.cfm). It provides the total number of teachers who earned certification in 2003–2004, as well as the total holding certification within each state.

According to www.nbpts.org, the highest number of National Board-certified teachers is currently found in North Carolina (8,283), followed by Florida (6,359) (NBPTS, 2004a). Both states also financially compensate teacher mentors, which suggests that more teachers pursue certification if they see financial gain and that more mentors help teachers achieve certification in part because they are being paid. The National Board Web site reports states in which the fewest number of National Board-certified teachers are located—South Dakota (32), North Dakota (23), and New Hampshire (16)—provide no information regarding mentoring services available to candidates (2004a). This implies that none are available and, furthermore, that teachers are less likely to feel motivated to undertake the rigorous certification process. The inference can be drawn, then, that offering mentoring to candidates, and paying mentors for their services, increases the odds that a teacher will initiate the steps to certification.

SURVEYING NATIONAL BOARD MENTORS

As an educator who has participated in the NBC process (both as an applicant and as a mentor), working collaboratively with my coauthor, I drew information from two sources: the relevant educational literature and surveys of teachers in a Florida county—participants of the mentoring process associated with NBC. The survey instrument, my own original development, peer reviewed before distribution, was electronically distributed in May, 2005. Seventy National Board-certified educators in my school district completed it, providing information about their role and experience of mentoring National Board candidates.

National Board-Certified teachers were asked six questions, three pertaining to their experience as teacher mentors:

1. What intrinsic benefits have you gained from participating in the mentoring program associated with NBC?
2. What extrinsic benefits have you gained from participating in the mentoring program associated with NBC?
3. What drawbacks have you experienced from participating in the mentoring program associated with NBC?

Concerning the teacher mentees they assisted, this group of NBC teacher mentors was asked:

1. What intrinsic benefits do you believe mentees have gained from participating in the mentoring program associated with NBC?
2. What extrinsic benefits do you believe mentees have gained from participating in the mentoring program associated with NBC?
3. What drawbacks do you believe mentees have experienced from participating in the mentoring program associated with NBC?

Intrinsic Benefits for Teacher Mentors

When asked, "What intrinsic benefits have you gained from participating in the mentoring program associated with NBC?" the respondents answered in similar ways. One teacher wrote,

> By mentoring, I feel that I can have an effect on our profession. I've learned a lot from the candidates that I have helped. I like reading about the teaching methods that other people use in their classrooms. It helps me to grow in my own practice.

Another individual commented,

> Great relationships with new colleagues, knowledge of other subject areas, experiencing pride when asked to assist a teacher, and feeling good about being able to make a difference with other teachers and ultimately affecting their students are all gains for me.

Someone else noted,

> I enjoy working with teachers and being able to help them in some small way be successful. It gives me great pride to be able to assist someone in their successes as well as provide them an avenue for becoming reflective thinkers.

Another added, "I feel honored and have gained confidence in myself as I learn more about my own teaching and how to better it through reading the accomplishments and methods of others."

Extrinsic Benefits for Teacher Mentors

All of the teacher mentors disclosed that financial remuneration was the greatest extrinsic motivator behind their mentoring commitment. However, other comments included, "Of course, the money is nice, but I was already doing mentoring so the personal pride in being asked by my supervisor is considerable. When your efforts are recognized, it is very rewarding." Another concurred, "The bonus is definitely the most rewarding benefit. I also appreciate the 'thank you' I receive from candidates as they achieve a new step in the process." In addition, someone else shared, "The financial rewards I receive from mentoring are important to my life as a single parent. The ability to list mentoring as an accomplishment on my resume is also powerful in reflecting my professional work with peers."

Drawbacks for Teacher Mentors

When asked to identify any negative aspects related to the National Board mentoring process in this district, the overwhelming response concerned the log that teachers must keep to verify their mentoring hours. Feeling troubled, someone shared, "So far, only the paperwork has proven somewhat daunting. After putting in so many hours, I always worry about not 'dotting the i's and crossing the t's correctly and putting the bonus money in jeopardy." Another elaborated on "the 'hoops' that you have to go through to qualify for the bonus" as a drawback. And one respondent complained, "Tediousness of the mentoring log—too time consuming—too many restraints (you can do this, but can't do this; entries must be worded in a certain way, etc)." Another shared a similar point of view, expressing the desire to be treated professionally: "I feel uncomfortable asking the teachers I help to sign my mentoring logs as evidence of teaching. I'm a professional, and I'd like to be treated like one."

Intrinsic Benefits for Teacher Mentees

Mentors in the large Florida district studied were also asked to comment on how teacher candidates feel about the mentoring program. They were informed that this question could be interpreted from the teacher's own perspective (as in when he or she went through the application process) or from the viewpoint of a mentee that one had assisted the previous year. One teacher mentor wrote,

> This is the best part for mentees. In the media field, there is so much to learn that is specific to our district. Consequently, a newbie will need to have someone to turn

to. When trust is established between teachers the professional relationship becomes formed.

Someone else responded,

I believe candidates appreciate the knowledge that is shared with them, as well as the boost of confidence we provide as a mentor. If they are questioning their lessons, for example, and we compliment them or show how to make a good lesson even better, it provides a feeling of accomplishment or security in their own ability.

And someone else added, "Sanity and satisfaction, as well as camaraderie, are intrinsic benefits for teacher applicants."

Extrinsic Benefits for Teacher Mentees

When asked to identify extrinsic benefits for teacher mentees (applicants), the mentors offered a variety of responses. Someone wrote, "I believe mentoring helps teachers accomplish the certification. Some teachers would not pass if it were not for mentoring." Another reflected on the issue of future benefits, saying, "The knowledge gained and recognition of becoming a National Board Certified Teacher—the certificate, letters of congratulations from various regional, state, and national leaders and organizations, and personal cards and notes from friends and colleagues." Finally, one person described extrinsic benefits for mentees as including "recognition when they accomplish something wonderful, such as a lesson that goes well, increased student achievement, and increased parent involvement."

Drawbacks for Teacher Mentees

Most respondents did not identify any mentee-related drawbacks. The minority who did expressed such sentiments as, "Sometimes mentees solicit too many opinions from [board-certified mentors] and so things can become confusing for them. Some sort of formalized mentoring, where mentors are assigned to candidates, might be beneficial to the process." Another agreed, "Mixed opinions, too many to know which ones to follow even from mentors. Sometimes confusion occurs—one mentor will guide in one way whereas another will oppose that direction."

FINAL REFLECTIONS

Based on the national data we examined, the early but tentative determination can be ventured that most state legislators and school district personnel are active in their encouragement of teachers to pursue NBC. Be it through providing mentoring sessions led by district personnel or through paying National Board-certified teachers to work one-on-one with candidates, most states are encouraging teachers to participate in this rigorous process. Moreover, when reviewing the data obtained from a large sample of participating certified mentors within my own Florida district, it appears that the mentoring experience is overall positive, leading to benefits for both the mentor and the mentee.

In addition to the obvious gains of financial reward and well-being that come from affirmations for doing a good job, the intrinsic gains identified by teacher mentors were impressive. These highlight feelings of personal pride and satisfaction in having helped teacher candidates succeed in the application and growth process. The mentors agreed that not only had their own teaching and learning improved as a result of this commitment but also that they were given an opportunity to make a difference to the teaching profession. Time-consuming paperwork, including the logging of activity, was the overwhelming negative cited regarding their experience of the mentoring program. The relevant authorities governing teacher certification should review this area of concern, especially as suspicion regarding teacher professionalism was raised.

As a cautionary note, the applicant group was perceived as having experienced unnecessary confusion during their learning cycle, which teacher mentors attributed to a lack of formalized mentoring. It was recommended that mentors be consistently assigned to the same candidate to reduce the latter's information overload. This is an excellent pointer for the National Board, as well as school administrators.

Finally, researchers' claims about the value of teacher mentoring as a professional development tool appear to have validity within the context of professional teaching standards for educators seeking board certification. As schools, districts, and states continue to look for ways to better the education system, they might find that the NBC process and its corresponding mentoring programs could serve as a viable pathway for promoting curriculum leadership among teachers.

PRACTICAL, REFLECTIVE ACTIVITIES

- Read current federal and state legislation dealing with the NBC process. Take notes covering your areas of interest, such as compensation, mentoring, and leadership. Share what you have found with colleagues in your building or at a university.

- Talk to National Board-certified teachers and applicants in your own school or district. Ask about the benefits and drawbacks they have experienced and compare what you learn to the results reported in this chapter and anywhere else.
- Distribute the survey questions provided here to the National Board-certified teachers in your own district and analyze the responses. Use or amend the list, noting the publishing attribution. Or develop a new instrument for the teacher applicants or school administrators involved in this process. (Leaders are central to encouraging teachers' professional and curricular development.)

10

Administrator Walk-Through as Instructional Aid for Classroom Teachers

Cindy Dowdy
Jennifer McCrystal
Robin Snyder
Carol A. Mullen

New trends in education, often pitched as magic elixirs, promise to be the "cure-all" for every problem that arises. In an effort to meet the mounting demands of the public and federal government, teachers, administrators, and district personnel are easily enticed into endorsing such panaceas, one of which is the administrator walk-through. Administrators use this practice as an observation tool and to support a school's most important resource, its teachers.

According to Downey, Steffy, English, Frase, and Poston (2004), all too often, the latest programs or reforms do not have a sound research base:

> Today, when all educators are under tremendous pressure to make dramatic test score improvements, many hurry to grab the new products and programs parading at educational conferences and in the literature. These products are selected based on their promises and slick packaging, not on demonstrated results. (p. 141)

The administrator walk-through is one of such trends on the horizon. It is an informal classroom visit designed to support the curriculum development and leadership of classroom teachers and the understanding of administrators. Differing from the traditional formal evaluation, it offers administrators the opportunity to frequently visit all teachers during the course of the academic year. The underlying premise is that these brief, unannounced observations will immerse the administrator in day-to-day instructional practices, lending to his or her skills as an instructional or curriculum leader. By being in the classroom on a more regular basis than is allowed by traditional formal evaluation processes, administrators can see first-hand what best practices look like in action as well as stay grounded in the day-to-day challenges that the regular classroom presents. By doing so, they can more readily develop rich insights into teaching and learning that can only be attained by intentional, purposeful visits.

Here, we briefly describe variations of the walk-through model, focusing mainly on the Three-Minute Walk-Through as developed by Carolyn Downey (see Downey et al., 2004), and share what we have learned about its strengths and weaknesses. Finally, we consider whether the administrative walk-through model constitutes valid site-based reform or passing fancy.

This examination of walk-throughs was sparked in 2005 by the possibility that a Florida school district was ready to begin implementing Downey's Three-Minute Walk-Through. Initially, we perceived the walk-through method as enabling administrators to become more involved with everyday teaching practices, thus making them an integral part of school improvement. We imagine the Three-Minute Walk-Through as a way in which teachers can collaborate with administrators to propel their own professional development, and it has created a vision for us of how a professional community of learners can be of mutual benefit.

CLASSROOM WALK-THROUGH VARIATIONS

Informal Classroom Walk-Throughs

The coaching and assessment literature we consulted portrays the informal classroom walk-through as an alternative and potentially empowering form of teacher evaluation. Kim Marshall, leadership coach for new principals and a former public school principal in Boston, describes this approach in a series of articles. His program consists of frequent unannounced classroom visits based on the following questions:

- Are teachers on track with the curriculum?
- Are the students learning?
- Are teachers "happy campers" in terms of their jobs and lives?
- Do some teachers deserve special praise?
- Do some teachers need redirection, emergency support, or a negative evaluation? (Marshall, 2003, p. 702)

Written feedback or follow-up conversations complete the observation.

More recently, Marshall (2005) claims that administrator visits have the potential to spark the development of active learning communities. As a proactive curriculum leader, Marshall (2005) has adopted the stance that educational supervisors "want individual teachers and teacher teams to be thinking constantly about whether students are learning and what can be done to get better results" (p. 734). He explains that the principal should be the "chief learner" in this respect, incorporating research and knowledge into such activities as study groups, article and book groups, peer observations, and lesson videotapes. Through such practices, a culture can be created in which analyses of student learning proceed nondefensively and thoughtfully. Marshall (2005) adds, "Principals are ideally situated to start this team-driven 'engine of improvement' and keep it humming" (p. 735).

As instructional leaders invest in teacher improvement, it is beneficial for principals to have the necessary support from their central administration office. Burdensome expectations for supervision and evaluation must be streamlined if principals are to be given the chance to campaign for the growth of teacher-led professional communities. Mindful site-based administrators should

> ... spend their time doing what will make the most difference: quickly and efficiently keeping tabs on what is truly happening in the classrooms, giving teachers constant feedback, making fair judgments about teacher performance, and getting teams invested improving student learning and focused on results. (Marshall, 2005, p. 735)

The Administrative Observer

Bill Craig (n.d.), secondary principal in Illinois, endorses the Administrative Observer classroom walk-through software. This leader states that "after many years and many approaches, I find that walk-through observations documented using my handheld computer are particularly effective and efficient" (p. 1). He presets criteria into the program and then records his observations during the 8- to 10-minute classroom visits. Using this device, the administrator is also able to take observational notes. On returning to his office, he prepares a report that is shared with the teacher and kept on file. It is worth noting that this particular process turns the walk-through into a teaching evaluation.

The teacher qualities and classroom variables Craig (n.d.) highlights include

- Quiet, orderly atmosphere in the room.
- Students appropriately engaged in meaningful activities.

- Meaningful recitation from all students every day.
- Teacher skillfully guiding direct instruction.
- Friendly, welcoming classroom environment.
- Skillful classroom management.
- Accommodations for special needs students.
- Appropriate use of graphic organizers. (p. 1)

Another high school principal from Florida led the development of a guide listing observational criteria and examples to assist in the walk-throughs of administrators and teacher mentors at her site (see Table 10.1). A carbon copy of the completed form is left with teachers who have been observed.

One of the school's teacher mentors described the merits of this walk-through checklist for the assistance it provides the observer and the observed. However, consistent with the Downey method, a checklist should be bypassed, at least for the first few visits. Also, on this particular form there is no place for the administrator or teacher mentor to jot down any reflective questions for the teacher to think about before meeting to discuss what was observed. The coaching/reflective questioning component that the administrator initiates is intended to take the walk-through intervention to another level.

The Three-Minute Walk-Through

Similar to the walk-throughs previously described, Downey's Three-Minute Walk-Through is a brief, unannounced visit that the principal makes for the purpose of observing the teacher in action (see Downey et al., 2004). However, this version differs from the others in that a reflective conversation between the administrator and teacher follows, not a checklist (as executed by Craig) or written comments (as in Marshall's model). We discuss the reflective conversation in more detail later on in this chapter. In fact, this walk-through model is unique for its focus on "a cycle of self-analysis and improvement" for all staff (Downey et al., 2004, p. 13).

History and Development

Downey developed the Three-Minute Walk-Through in the 1960s when she was a practicing school administrator. The first version of her model involved a simple walk-through and meaningful dialogue with teachers. As a beginning leader influenced by the work of Madeline Hunter (see Downey et al., 2004), Downey began incorporating suggestions for improving teacher practice and behaviors. During the 1970s, she studied the work of Sue Wells

TABLE 10.1
Administrator/Teacher Mentor Walk-Through Reflection Sheet

Teacher:_____   Date:_____

Period and Time:_____   Observer:_____

Elements of Effective Teaching Recorded During Visit

Circle the observed behaviors under each learning element—check each surveyed category.

____ *Prior knowledge*: Examples: think-pair-share; prereading journals; anticipation guides.

____ *Defined purpose*: Examples: anticipation guides; stated and written objectives; lesson plans; agenda (including benchmark [Sunshine State Standard]) posted on board/wall.

____ *Active learning*: Examples: two-column notes; support on anticipation guides; opinion/proof notes; graphic organizers; free-form mapping; learning logs; postreading journals; selective underlining; highlighting; cooperative teams; reciprocal teaching; class discussion. Number of students not engaged ____

____ *Writing*: Examples: journal responses; free responses; pre/postreading journals; maps; problem-solution formats; two-column notes; five-step or one-sentence summaries; spool papers; concrete definition maps; word keys; sentences and word expansion; writing planning sheet; rough drafts; editing.

____ *Reorganization*: Examples: sequence map; power thinking; pattern puzzles; Venn diagrams; five-step summaries; one-sentence summaries; framed paragraphs; two-column notes; problem–solution guides; graphic organizers; story plans; semantic feature analyses.

____ *Metacognition*: Examples: four instruction steps (introduction, modeling, guided practice, independent application); reorganization of read information; re-reading; self questioning; organizing information; understanding; adding needed information; self-testing; 12-minute study activity.

____ *Classroom management*: Examples: Class begins immediately-bell work or thinking activity begins the class; teacher takes roll quickly and quietly; discipline plan and assignments are posted; teacher has routines; class is brought to attention easily; teacher praises and encourages students; teacher dismisses class—not the bell.

____ *Classroom environment*: Examples: Information is posted on the door (name, room number, period/subject); teacher stands at door and greets students; student desks have a view of the teacher and the teacher can see all students; a bulletin board or wall space displays student work; discipline plan is posted; procedures and assignments are in a prominent place—topic or skill for the day is written and defined; word wall is displayed; exit slip and are posters displayed.

____ *Strategic Reading*: Examples: surveying the text; selective highlighting; chunking; margin notes.

List the specific reading skill taught and the strategies used to teach the skills:
Comments:

Note. From Laura Zavatkay, principal, Robinson High School, Tampa, Florida. Revised by Carol A. Mullen.

Welsh and added a self-analysis component. This revision shifted the administrator away from extending observations of teachers with compliments toward engaging them in reflective conversation.

Inspired to allow the teacher to lead in the reflection process, Downey further refined her approach in the early 1970s after studying Costa and Garmston's work (as cited in Downey et al., 2004). This initiated a more collaborative and interdependent framework. Later, the work of Stephen Covey led her to identify three different levels of reflective interaction—direct, indirect, and collaborative/reflective dialogue. This model, coupled with Eric Berne's transactional analysis, shaped Downey's thinking about administrators' supervisory–employee relationships.

Moreover, Fenwick English's (as cited in Downey et al., 2004) research on the alignment of the written, taught, and assessed curriculum also inspired Downey. She changed the focus of teacher observations so the emphasis would be on what educators were teaching, not how they actually taught. Consequently, the curriculum and instructional emphasis has been pivotal to the Downey observation model for more than 15 years. She has since revised her model to stress not the actions of the teachers, but rather the instructional decisions they make.

As Downey began to teach others her approach, she also further refined the components of the reflective question and conversation (see Downey et al., 2004). The ultimate goal of this process is the active involvement of the teacher in a cycle of self-analysis and improvement. The role of the administrator becomes that of curriculum leader in the form of supervisor/coach. Downey realized that her original assumption that she could help teachers become more effective by telling them how to change their instruction was false. Even though they would make some improvements, significant and sustained change in instructional practice was not evident. At the time, teachers remained dependent on Downey's thought processes as opposed to developing the ability to independently reflect on and analyze instructional decisions.

Why Implement the Three-Minute Walk-Through?

Mullen (2004a) designed an administrative survey and circulated it throughout Florida to assistant principals and principals in their first 3 years on the job. Participants rated the importance of certain tasks using a Likert scale of 1 to 5, with 5 being "most important" and 1, "least important." Forty-seven percent of those surveyed ranked assisting teachers with instruction as most important. In most of this state's K–12 public schools, instructional leadership has also been identified as one of the primary expectations for administrators. In order to successfully implement any walk-through program, principals must commit to scheduling visits and analyzing the data collected. This focus on instruction elevates the principal's role from mere manager to curriculum leader.

Many schools have also implemented peer coaching, which is a "simple, nonthreatening program designed to help instructors improve instruction or learning situations" (Gottesman, 2000, p. 5). Though the Three-Minute Walk-Through incorporates some of the key ideas of peer coaching, it also differs. In the peer-coaching model, assistance for learning is provided by a teacher colleague, not someone in an administrative or evaluative position. Marshall (1996) explains that although peer coaching can be an invaluable process wherein teachers lend crucial support to their peers, "it is also important that teachers be observed regularly by their principals who have a school-wide perspective and input into the formal evaluation process" (p. 343).

Components of the Walk-Through

To paraphrase, five key ideas are pivotal to Downey's walk-through:

1. Short, focused, yet informal observation—the informal observation usually lasts 2 to 3 minutes and is used to gather information about curricular and instructional teacher practices and decisions.
2. Possible area for reflection—the ultimate goal of the observation is to engage the teacher in reflective thought about teaching practice.
3. Curriculum as well as instructional focus—data are gathered concerning curriculum and instructional decisions made by teachers and their impact on student performance. Time does not permit the observer to examine for completeness and content accuracy.
4. Follow-up occurs only on occasion and not after every visit—8 to 10 classroom visits may occur before the observer is ready to initiate reflective conversations with the teacher. Feedback should be given in a meaningful and timely manner.
5. Informal and collaborative—there are no checklists or judgments, which resemble an inspection. (Downey et al., 2004, pp. 2–4)

Reflective Thinking Models

Direct, independent, and interdependent types of interaction occur between supervisors/coaches and teachers. The instructional leader determines which conversational style to use based on the teacher's level of experience and willingness to participate in self-examination. What follows is a paraphrase of the three levels of interaction inherent in Downey's Reflective Thinking Model:

- Direct (lowest level)—in this approach, the supervisor/coach assumes more of a mentor role and provides the teacher with direct feedback and instruction. (This intervention is usually used with novice teachers and educators who might otherwise be ineffective.) Following an observation of a lesson where classroom management and teacher frustration regarding interruptions is a concern, a novice teacher might be asked about the types of procedures she expects students to follow during lessons. The teacher's response could lead to a discussion of effective classroom strategies, as prompted by the supervisor/coach.
- Independent (middle level)—at this stage, the supervisor/coach engages the teacher in reflection focused on the observed part of the lesson. The teacher is left with a carefully phrased question so that attention can be given to how instructional decisions were made during the lesson, for example, "What thinking went into your decision as to which children should share their writing at the end of the lesson?"
- Interdependent (highest level)—the supervisor/coach uses reflective questioning with the teacher based on the latter's instructional practices. The aim is to continue this dialogue in future conversations at the discretion of the teacher. (Downey et al., 2004)

Principal–Teacher Dialogue

With reference to our personal experiences as seasoned teachers and instructional coaches, we offer the following example of principal–teacher dialogue. In this scenario, the principal asks the novice teacher a question that is not focused on a particular lesson but rather covers a variety of instructional situations.

Principal: I'd like to ask you a question if you have a moment.
Teacher: Yes, I've got a few minutes before my students are finished with their music lesson.
Principal: I've observed your work with struggling readers. Based on this, I can see that they often need a great deal of support. Think about how you decide the appropriate amount of support to extend without giving them too much help.
Teacher: Many things go through my mind as I decide how much help I need to give each student. I'd like to talk with you about that.
Principal: Good. Let's set up a time then.

According to Downey et al. (2004), it is critical that an educator have the freedom to accept or decline such an invitation. In this brief exchange, the teacher accepts the opportunity to reflect, learn, and improve and requests further discussion.

David Schumaker, a veteran principal, cites the merits of this type of learning and growth among his staff: "Every time I have engaged staff members in a reflective dialogue, they have gained new insights, developed a new plan for the next time they teach, and increased their competence and confidence as a teacher" (cited in Schumaker & Sommers, 2001, p. 95).

Implementing School-wide Change

The success of any change effort depends greatly on how much time and preparation is given to its introduction and implementation. Downey (in Downey et al., 2004) cautions that teachers should be aware of the purpose and procedure of the Three-Minute Walk-Through. Not preparing the teacher for walk-throughs can result in interruptions in the observation, unnecessary anxiety, miscommunication, and even calls from the teacher's union (see chap. 8). Teachers who have not been informed of the purpose behind their administrator's visit will likely stop the flow of instruction to greet the observer. Students also need to learn to ignore the administrator so the observer can focus without interruption. Informing parents and the community of the nature and purpose for such walk-throughs is also a good idea, as this can change the perception of principals as school managers and teachers as instructional isolates.

Downey and her program codevelopers (2004) indicate that preconditions must be met in order to determine the readiness of any particular school to improve. Most importantly, administrators should examine their relationships with teachers: "Your presence in the classroom may be perceived as a threat, especially if your teachers know you only as an inspector or critic" (Downey et al., 2004, p. 112). Establishing positive relationships with faculty and staff is critical and should precede the implementation of unannounced walk-throughs. These types of visits allow the administrator to view authentic teaching practices as opposed to staged "performances," also known unfavorably by teachers as "dog-and-pony shows" that are the usual platform for formal evaluations (Danielson & McGreal, 2000). Teachers need to understand that the motive for the unannounced visits is not negative or punitive, just the opposite. Zepeda (2003) explains,

> The supervisor conducts informal classroom visitations *not* to catch the teacher off-guard or by surprise, *not* as "snoopervision," and *not* to interrupt classroom activities. By taking the time to observe the work teachers do on a daily basis *in their*

TABLE 10.2

Comparing Formal and Informal Walk-Through Models

The Downey Approach	*Other Walk-Through Approaches*
Informal	Formal
Brief—2–3 minutes	Longer—5–15 minutes
Sample of data gathered to explore teacher decisions.	Gather data about teacher effectiveness.
Walk-through time can occur throughout the day and is unannounced.	Walk-through time is typically known and scheduled (e.g., to watch a teacher's use of shared reading strategies).
No checklist of teaching practices to use; focus is on teacher's curricular and instructional decisions.	Specific checklist (rubric) to use for gathering data about specific practices.
Nothing to put into teacher personnel file.	May be put into teacher personnel file.
Focus on professional growth.	Focus on evaluation and assessment.
Ultimately leads to reflective conversation between the principal and teacher.	Usually leads to direct feedback from the supervisor to the teacher.
Coaching focus—intended to be supportive.	Judging focus—often inspectional.

Note. From Downey (2004). Adapted by Cindy Dowdy, Jennifer McCrystal, Robin Snyder, and Carol Mullen.

> *classrooms*, instructional supervision can exert informed effort and energy to assist teachers beyond formally scheduled observations. (p. 35)

COMPARISON WITH OTHER WALK-THROUGH MODELS

As previously mentioned, one Florida school district adopted the Downey Three-Minute Walk-Through model. For an overview of how this approach differs in intent and form from the other approaches educators implement, refer to Table 10.2. It lists the key components that differentiate the Downey approach from its "competitors."

Initially, our impression of the walk-through as professional teachers was that it was an evaluative method. We imagined teachers' practices being put under a frequent and unexpected microscope in which the administrator would establish opinions on an educator's effectiveness and within an impossibly limited time-frame. As teachers, we have found most walk-through methods to be just that—a miniature form of the formal evaluation. However, Downey's approach seems to offer an entirely different purpose. The focus is on coaching, not evaluation. It offers teachers of any instructional or subject area the opportunity to reflect on their practice free from the pressures of formal evaluation. According to Gottesman (2000), the current system of teacher evaluation tends generally to be ineffective anyway and perpetuates the isolation of teachers:

> The failure of our current evaluation systems is well documented. ...During any given day, most teachers will make hundreds of highly subjective decisions involving teaching and learning. To further complicate this matter is the fact that most teachers work in isolation. Therefore, many critical decisions about teaching and learning are made in total and complete isolation. (p. 3)

The Downey walk-through model goes beyond the managerial aspect of walking around from one classroom to the next. According to the studies Downey and her colleagues (2004) cite, when the principal courageously steps into a coaching mode by adopting the Three-Minute Walk-Through, he or she:

- Develops focus on curriculum;
- Increases visibility in classrooms;
- Stimulates rethinking of the principal's role;
- Clarifies and helps overcome time and politics as reform obstacles;
- Further develops positive school culture; and
- Enhances comfort level with reflective questions. (p. 155)

"The principal's primary purpose when making a walk-through" is to "[assess] whether what is being taught aligns with the written curriculum" (Downey et al., 2004, p. 155). The idea here is that the written, taught, and tested curriculum must be thoroughly aligned by curriculum leaders for students to excel.

After reviewing a variety of checklist models, we developed the following instrument (see Table 10.3). It incorporates the required checklist as well as a reflective questioning component, as suggested by Downey.

AFTERTHOUGHT

After considering the Downey walk-through model, we determined through analysis, research, and reflective discussion that this approach has the potential to greatly assist schools in improving from within. So often improvements are mandated by organizations outside of schools or through the implementation of specialized programs and/or materials, yet this approach utilizes resources *already* in the possession of schools—their own leaders. The walk-through tool can be used to address a number of cultural issues that continue to erode public education, such as teachers' isolation from colleagues and leaders, principals' evaluative approach to instructional leadership,

TABLE 10.3
Classroom Walk-Through Checklist

Teacher _____ Date _____ Room Number _____

Subject area being taught

Safe and orderly environment
Room arrangement is conducive to instruction
Classroom is welcoming/visibly appealing
Classroom discipline plan/rules visibly posted
Daily schedule visibly posted
Areas are organized for small group instruction
Material being taught is age/grade appropriate
Teacher is actively engaged in the teaching process
    Teacher's Role:

Students are actively engaged in learning
    Student's Role:

Other items to be added

Classroom equipment/building notes

Reflective Questions

Observer's Signature

Note. From Cindy Dowdy, Jennifer McCrystal, Robin Snyder, and Carol Mullen.

and schools' lack of professional dialogue. The reflective questioning piece of the Downey method is the distinctive feature that, when practiced effectively, lifts the observation tool out of the mundane realm of evaluative routines into that of metacognition.

One of us has attended a school improvement conference conducted by the Florida district mentioned at the outset. During this conference, school personnel were informed that walk-throughs would be mandated as of 2006; the intent was to ensure the implementation of school improvement goals and strategies. Contrary to the Downey approach, a required aspect of these walk-throughs involves a checklist of teaching indicators. This is to be developed not by site-based curriculum leaders and instructional coaches but rather by the district.

We see the mandatory mentoring twist on this program, complete with a formal observation tool, as potentially limiting if not outright illogical and disempowering. The philosophy inherent in the walk-through model is not one of vigilance and accountability but of partnership and growth. The district's focus on the direct form of principal–teacher interaction enacts the lowest level of reflective thinking, as outlined in Downey's model. Whereas some of the claims in the literature promote walk-throughs as a means of opening classroom doors, this district's model may very well close the doors it intends to open. The way in which the district has chosen to implement this initiative seems to rob it of the reflective questioning component—the very piece that empowers teachers as curriculum leaders and as partners joined with principals in authentic professional development.

PRACTICAL, REFLECTIVE ACTIVITIES

- (a) Review the three levels of reflective questioning in Downey's Reflective Thinking Model and choose the level of reflective conversation that would be appropriate for each of the following types of teachers:

    Novice or at-risk teachers who have complained that students cannot read the text in their content area;

    Experienced teachers with satisfactory performance who are working to incorporate higher order questioning in their lessons; and

    Master teachers who are trying to implement a new math program based on the inquiry method

    (b) Practice developing direct questioning or reflective questioning that curriculum leaders who are instructional coaches might frame for these groups of teachers.
- Compose a list of indicators (checklist) that you could use for observation in an effective teacher's classroom. Reflect on this list: To what extent is it clarifying? Limiting? Refer to the Downey model (or any other) to develop a critique of such checklists.
- Walk-throughs by curriculum leaders can enhance a school's culture. If teachers are not sufficiently informed of the purpose and nature of the walk-through, the culture could be affected negatively. As an instructional leader, how might you best prepare your staff for the purpose and implementation of administrator walk-throughs?

11

Transformation of an Inner City Elementary School Into a Magnet School

Mary Schmitz-Phillips
Susan King
Carol A. Mullen

WHAT ARE MAGNET SCHOOLS?

Emerging in the 1970s and quadrupling nationwide (from approximately 1,000 in 1981 to almost 4,300 in 2000; Morrill & Ryan, 2004), magnet schools are thematic curriculum schools within a traditional district assignment or controlled-choice plan. The sites for these schools are usually located in or border the inner city and face such challenges as poverty, high crime rates, teen pregnancy, and illiteracy. A federal grant that addresses educational and ethnic outcomes is the initiating event that typically allows these urban schools to be transformed (U.S. Department of Education [USDOE], Magnet Schools Assistance Program Grant [MSAP], 2004).

Magnet programs were established to promote racial diversity, improve scholastic standards, and enhance curriculum through a range of programs that satisfy individual talents and interests (Goldring & Smrekar, 2002, p. 13). They are characterized by the empowerment of staff to transform their school to respond to client preferences (Goldring & Smrekar, 2005), and the effectiveness of the school's curriculum leadership is key to the success and infusion of a magnet curriculum.

The curriculum at a magnet school is infused with a special theme. For example, a regular public (traditional) school might offer a music and an art class, but at a magnet performing arts school, the curriculum would be steeped in the visual, performing, and communication arts. An elementary magnet school would have its own art gallery and dance studio. Similarly, international studies schools can be expected to videoconference with other schools around the world, and students would share their culture with others in other countries via web pages and digital movies and pictures.

In a traditional school, students are assigned based on their home address, whereas in a magnet school, students apply and are selected to attend. A magnet committee hires all staff members, including the principal, who is charged with seeing that the school's particular theme is integrated in all aspects of the curriculum.

WHY TRANSFORMATION, NOT CHANGE?

We prefer to use the word *transform* over *change* to describe the development of existing elementary schools into magnets because it connotes change that is intentional or deliberate. Although *Merriam-Webster's Collegiate Dictionary* presents *change* and *transform* as synonymous, synonyms for *transform*— *transmute, transfigure,* and even *metamorphose*—reveal high intention. The magnet school leader is the change agent for the transformation, and the principal must establish the climate that sets the tone for high intention, as in the commitment to high-quality teaching and inclusion of all students in learning.

ADVANTAGES AND DISADVANTAGES
OF MAGNET SCHOOLS

Advantages of magnet schools include the "variety of specialized programs that students can choose from" and the encouragement students receive "to be creative and to hone their skills in their area of interest" (Morrill & Ryan, 2004, para. 5). Morrill and Ryan (2004) also clarify that some of these schools have adopted different teaching styles. Magnet schools are usually designed to bring students together from different ethnic, socioeconomic, and racial backgrounds. These schools are particularly important in districts that are trying to desegregate its schools. As outlined in federal magnet grant information, the purpose of magnets and the advantages that they bring to the district are the elimination of minority group isolation, instruction that strengthens knowledge of academic subjects and vocational skills, and the development of innovation educational methods and practices. In addition, magnet programs promote systemic reforms and provide all students with the opportunity to acquire challenging state content and performance (U.S. Department of Education, 2003).

For example, the University of Hartford Magnet School, an elementary school in Connecticut, uses psychologist Howard Gardner's theory of multiple intelligences, which enables students to learn and develop their own strengths. The New York Yonkers Public School District (2005), New York, espouses that the advantages of magnets are "far-reaching" (para. 2): Magnets provide more incentives for student learning and parents and children can choose learning based on the student's interests and needs. In fact, this district's belief is that "Magnet programs provide a quality education for all students at every level of ability" (para. 2). Although a great deal of research is available on magnet schools, choice schools, city schools, and more, there is no uniform agreement that magnet schools produce better results than these other alternatives or even regular public schools.

However, many argue in favor of magnet schools, saying that schools that compete for students should be better places of learning than attendance-area schools (Rouse, 1998). A report by the Citizen's Commission on Civil Rights claims that inner city students who attend a magnet school may benefit from an atmosphere of higher expectations for school performance and higher education (Yu & Taylor, 1997). In the Hillsborough County Public School District, west-central Florida, the magnet office, using the scores recorded on the district Web site (see http://apps.sdhc.k12.fl.us), calculated that more than 62% of the district elementary magnet schools made "A"'s on the Governor's A+ Plan, exceeding the district's average of 44%. If fact, using the district Web site information, the office calculated that all of Hillsborough's elementary magnet schools have made an "A" or a "B" on that rating since the plan began. And almost half of the elementary and middle school magnets made Adequate Yearly Progress (AYP) on the NCLB Act of 2001 (U.S. Department of Education, 2002).

Many researchers, including Patricia Bauch, Ellen Goldring, and Claire Smrekar, have found that magnet schools promote school improvement by, for example, "provid[ing] more opportunities for parental involvement and effective communication between home and schools (Smrekar, 2004, para. 6). According to Smrekar and the sources she cites, magnet principals usually have more autonomy in choosing faculty and magnet teachers, and teachers tend to have greater freedom in curriculum instruction and involvement in decision making about curriculum issues. Shared governance combined with team-based curriculum leadership have been known to improve classroom instruction and enhance student learning (Smrekar, 2004, para. 6).

Disadvantages of magnet schools include the time-consuming application process and "the selective admissions criteria" that "create firewalls" for low-performing students (Morrill & Ryan, 2004, p. 8). A traditional principal is at liberty to hire immediately but a magnet principal must call together a faculty committee and screen all applicants. And, in most districts, students are placed by the magnet office and the names are then submitted to the school. These procedures are outlined in the federal grant; they must be followed even though additional steps are included. Furthermore, given the thematic concentration and curriculum of these schools, students can be shortchanged on academics. The students can have lower grade-point averages than their counterparts attending neighboring schools, and the courses they take can be less demanding as well. Parents and students often have to make the time commitment of a long bus ride to school each day and a longer commute for evening events and school conferences. Students and families in competitive magnet programs, such as International Baccalaureate, have a rigorous academic schedule and often feel overwhelmed as they strive to participate in both academics and extracurricular activities.

Another issue involves the lack of research about the benefit of the magnet school experience to students once they leave this environment. According to Gaines, "The evaluation of achievement in magnet programs is uninterpretable when there are no comparisons of magnet students with nonmagnet students or with scores district-wide" (cited in Douzenis, 1994, p. 15). Because the magnet school program is a new concept, more research is obviously needed to validate its success and as well to assess its shortcomings.

STANDARDS AND DIVERSITY

As district personnel assess the community needs and consider redrawing boundaries, advertising for staff, planning workshops and training, and ordering equipment and materials, many factors will need attention. They must first identify the academic goals of each magnet school, in order to promote excellence for all students, and then ensure diversity amongst staff and students. They must also identify goals that promote excellence for all students and that serve to increase diversity within the district. Throughout the process, staff must be sensitive to parent and teacher concerns about the students selected to attend. Further, the community needs assurance that students will have full access to the new program and curriculum.

The school district featured in this chapter was awarded unitary status in 2001, meaning that the district has satisfied the federal requirement that racially segregated schools be eliminated in the county. The measures used by the courts to determine if this social justice goal has been achieved are transportation, extracurricular activities, administrative staff assignment, quality of education, faculty assignment, facilities and resources, and student assignment (Terry Sanford Institute of Public Policy, Duke University, 2004). Evaluations are prepared annually by the assessment office to monitor the progress of these outcomes. Before this important change in desegregation occurred, minority students were automatically bussed to suburban schools. Under the recent offering of choice plans, these students may now seek placement in schools closer to their homes or apply to magnet schools.

As Archbald (2004) explains, magnet schools are built on the premise that school choice provides impoverished children a way to escape inferior-zoned schools. Magnets promote innovation and voluntary racial integration through specialized schools.

Magnet programs are designed to entice students in the suburbs to attend schools in the urban area. Choice attractor programs, on the other hand, are designed to attract urban students to schools in the suburbs. Using both of these methods, the district can then achieve diversity on a voluntary basis. By providing a magnet program in urban areas, and choice attractor programs in suburban and rural areas, these schools work together to achieve a district's diversity goals.

The magnet school office staff in the Hillsborough County Public School District in Tampa, Florida prepares reports to identify patterns for student applications to target areas and themes for recruitment. Based on the number of applications and acceptances, the most popular themes are based on advanced academics and the performing arts. Because magnet schools offer a specialized curriculum to entice parents and students out of their neighborhoods into a magnet school, curriculum becomes the driving force.

PRINCIPALS AS ORGANIZATIONAL CHANGE AGENTS

Schools that are transformed into magnets reflect investment in the notion that organizational change is necessary if student achievement is to improve (Schumaker & Sommers, 2001).

Before making this wholesale commitment, principals must collect and analyze data for that particular site and develop a plan to determine if the change makes sense. At this point, the process of change becomes site-based, in that school leaders are responsible for marketing that change to teachers, parents, and the community (Schumaker & Sommers, 2001).

Because students, parents, and staff have chosen to participate, parental involvement, student interest, and staff investment are all factors that work toward creating an academically challenging, safe environment. Once a theme is determined, magnet instructors are hired through a rigorous process, ensuring excellence and expertise within the collective focus. Comprehensive in-service and professional development programs are integral for the most up-to-date practices in the content areas. This includes the principal's direct involvement in training and development programs—modeling needs to come from the top of the school's curriculum ladder.

BACKGROUND AND RATIONALE

The large Florida district that constitutes the context of our study opened the first magnet program in 1990 and it currently operates 25 programs in 23 schools. Using funds from a federal MSAP, the district has committed to transforming a traditional elementary school into the Academy of World Studies. Each school included in the grant has a specific budget for its opening that covers personnel, equipment, supplies, dues and fees, and contractual personnel (responsible for helping to infuse the magnet's theme through the curriculum).

Students' academic performance at what we refer to here as "School X" has declined in the past 10 years, but AYP (for a definition, see chap. 14) baseline data is expected to show gains during the 3-year grant project (USDOE, MSAP, 2004). Other data included in the grant indicate that minority student percentages are at or above 60%. Because of participation in this project, and based on projected enrollment through Year 3, the school is projected to achieve a minority percentage of approximately 55%. One of the anticipated outcomes, as stated in the grant, is that minority isolation will not occur in the magnet school or any of the sending schools. As in most of the districts operating under a MSAP grant, the administrators must submit annual reports specifying the ethnic status of each school.

School X is currently being changed into the Academy of World Studies in order to improve the racial balance of the school and prevent minority isolation. The latter goal will be met by building a strong academic program based on language and multicultural experiences. The curriculum will implement the Foreign Language Experience (FLEX) model (FLEX: Foreign Language Experience Programs, 1996), which provides children with the opportunity to learn languages other than English.

Key features of the new school's theme are accelerated curriculum, interdisciplinary units of study, communication technology, summer communication institutes, and community partnerships with those interested in global communications and foreign-language education. The language arts curriculum will provide students with opportunities to use their language skills to read and write stories as they share information with their e-pals in other countries. Sixty minutes of daily intensive reading instruction is also included. Throughout the school, all teachers, using a Latin-based program, will teach language. Students will have Spanish every day, and those who complete first through fifth grade will have had the equivalent of instruction received in a Spanish I course. In addition, the summer institute will feature a month-long exploration of languages and cultures. Projects will include an international cookbook and the study of foreign language, e-pals, story-boards, and a final celebration in the International Café.

The curriculum will be accelerated and compacted with such specialized programs as the Math Academy. World science issues will be investigated through hands-on learning in the Spectrum Science Lab, and the global issues of economics, environmental, and cultural connections will be woven into the curriculum. Technology will be used as a gateway through which students will develop analytical, critical, and evaluative skills, and assessment and evaluation will be ongoing and vertically aligned within the curriculum.

Teachers will design the curriculum using a three-tier model that will allow students to experience success through research, contact, and presentation. As an example, the first tier might consist of researching basic facts about a culture or site (e.g., a virtual field trip to the Louvre). In the second tier, students would develop a deeper and more personal appreciation for French culture by connecting with Francophone students using the Internet. And in the third tier, students would create a multimedia presentation using PowerPoint and other software to share their culture with French peers.

The Parent–Teacher–Student Association (PTSA) will be involved in school fundraisers to assist in providing student materials, and regular parent meetings should encourage greater parental involvement. The school will explore before- and after-school options that are theme related. More student contact time will likely be provided to assist parents with childcare in program areas that explore different cultures using recipes, computer language, costumes, dances, and more.

Each MSAP grant highlights specific outcomes. Anticipated funding-related outcomes for the academy include elimination of minority-group isolation, academic excellence for all students, and promotion of student achievement through innovative curriculum, professional development, and sustainability (USDOE, MSAP, 2004).

PROCEDURAL STEPS FOR THE TRANSFORMATION

Selection of Principal and Staff

A crucial step at the organizational level involved in making a successful transformation as a new magnet school is to select a highly effective principal.

Magnet principals are charged with the implementation of all magnet objectives; for example, they are the key leaders with respect to the marketing of the school and assessing the success of all projects. As the instructional leaders of their sites, these individuals are expected to facilitate the development, articulation, and implementation of the vision of the school and its curriculum. The principal is also responsible for collaborating with families and community members to nurture and sustain a school culture that promotes student learning and staff professional growth (Office of Superintendent of Public Instruction, n.d.).

District advertisement for the magnet principal occurs in December of each year so he or she can be appointed before the school opens in the fall. The next step is for the principal, along with magnet and district staff, to conduct interviews for an assistant principal. After that, the principal, assistant principal, and magnet staff interview for key positions, including classroom teachers. Together this team will recruit teachers committed to creating a strong student-centered environment where ideas and talents are treated with respect and dignity (Riley, Wilson, & Fogg, 2000). This process proves time consuming, as the hiring committee is not only searching for quality teachers but also for those who can identify with the magnet theme and the philosophy of the school (Hudson, n.d.).

Figure 11.1 depicts the transformation of an inner city elementary school into a district magnet school. As conveyed, specific tools (e.g., the budget and theme) in the "toolbox" are needed in order to create a theme-specific magnet school. First, the principal and his or her team will need to identify a school theme and then follow the other steps (1 through 8), as illustrated by the ladder, to achieve student success.

Recruitment and Selection of Students

Teacher author Susan, the current supervisor of magnets for her school district in Florida (who previously worked as a magnet marketing and recruitment specialist), has developed procedures briefly discussed here for recruitment and selection. The following marketing and recruitment strategies used by the district magnet office for advertising programs to parents and students are modeled after ideas and strategies outlined in various federal MSAP grants. Most MSAP grants are based on the assumption that the new program will eliminate minority isolation in inner city areas. The success of a magnet program is directly related to a district's ability to recruit non-Black (federal language) students from traditional schools located beyond the urban center. Magnet personnel in the district use a combination of brochures, mailers, television ads, parent information meetings, open houses,

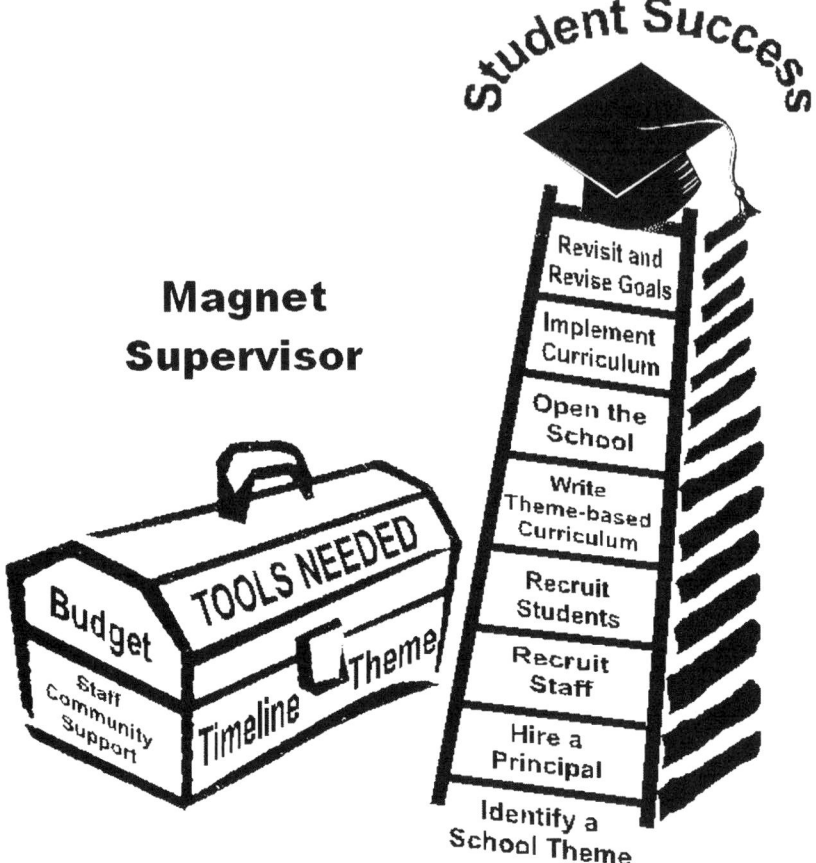

FIG. 11.1.   Transforming a regular elementary school into a district magnet school.

neighborhood canvassing, and telemarketing to ensure that parents are aware of their magnet choices. In this particular district, the initial recruitment for lottery selection is conducted for a certain period, usually early Fall, but secondary recruitment is ongoing.

Students enrolled at this new elementary school are selected in the same manner as the other elementary and secondary magnet schools and programs. Based on national, race-neutral factors (interest, geography, school culture, and language spoken at home), students in this district are placed in their first, second, or third choices by a computer lottery program. Offer letters are then mailed to parents, and if there is no response, phone calls are made. The district office sends each accepting student a letter of congratulations with directions on how to enroll at the school. Applications accepted after the deadlines are entered into secondary recruitment for the next lottery. Lotteries from secondary recruitment are conducted until all schools are filled to capacity, and the district office continues to fill all magnet schools throughout the year.

Implementation and Staff Development

After all staff have been hired, it is crucial that the magnet administrators and staff are given the opportunity to develop expert knowledge about the theme or philosophy that makes the school unique (Hudson, n.d.). Having the capacity to implement effective innovation programs staffed with the most capable teachers available is integral to the success of the school, as is continuous staff development. Start-up costs can include renovations to facilities, additional personnel, more training, and new technology and, although these costs are high, the increased student achievement, more choice for parents, and district diversity are clearly beneficial to the students, the district, and the government. A major goal of magnet schools is to provide specialized niches of learning for students. The efforts of individual teachers combined with their passion for teaching children is what makes possible this unique learning environment (Schumaker & Sommers, 2001).

ADMINISTRATORS' INSIGHTS INTO SCHOOL LEADERSHIP

The transformation of a magnet is not complete without instructional leaders—traditional school administrators are transformed along with the school. We interviewed both magnet and regular school administrators to inform as well as to personalize this process. Interview questions for all of the principals included the pros and cons of school administration, their interaction within school communities, and the role of magnet schools in leadership. Magnet principals reflected on whether their leadership style had changed, whether they felt more empowered at a magnet school, and whether they would recommend the job of magnet leadership to others. Traditional administrators discussed the important characteristics of leadership, their perceptions of magnet schools, and whether they would consider making a professional move.

Specifically, the teacher authors developed the following interview questions for magnet principals:

1. Do you feel more empowered as a magnet administrator?
2. What are the pros and cons of being a magnet administrator?
3. Has your leadership style changed and how?
4. Has the community around your school changed?
5. Would you recommend an administrator from a traditional school to make the change to a magnet school?

Adapting the questions we developed for administrators of regular schools, these principals were asked:

1. What is your perception of magnet schools?
2. What do (or did) you see as the pros and cons of being an administrator?
3. How do (or did) you reach out to the community in order to bring positive attention to your school?
4. Would you ever consider making a change and becoming an administrator of a magnet school? Why or why not?
5. What leadership characteristics do you feel you need to be an successful administrator?

We spoke with a former traditional school principal who has since moved to the district level, as well as the current assistant principal at the same school. The principal had served for 4 years, whereas the assistant principal was serving her 1st year in administration. We also interviewed two magnet school principals, one of whom had moved back to a traditional school. These magnet principals had worked as school leaders for more than 5 years, one in a successful performing arts programs and the other a technology magnet. The performing arts magnet had grown more successful each year, whereas the technology magnet had suffered declining enrollment for the past few years but had recently added a new theme of foreign language and global studies. In addition, in 2003, a custodian was murdered by a passerby at 11:00 p.m. at the technology magnet, and the school suffered significant teacher turnover. However, it was difficult to determine if the declining enrollment and teacher turnover resulted from the lingering fears regarding this late-night crime.

Our interviewees all saw professional growth as a positive aspect of school administration, and most of them listed lack of control as a con. Magnet principals discussed the extra layer in the application process using a district committee for hiring, but only one of them considered this a hindrance. One of the magnet middle school principals shared that she enjoyed "the icing" of a magnet school and that a magnet principal is able to attract teachers willing to go beyond the official duties of the job. She elaborated,

It takes a special heart and a devoted principal to understand that magnet is empowerment! This is not a con for me—only a loop that helps to identify those highly interested and talented teachers with a sincere desire to work with magnets.

Like the magnet principals, the traditional principals reflected on opportunities that leadership had afforded them both personally and professionally. The principal who has since become the supervisor of school improvement identified as a positive the "ability to create a common vision, goal, and focus and to influence the staff to buy into it and help obtain a common product."

The other magnet principal commented that his leadership style had become more consensual over time. He attributed this change to the committee interview and the collaborative efforts with the magnet school office. Such magnet procedures as the committee interview and the assignment of students were attributed to the magnet office's support of a democratic style. The first magnet principal believed that her leadership style had improved with the experience afforded her as a magnet leader. She also mentioned that magnet principals reap the benefit of the support and services from the district level. Although she was leaving her position, she took what she coined "the magnet phenomenon" with her. Both magnet principals said that the community housing and businesses around their schools had improved, but only one attributed this to the fact that the school changed from traditional to magnet.

One of the magnet principals indicated that she would recommend making a leadership change to a magnet because of the smaller, more diverse populations. One traditional administrator responded to the question more personally, saying that she would not move because she was content with being the leader of a Title I school. (Title I is a federal program designed to improve academics for the disadvantaged; U.S. Department of Education, 2005). Both discussed the different ways they had reached out to the community, with the support of their partnerships with a local university and a science museum.

All four administrators talked about the importance of their leadership roles, but the principals focused more on instructional leadership, whereas the assistant principal discussed student management at greater length. One administrator who had been an assistant principal at both a magnet and regular school explained that her leadership style had improved through experiences with the highly skilled, optimistic people who are attracted to magnets.

Based on the interview results we generated, the administrators all viewed leadership as a source of personal growth. The magnet principals viewed the themed curriculum at their schools and their own personal leadership as intrinsically connected. Because teachers were teaching to the personal strengths and interests of their student populations, the magnet teachers were perceived as more successful. The magnet principals appeared to have an elevated sense

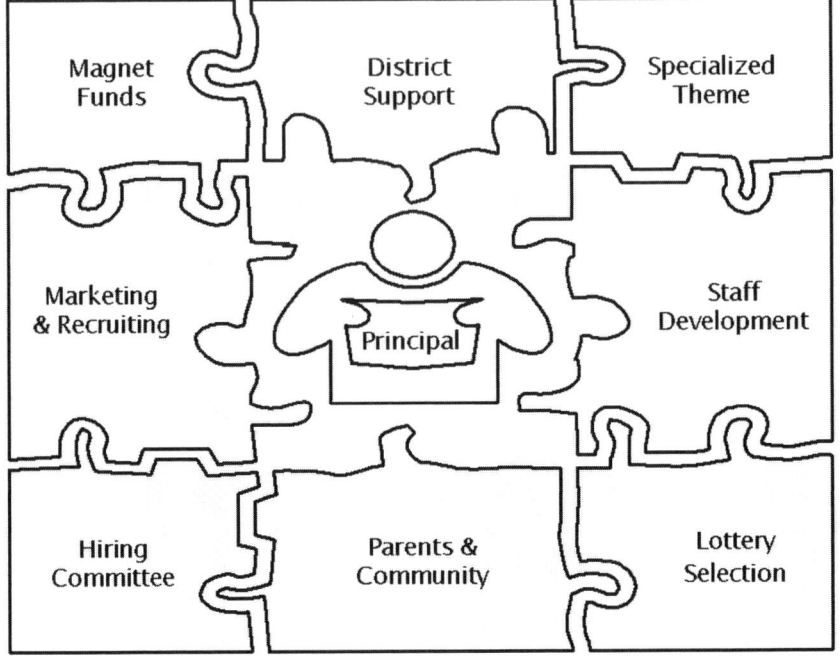

FIG. 11.2.   Fitting together the pieces of a thematic curriculum.

of pride as an outgrowth of building and developing a theme-based curriculum, as chosen by the student and his or her family. They expressed great satisfaction about having the necessary curriculum tools to steep children in learning through a theme of inherent and collective interest.

We learned from our interviews with the principals and from the literature we read that various "pieces" or components need to fit together to create a successful magnet school. Everything revolves around the principal's capacity to fit together the pieces of a thematic curriculum while making sound decisions. For example, this leader will have to support the school's curriculum theme, make connections between the district and him or herself, and hire teachers with expertise and confidence in their abilities and knowledge of the theme. (See Fig. 11.2.)

FINAL THOUGHTS

The transformation of a traditional into a magnet school ultimately offers parents educational choice with regard to public education. Magnets have been linked with the reduction of school violence, the improvement of student attendance, and positive attitudes about learning. Research studies tell us that magnet sites have matured beyond serving as basic tools for desegregation and, among other contributions, take an important step toward full racial and ethnic equity. The role of magnet schools under unitary status is to provide options for public schooling, as well as to maintain voluntary integration. This complex process of organizational transformation can benefit an entire school district and the nation as a whole.

From having studied the history of magnet schools in this district and others, we believe that a strong leader is a key element in this transformation. Those interviewed admitted that as a school leader they had faced many challenges, but magnet principals seemed to feel more empowered by and responsive to the myriad of challenges they dealt with, largely because of the support provided by the magnet office. Principals of magnet schools described these organizations as more student-focused, emphasizing the reasoning behind the development of this type of innovation. Some shared that these programs do not have to change teachers, but rather provide an environment that encourages professional teaching and returns the responsibility for teaching to these curriculum experts (Riley et al., 2000). If the major goal of a district is excellence in education for all, school choice and magnets are an important aspect of the plan. Magnet schools potentially allow the personal strengths and talents of students to shine as they thrive in theme-focused curriculums.

Magnet schools were the nation's first schools of choice and are now leading the field in providing alternatives to traditional public schools. Because the education field is crowded with additional choices, magnet schools must depend more and more on the specialized curriculum and school leaders for providing parents with the education that best meets the needs of their children. Magnet schools must also allow the selected curricular theme to stand out in order to gain recognition for teaching children in a style different from conventional teaching. It is important for administrators of these schools to remember that parents and students who *choose* the magnet school environment expect a higher quality of teaching. Great care must be taken by the district and magnet leaders to make choices that will ensure strong leadership in these innovative sites. Schmitz-Phillips wishes to share a poem she wrote that honors the voice and reality of some magnet students.

I am a child.
I am a child they say is hard to reach,
Have you really tried?
I am a child they say is hard to teach,

I just can't learn the way you want me to.
I am a child they say is not in the right placement,
Why not? Where should I go? Who wants me?
I am a child who chose to switch to a magnet school.
I am a child they say is easily reached, readily taught,
I guess there are things that I'm good at.
I am a child they say who has learned a lot.
Here I can learn they way they teach me,
I can succeed because they know how to reach me.
I am a child they say has found her home.
I've finally found where I belong.
I am a child who wants a chance!

PRACTICAL, REFLECTIVE ACTIVITIES

- Imagine that you are the principal of a magnet school. Based on your chosen specialized theme, select the "puzzle pieces" around you, the leader, to make the school successful. Such components include sources of funding, criteria for hiring teachers, the kind of community that would best fit, and strategies for drawing families to the school.
- Interview magnet school leaders in your locale. Devise questions that address these areas of leadership: demonstration of leadership in innovative curriculum, customer service, and commitment to excellence in education.
- Write an essay that compares the advantages and disadvantages of magnet schools to public schools. Consult Morrill and Ryan's (2004) article for this purpose.
- Read about magnet schools in areas of personal interest. Morrill and Ryan's (2004) source contains a list of web-based resources (go to the end of the article). Each source is briefly annotated, covering such issues as racial integration, magnet school goals, and student profiles.

12

Career Academy Trends in Modernizing Curriculum and Infusing Technology

Annie Hunter Clasen
Carol A. Mullen

TECHNOLOGY-RELATED LEGISLATION AND SCHOOL REFORM

Influential educational policies such as the Technology Standards for School Administrators (TSSA) have mandated program changes for schools and universities (TSSA Collaborative, 2001). These specify that aspiring leaders be familiar with advanced learning technologies and adapt to the new high-powered, technology-infused curriculum leadership (National Policy Board for Educational Administrators for the Educational Leadership Constituent Council, 1995). Administrators, in turn, must be capable of making informed data-based decisions affecting technology infusion and curriculum reform (Chen et al., 2005). Even "the most basic uses of technology have a vital function beyond their apparent application" (Mullen, 2004a, pp. 135–136). Hence, course and program offerings that match the real-life experiences of students and staff outside of school support the modernization of school curriculum.

The National Education Technology Plan, released January 2005, addresses the need for technology to be incorporated in educational delivery systems. As Curtis (2005) explains, this report, commissioned in 2003 by the U.S. Department of Education (Office of Educational Technology), identifies America's students as our ultimate constituents and encourages educators to listen to and learn from this "IM" (instant-messaging) generation. In fact, students often better comprehend many of the intricacies and opportunities inherent in the technological revolution than many of their elders, including teachers and administrators, who lack the "advantage" of growing up with the Internet and advanced technologies.

School reform across the nation accounts for dramatic changes in technology and curriculum leaders' perceptions of school and business. Technology developments and innovations require revised curricula, entirely new programs, different approaches to instruction, fresh staff development strategies, and updated administrator education programs, as well as the commitment of educational leaders. Technology advocates argue that it is crucial to stay abreast of technology and, when appropriate and desirable, to integrate into the school curriculum such developments as palm-sized, wireless, or voice-controlled computers, virtual reality (Cunningham & Cordeiro, 2003), voice-recognition software, e-mail programs, homework Web sites, and online grade books (Mullen, 2004a). School leaders must exercise discretion, however, as they are inundated with sales promotions offering the newest gizmo that promises to revolutionize the classroom and school community. They must thoroughly research products to make informed decisions as to what best suit the needs of their constituents and will have future viability. Unfortunately, a limited budget for such expenses is a constant worry for most school administrations. These days, equipment is nearly outdated by the time personnel deciphers the accompanying instructions.

Education leaders also face the challenge of engaging technology-sophisticated learners at their level. These "millennium students" effortlessly communicate, work, and play using cell phones, e-mail, video games, and a host of other gadgets (National Education Technical Plan, 2004, p. 16). A running joke in most households is that teenagers are indispensable, at least when it comes to programming, operating, and fixing the technological devices.

THE NEW MILLENNIUM HIGH SCHOOL: OVERVIEW

New Millennium High Schools (NMHSs) commit to comprehensively restructuring their curriculum offerings to integrate academic courses with career education and the business community (Mullen, 2002c), training high school students as apprentices, interns, and on-the-job trainees, and matching the workforce needs of a quickly changing global business environment (Florida NMHS academy coordinator, interview, 2005).

In the 1990s, Florida legislative support for NMHSs came from the commissioner of education, Ed Brogan, and legislator Jim Horne, financing grants for a 2-year period, from 1999 to 2001. Originally, 10 schools were selected for the NMHS designation because of their collaborative approach with technical career programs, academic teachers, and the business community. The grant supporting the development and implementation of the NMHS model led to school-wide program development being sustained at the 10 original sites, and 4 additional schools we studied for 2 years. The funding changed in 2002 to support career academies instead, requiring that administrators at these sites adapt to this new reform initiative. Educational researchers of the Council for Educational Policy, Research, and Improvements (CEPRI) shared that these funding changes occurred because of shifts in state legislation and the perceived need for students to connect to a small group within a large school.

The main change in the NMHS designation is different curriculum offerings, but this change in status from NMHS to career academy is probably confusing to the public, in that the NMHS designation, familiar in Florida, is still being used in promotional materials, Web sites, and as a seal on graduation certificates. The experience that NMHS personnel had with curriculum development in their former role as millennium overseers gave them the necessary framework for rebuilding their career-academy curriculums. However, these leaders favor the NMHS designation for the reason that it makes public the school's commitment by both administration and staff to meet student and workforce needs.

"Once a New Millennium High School, always a New Millennium High School," a school administrator uttered when I (Annie Clasen) inquired whether her school was still designated as a NMHS site. When discussing its status, this leader clarified that "there is no funding specified for that designation now. Career academies are the new source of our grant funding" (Florida NMHS school administrator, personal communication, June 2005). She further explained: "We continue to use the NMHS designation on our diplomas. We are proud of the designation."

Career Academies

Career academies are small learning environments within a school that connect relevant and rigorous curriculum to real-life experiences, with students, teachers, and employers working together in job-related subjects (Mullen with Sullivan, 2002). These state-funded programs are available to middle-grade students matriculating to secondary schools, as well as to high school students. Although school leaders structure the career academy programs in different ways, the method of grouping students into academic and career-orientated electives using the school-within-a-school format is the main delivery. They reorganize school programs using three major conduits: small learning communities, college preparatory curriculum with a career theme, and partnerships with the community and organizations; these offer such varied curricular options as environmental science, health and human services, communications, informational technology and management, finance, and leadership and international studies (Florida State University Schools, 2005). An integral part of career academies is the focus on career goals and the connection of learning to real-life experiences. Partnerships with the business community are also stressed (Mullen, 2002c). A primary goal is to prepare students to exit the academies with marketable skills and to take the next step following graduation, whether a 4-year school, a 2-year school, a vocational program, the military, or a paying job (Florida State University Schools, 2005).

As noted, curriculum development involves the business community's input. Each career academy is expected to have a functioning advisory committee composed of community leaders, business leaders, parents, students, and academy staff. Students are involved in various cooperative learning opportunities, including mentoring, job shadowing, internships, field trips, guest speakers, curricular-based clubs, competitive events, and part-time employment (Mullen with Sullivan, 2002). The career academy program manager I spoke to commented,

> Having a strong advisory committee is a key to success for our programs. I am able to call various members to ask questions, receive input on what is happening in the business world, invite them to my classroom as guest speakers, and have job placement opportunities for our students. It takes extra effort to have this committee up and running, but the payoff is big for our programs.

Curriculum objectives at these academies focus on enabling students to both understand and apply, to the world of work, the knowledge and skills learned in the classroom. As an example of this transition to the workplace, we learned about a career academy for health sciences at a high school wherein students work as emergency medical technicians. The students integrate classroom subject matter by volunteering at local health facilities until they reach the age of 18. In the classroom, they receive "First Responder" certification, pass a national certification exam, and practice on computerized dummies programmed with various ailments (Florida NMHS academy coordinator, interview, 2005). This exemplary model certainly seems to connect students to today's changing workplace.

Another academy coordinator, from an original NMHS site, shared that once the New Millennium grant had reinitiated the senior capstone project, twelfth graders received intensive, real-world learning. This involves a 4-year career planning process, a career-related research paper, and the development of a career portfolio. Students make final presentations to a panel of industry representatives that provides evaluative feedback. The senior year is more meaningful for these students than traditionally because they are able to connect with potential employers (Florida NMHS academy coordinator, interview, 2005). In one New Millennium High School that received state-level recognition for demonstrating exemplary leadership and curricular reform, the seasoned principal enthusiastically reported that students were being challenged as never before. By completing the senior career capstone project at this Florida school, students were accountable in the present for their future (Mullen with Sullivan, 2002).

TECHNOLOGY ISSUES AND CHALLENGES

As previously mentioned, the increasing availability of technology has changed the way students communicate with one another, with their parents, and their school community. In a Pew Internet Project Surveys (2004) study analyzing Internet users' online activities, more than two thirds of the 18–29 age group used the Internet for research. More than half sought new job information, used IM, listened to music online, and consulted sports scores and information.

The Pew Internet and American Life Project Report (2004) found that the web has become the "new normal" in America. On a typical day in 2004, some 70 million American adults logged onto the Internet to use e-mail, access news, obtain government information, retrieve medical information, participate in auctions, book travel plans, research genealogy, play games, and engage in countless other activities. This figure represents a 37% increase from 2000.

Contacts at the four high schools we investigated thought that reliance on the Internet for researching job information and completing the career research paper was a positive trend. A career academy program manager at a large urban school shared how her employability curriculum now includes creating electronic resumes, completing online job applications, and producing digital portfolios. She is challenged to stay updated with respect to the continuous changes in the business world and thus finds it necessary to spend many hours each week researching via the Internet. In addition, the senior capstone projects that were once delivered using science project boards are now presented using advanced technologies. Modernizing curriculum means using such updated delivery methods as PowerPoint, video, and web pages (Florida NMHS academy coordinator, personal communication, 2005). Based on national reports and the data we collected, such trends will continue to influence curriculum content and program delivery.

"High-Tech" Schools

More and more high schools in Florida and across the nation are going high tech. E-learning classroom environments have laptops, Internet access, multimedia software, interactive web-based discussion boards, and virtual and online classrooms, and many elementary-, middle-, high school, and especially postsecondary, classrooms today have electronic whiteboards, electronic digital animations, virtual labs, threaded discussion groups, and IM. NMHSs are using these technologies and others to update or completely change their traditional curriculum and classrooms.

Wood (2005) explains that blended or hybrid classrooms are becoming the norm within secondary schools in North America. These offer students a classroom environment with instructional support; however, the curriculum, with respect to instructions, content, assignments, resources, and so forth, is provided online. The teacher, in the role of coach or facilitator, assists with real and virtual labs, taking students on actual field trips and guiding them to investigate topics with support of the Internet. A career academy program manager at a rural school was excited about an interactive lab that was coordinated with a local university using video conferencing technology. Her students engaged in invaluable learning within a university-based cancer research lab, and without ever having to leave their school site.

Although such technology is extremely beneficial, it is compromised by socioeconomic realities with respect not only to purchases but also to adequate technological training for students, teachers, and parents. Furthermore, inequitable distribution of resources to poor students and schools is still an obstacle nationwide (Bravo, Gilbert, & Kearney, 2003; Mullen, 2004a; Wiburg, 2003).

NEW MILLENNIUM HIGH SCHOOL
TECHNOLOGY REPORTS

In 2000, Florida's NMHSs were recognized as innovative curriculum and technology "showcases." The School Technology and Readiness (STaR) survey solicits responses from K–12th-grade principals specifically about technology and its utilization at their respective schools. Questions cover infrastructure and available equipment for teachers and student use, and school administrators input their school's technology scores based on technology planning, support, availability, funding, teacher use, and student access, as well as the application of such learning tools as virtual classrooms, interactive whiteboards, computerized labs, discussion boards, and chat rooms.

On examining the Web site data for the four NMHS sites, we learned that these had received scores of only 1 to 2 from the Florida Department of Education (FDOE) (2004) on a 4-point range for meeting the needs of the 21st-century classroom. These low scores emphasize not failure but rather the challenge that such innovative sites face trying to keep pace with the rapid growth in technology. For each of the four high schools, in 2005, scores of 3 and 4 were assigned for technology planning, support, funding, teacher and administrative use of technology, and student/teacher access to technology. Importantly, these high scores show the commitment of the site-based school administrators for modernizing their curriculum and programs with the support of advanced technologies.

Another challenge that the four NMHS sites experience is using technology to enable students to develop, as well as apply, higher level thinking skills (FDOE STaR Survey, 2004). The Florida state government's Web site provides the results for all Florida schools and at all levels regarding the primary way students use technology in their class work. It was found that testing and practicing for skill mastery was, overall, quite high (59%). Technology use for researching and presenting by individual learners was 33.84%, which suggests that students are using the Internet and computer programs for research purposes, a trend that will likely increase.

With respect to the 2004–2005 school year, the four career academy leaders contacted each reported technology use by their students and on a daily basis in every classroom. More public school media centers have computer access with Internet hookups (see chap. 5). However, there exist the challenges of having students use more advanced applications of technology data and collaborating to propose solutions to real-world problems. The FDOE STaR Survey shows a low rate of 5.1% of Florida high school students' overall use of advanced applications of technology for analysis purposes. Although the report did not break down the actual percentages for the NMHS sites, it is worth noting that the integration of critical thinking skills into the curriculum occurs as students get exposed to various skills-building opportunities—interactive activities, test banks, research, and individualized study aids, all available online.

The four career academy program managers also shared that many of the textbooks they used contained web pages dedicated to enhancing the curriculum. After students log onto a publisher's Web site with their school code, they can access practice tests, interactive activities, and reference material. While examining textbook purchases, these curriculum leaders stressed that the technology-enhanced textbook packages are increasingly expensive and that the ability to use a publisher's Web site to gain current and interactive material is indispensable.

VIRTUAL HIGH SCHOOLS AND THE NMHS

The four NMHS educational leaders interviewed more in-depth for this study shared that their student populations are encouraged to take at least one online course offered through the Florida Virtual High School (FVHS). Operating out of a central office in Orlando, Florida, this strictly virtual high school had an enrollment of more than 33,000 students in 2004–2005 and a staff of 200 teachers. FVHS is a part of the Florida public education system, and it serves students in all 67 Florida districts. It is the only virtual high school endorsed by FDOE. It offers more than 80 courses—everything from General Equivalency Diploma (GED), to honors, to 11 advanced placement courses—all delivered over the Internet (Florida Virtual High School, 2004). The availability of Scholastic Achievement Test (SAT) preparatory classes online, cost-free, is an added benefit to students on the roster. In addition, advanced placement exams are administered in April each year, even for students who missed taking the course through FVHS.

This SACS-accredited (Southern Association of Colleges and Schools) institution also offers courses not typically provided at the student's own school, and they are transferable to other institutions. A career academy program manager recounted the situation involving a student who was unable to study Latin at her small rural school. This student felt that knowledge of this language would help with her medical coursework, as well as assist with preparation for the SAT. She would have had to travel 50 miles each way to a community college in a neighboring county to take the course, but through FVHS she accomplished this goal online, and without the cost of travel. E-learning (also called *distance learning*) is generally accepted by faculty and guidance at the NMHS study sites. Understandably, the appropriateness of e-learning for subjects that require hands-on application is a concern, just as it is at any school. We contacted an education professor who teaches online graduate courses at her university in Florida to ask about the value of virtual learning for high school students (personal communication, June 2005). I (Annie) decided to interview this individual because, after working with her for more than 15 years on state organizations and curriculum committees, I had confidence in her expertise as someone who, for years, has spearheaded distance learning and curriculum development at secondary and postsecondary sites.

The professor shared that virtual online courses are important to the future success of students and that most major companies use online courses to update their workforce. Colleges rely on distance delivery systems these days, and students continuing their education will turn to online modalities, she added. To be successful in the virtual classroom environment, though, students must be self-directed and motivated, possess technology know-how, and have access to a computer. Such realities prevent online learning from being an effective curriculum delivery for every adult student at every level of the socioeconomic ladder (Bravo et al., 2003; Mullen, 2005a; Wilburg, 2003).

The professor we consulted felt that students, whether younger or older, are generally excited about or at least receptive to online learning. She experiences greater involvement now by her student populations than previously in the traditional course structure. Electronic discussion groups allow even the quietest student to have a voice. But we know from our reading and personal experiences with online courses that time management and frustration hamper students who cannot or will not adjust to the demands of electronically delivered programs. Moreover, the time it takes to develop and deliver an online course is estimated to be as much as four times that of a traditional course (Mullen, 2005a). Responding to these drawbacks, the professor stressed that instructors must be motivated and ready to meet the demands of online instruction.

The FVHS Stakeholders Survey (2004) solicited input from students, parents, school officials, and district personnel, and results from the survey mirrored what NMHS staff members described about the use of online classes. Site-based guidance counselors have increased workloads because of student enrolment in the FVHS, and the registration process has apparently not been easy to manage—our respondents recommended a streamlined and simplified registration process.

FINAL REFLECTION

Technology changes have certainly influenced the way career academies manage curriculum and leadership decisions. However, they must find creative ways to finance the needs that are part of a constantly changing technology-based curriculum. Legislative support in funding changes yearly, so the financial health of career academies is not certain for the future. Related difficulties involve teachers' and students' changing interests and abilities, as well as staying current with the business and postsecondary environment. Nonetheless, school administrators and instructional staff are committed to offering innovative curricula that prepare students for both careers and college, with the assistance of technology and online programs to modernize their curriculum.

PRACTICAL, REFLECTIVE ACTIVITIES

- Research the concept and practice of a career academy within your own state and compare your findings to the results provided here. If you live in Florida, you can select aspects of the discussion you find most interesting.

- Investigate software packages (e.g., SchoolSpace) that enable administrators to manage information and teachers, parents, and students to communicate. They offer a streamlined approach to report analysis, grading, attendance, and information organization and storage. In addition, such software provides different online modules for administrators, guidance counselors, and teachers to record and store information (see Mullen, 2004a).
- Experiment with digital portfolios by storing "samples of student work and performance" in a select "range of media, including text, image, video, and audio" (Chen et al., 2005, p. 317). You can post selections from students' portfolios at school Web sites to highlight excellence, or you can better study the difficulties of academically struggling students by sharing the portfolio, or portions of it, with colleagues for input.

13

Early Reading Intervention Through After-School Tutoring Programs

Valorie L. Fish
Carol A. Mullen

LITERACY-RELATED TRENDS AND EXTRAMURAL PROGRAMS

The ever-changing global society in which we live has contributed to the expectation of functional literacy for productive citizens. However, data on literacy levels in American society indicate that one fourth of the adult population experiences serious reading difficulties (Murphy, 2004). Under the NCLB Act of 2001 (U.S. Department of Education, 2002), the nation's schools and states are accountable for ensuring that all students reach or exceed proficiency in reading and mathematics by 2013–2014. Federal, state, and local governments have taken action to improve literacy education and increase educational standards more generally. Thus, schools are now placing more emphasis on information literacy (see chap. 5), and specifically on learning how to read.

Current findings reported by Murphy's (2004) exhaustive literature review confirm that the early years are critical, when the foundation for literacy learning is forming: "The message from all this research is fairly clear; those who are not on track by third grade have little chance of ever catching up" (p. 46). If an individual's foundation is weak, then later development will probably suffer, perpetuating a lifelong cycle of illiteracy.

Educators are seeking a variety of ways to assist such struggling learners. Remedial programs have been woven into the daily schedules at many schools. However, "when children fall behind in a content area or areas, there may not be sufficient time in the school day to offer the remedial instruction necessary to get them up to speed" (Miller & Snow, 2004, p. 1). Remediation, then, should be used as a strategy to prevent, not remedy, failure, underscoring the need for academically based after-school programs, such as Students of Utmost Potential, Excellence, and Respect (SUPERKids).

Importantly, the tutoring setting can provide the structure of a family while parents are working, so students do not seek it inappropriately elsewhere. Cooter (2004) claims that, within many low-performing schools, the connections among parents, schools, and communities are usually weak. Some students even confided that they belonged to gangs and other types of surrogate families. Hence, family structure is an "important variable," perhaps even more so than "poverty and discrimination" (Mullen, 2004a, p. 227). One longitudinal study examined how family structure affects serious crime (Harper & McLanahan, as cited in Gallagher, 1998). The lives of 6,403 boys were tracked, and it was discovered that boys who are raised without fathers are twice as likely to be jailed. Furthermore, Chung (2000), finding that "juvenile crime peaks in the after-school hours," explains that

> About 10 percent of violent juvenile crimes are committed between 3 p.m. and 4 p.m. Children are also at a much greater risk of being the victim of a violent crime (murder, a violent sex offense, robbery, or assault) after the school day. (p. 4)

After-school tutoring programs in reading and mathematics can help bridge the gap between the educational demands on society and needs of parents and children. Successful programs address both the academic and social concerns of today. Program support, in combination with family support, is instrumental in achieving success, as Hispanic scholar Gandara (1995) attests: "Greater parent involvement leads to higher academic achievement in children" (p. 47). Researchers and practitioners agree that all youngsters need exposure to, as Chung (2000) clarifies, "rewarding, challenging, and age-appropriate activities in safe structures and positive environments" (p. 4). In general, after-school programs help decrease juvenile delinquency while protecting children from violence, and they provide a much-needed foothold in literacy and social development.

OVERVIEW: THE SUPERKIDS PILOT PROGRAM

A History of the Program

The concept for the SUPERKids after-school program was formed during a Board of Trustees' (BOT) Engagement Working Group meeting at the university. Master's students in the university's public relations department were solicited to gather needs-based data on after-school literacy programs for the board. They conducted a literature review of after-school programs, distributed teacher and principal surveys, and interviewed parents in a focus-group setting. The student group analyzed all of this data and, in 2004, presented the information at a BOT meeting (Gonazalez, Llenza, Seligman, Vnuk, & van Loveren, 2004). (This is not the same project data we report here, as the student group responded to the BOT's separate request for background data to be collected.)

Brainstorming about after-school programs continued at the BOT level. One member had spearheaded the idea, leading to the concept of the SUPERKids pilot program, which was partially based on the Reading One-One model, as developed by George Farkas of the University of Texas (Schacter, n.d.). This format provides 30 minutes of instruction, 3 to 5 times weekly, on a one-to-one basis using phonetically decodable and leveled books. Lessons are based on the learner's independent reading level, with student assessment occurring every fifth lesson to determine growth and focus for future lessons.

The tutors were solicited from two sources—a sorority and the student government's electronic bulletin board. The university personnel involved did *not* specifically target relevant majors, and the program was not part of any course requirement. The tutors were paid modestly for their efforts. Funding for the program was donation supported through the local community, and a foundation with a specified tax status (501© 3) was formed. (The foundation was created to specifically hold and distribute the funds for this project.)

The BOT's chair presented the idea for SUPERKids to the local school district. Members of the district's Title I, Nutrition, and After-school Program departments began working with the university on implementation issues. Deciding that the pilot would be launched in three of the district's elementary schools, the principals of each were contacted in order to gauge their interest. It was at this time that I became involved in the pilot, accepting my principal's invitation to assume programmatic leadership at their school.

Tutored Students' Background

In 2005, approximately 700 students were enrolled at the focus elementary school; 85% were Hispanic, and 80% of the total student population participated in the free and reduced lunch program. The school received extra funding via the Federal Title I Program and Florida's Reading First grant, used to improve classroom reading instruction and prevent student failure. The school's state grade was "B", and, though it displayed growth, the school did not make AYP for the 2004 academic year. AYP is a performance standard set by the U.S. government to ensure that schools are meeting the academic needs of all students. The implications of not meeting AYP can lead to reduction or elimination of a school's funds or reorganization of its staff.

A typical family at this school was one in which both parents worked one or more jobs, but the extended family was actively involved. A relative picked up the majority of the students from school and provided after-school supervision, an action consistent with Gandara's (1995) account of home influence, specifically regarding Hispanic families, which notes that impoverished youth benefit from the extended family structure. Due to the high number of parents at this school who spoke only Spanish in the home, many students were not receiving much help with their language-related assignments. The school offered after-school academic remediation for grades 3 through 5 via the Extended Learning Program (ELP). Unfortunately, funding for this program was not sufficient to cover the literacy needs of struggling first- and second-graders. The offsite after-school programs that the younger students could attend were childcare centers only, which lacked an academic foundation. The great need for literacy-based, after-school programs for the primary grades was apparent to my colleagues and me.

Program Implementation

The pilot program operated from January to April 2005, 12 weeks in total. Eight university students tutored 24 elementary students, with 3 children assigned to each tutor. For the first week of the program, the site coordinator and lead tutor met with the students to acclimate them to the after-school setting and program expectations. The following week, the tutors met with their assigned students 3 days a week for 30-minute sessions. Lunchroom staff prepared the program's "smart meal," a nutritional element recommended by the BOT.

A daily schedule was finalized after the first few weeks. The children arrived to the tutoring classroom and ate, giving tutors 15 minutes to prepare for the day. Next, the tutors worked with their first student in an adjacent classroom or on a picnic table outside the tutoring room. The one-on-one lessons consisted of site word reading, phonics-based reading, and writing. The tutor then returned to select another student until each participant was tutored. The remainder of the students stayed in the classroom, completing homework under my supervision or receiving whole-group instruction. (The classroom lessons included teaching of a phonics skill, reading a book aloud to the students, a literacy extension activity, and facilitating journal writing. These lessons were based on a literature theme, such as an author, character, or subject.) At the end of the program, the tutors organized a celebration, consisting of food and games that rewarded the children for their hard work.

REFLECTIONS ON THE PILOT PROGRAM

Academic Gains

Throughout the pilot program, I collected data from school-based assessments involving the 24 tutored students and a control group of 25 students. The control group was comprised of first-graders whose teachers had recommended them for the program but who were not being tutored due to its constraint on numbers. Data on the students' reading achievement were collected using the Developmental Reading Assessment (DRA) and Dynamic Indicators of Basic Early Literacy Skills (DIBELS) formal assessments. I sorted the data to determine student percentages for each performance category, as measured by individual assessment, before and after the 12-week pilot. I then compared the two sets of percentages to establish the growth of the tutored students compared with the control group. My prior training on assessment data provided by reading experts from the district prepared me to analyze the data, in addition to numerous years as a primary teacher.

The DRA measures students' independent reading levels based on performance in the areas of accuracy, fluency, and comprehension (see http://www.pearsonlearning.com/dra). The results from the DRA indicate that tutored students had a 9% higher gain with respect to reading on level (as defined by the instrument). The DIBELS measures student performance in the areas of phonological awareness, alphabetic principle, and fluency (see http://dibels.uoregon.edu). Three subtests were administered to first-graders at the school site: Phoneme Segmentation Fluency (PSF), Non-Sense Word Fluency (NSW), and Oral Reading Fluency (ORF). For PSF, in which students break down words into individual letter sounds, the tutored students outperformed the control group by 6%. NSW calls for combining letters into words; here the tutored students showed a decline in performance, whereas the control group made gains. However, the percentage of students who met

TABLE 13.1
Performance Data for Tutored Students and Control Group

| | Tutored Students' Performance Data | | |
Assessment	Preintervention score	Postintervention score	Change
DRA	8% on level	29% on level	improvement of 21%
PSF	43% low/no risk	63% low/no risk	improvement of 20%
NSW	31% low/no risk	21% low/no risk	decline of 10%
ORF	52% low/no risk	25% low/no risk	decline of 27%
	Control Group's Performance Data		
Assessment	Preintervention score	Postintervention score	Change
DRA	20% on level	32% on level	improvement of 12%
PSF	36% low/no risk	50% low/no risk	improvement of 14%
NSW	16% low/no risk	20% low/no risk	improvement of 4%
ORF	36% low/no risk	12% low/no risk	decline of 24%

Note. From Valorie Fish.

the low/no risk mark was equal for both groups. The final subtest was ORF, which required that students read a passage within a specified time frame. Results indicated that although the achievement level of both groups had decreased, the tutored group had performed better on the skill itself. Table 13.1 displays the complete set of data.

Although the pilot proved academically effective, some fine-tuning of instruction is clearly necessary.

Program Effectiveness

As with the first attempt with any project, trial and error guided the pilot program. Many areas worked well for the program, such as the lessons and routine, whereas others faltered, particularly in the area of communications. Based on the evidence studied, we concluded that the pilot was successful at improving struggling students' reading ability. In addition to the promising story conveyed through statistics, many supporting comments were informally given. Six homeroom teachers of the tutored students had concurred that they noticed a difference. One teacher even remarked that her tutored students' confidence with reading had increased. Whenever a child experienced success at an independent reading level and advanced to a higher one, the teachers shared this news with me (Fish), who in turn let tutors know of the progress. In addition to the teachers' comments, three parents made a special visit to my own classroom to remark on the improvement they witnessed in their child's reading.

The most valuable feedback came from the tutored students themselves. Despite the long day they experienced, with an extra 2 hours tacked on, they expressed excitement about their tutoring sessions. The average daily attendance for the 12 weeks of tutoring was 92%. The students' joyful response to the program spilled over into their classrooms. Many times the students would relay to their teachers and friends what they had learned from their tutors. When administering end-of-the year assessments, the school's reading coach shared that the tutored students had told her that they found the DIBELS easy because they had learned the phonetic skills in tutoring.

Student Routine

Once a set schedule was established, the students' day went smoothly. They understood the daily expectations and routines. They were also better able to predict text using prior knowledge, use basic elements of phonetic analysis to identify unknown words when reading text, identify story elements in literary texts, and relate reading to their own experiences. Because the lessons were similar in content to those taught in the regular classroom, curricular connections were made and student learning was expanded. Research shows that tutoring is most effective when correlated to classroom learning (e.g., Chung, 2000; Murphy, 2004; Schacter, n.d.). Allington and colleagues concur, explaining "Remedial instruction is most effective when it supports and extends learning in the core classroom curriculum" (as cited in Murphy, 2004, p. 169).

Communications

Communications between and among stakeholder groups proved challenging due to the considerable numbers involved in the program. I exchanged communications during the course of the pilot with 47 different people. At the university level, involvement was represented by the BOT and multiple colleges, including various department chairs, professors, and students—one set for empirical research, another for project development, and yet another for academic tutoring. Various players involved at the school and district levels included supervisors of district offices, principals, teachers, cafeteria staff, and, importantly, parents.

On reflection, the communication links would have fared better had a contact person been established from the university, district, and school sites. Contact persons would have had familiarity with the responsibilities and policies for their level, and they would have fielded all communications to their own stakeholder groups.

SUGGESTIONS FOR PROGRAM IMPLEMENTATION

A brief guideline follows for anyone seeking to develop an after-school tutoring program in reading or in other academic areas of the curriculum. Suggestions build on ideas gleaned from the literature and our reflections on the SUPERKids program.

Assigning Leadership Roles

When undertaking the task of creating an after-school tutoring program in reading, establishing leadership is a crucial first step. Decide early whether one person will serve as the program coordinator or whether co-coordinators or a leadership team is preferable. Establishing joint leadership is advantageous when a school will be working with another organization on program operations, particularly for matters involving personnel, funding, diagnosis, and assessment. Coordinators must have effective communication skills and substantial time to commit to the project, which requires negotiation around job assignment, release time, and possibly salary. Additional and unrelated school and service tasks should probably not be assigned to these individuals unless agreed to at the outset. A person knowledgeable in curriculum and assessment is invaluable as a program leader.

Defining Program Mission

An initial task for the leadership is to define the tutoring program's mission, outlining its purposes, functions, and foci. Mission statements guide planners in the design, implementation, and evaluation of programs (Koralek & Collins, 2004). Once recorded, this information can be publicly announced. Goals and objectives follow. The goals should be broad statements and the objectives, specific and measurable learning outcomes: "All of the program's services, policies, and practices will be based on the mission statement and the proposed goals and objectives" (Koralek & Collins, para. 13). Assessments will need to be developed. Align these with the program's goals and objectives.

Determining Funding and Resources

An important step involved in establishing an after-school program concerns funding and determination of resources. Ask such questions as "How is the program going to be staffed—paid personnel or volunteers?" and "What curricular materials are going to be used?" Then determine how many adults will be needed for implementing the tutoring program. If using paid personnel, pay rate must be decided. How many hours a day and for how many days the program will last should also be calculated to accurately forecast personnel costs.

Next, choose which books, workbooks, audiovisual supplies, and computer programs to use. Find out whether resources are available at the school site; if not, decide which products should be purchased from where. Be sure that you have an up-to-date copy of the materials catalog, as prices change. In addition to academic materials, celebratory goods and other items (e.g., paper, pencils, crayons) may need budgeting, as well as field trips. Carefully track all expenditures throughout the program.

Another item to consider is food. Will students bring an after-school snack or will it be provided? If the latter, what will the snack consist of and who will the vendor(s) be? Be sure to consider food allergies and special diets. Once all of these factors have been accounted for, a final budget can be formed. By over-estimating the costs, you might avoid bureaucratic fallout later.

The next step focuses on securing the necessary funding. You can access funds already available at the school (i.e., Title I funds; NCLB funding). If you need to write grants or solicit funds via community donations, plan well ahead. Consider partnering with a foundation that has 501© 3 tax status, designating it a nonprofit organization. As soon as funds are secured, materials should be ordered.

Choosing Curricular Materials

Materials for the program should be chosen based on your objectives for the tutoring program, as well as the students' learning needs. An evaluation of available materials will determine what is most beneficial for your program. Remember that there needs to be congruence and integration between classroom instruction and tutoring activities (Murphy, 2004). Review the supplemental materials offered by the publisher if you have an adopted textbook series, as those might provide good support. Also, when selecting curricular materials, search for items that tutors will find user friendly: "In the adaptation, it will be essential to ensure that the curriculum is suitable for use by tutors with the level of skills and amount of training that are likely to be characteristic of those participating in the program" (Koralek & Collins, 2004, para. 24).

I suggest that you use materials with a strong phonics emphasis that incorporate authentic literature. I utilize the *Sing, Spell, Read, and Write* materials developed by Sue Dickson for remediation in my classroom. (This program has a phonics theme for each story in the series and multisensory follow-up activities.) Research indicates that a crucial element in learning to read is phonics instruction, which is comprised of both phonemic awareness (knowledge that words are made of sounds) and the alphabetic principle (written letters make sounds). As Murphy (2004) eloquently explains, "Wherever one looks on the literacy landscape, the terrain is covered with evidence that phonics is both a necessary element in the process of literacy acquisition and an especially effective method of enhancing achievement" (p. 115). Thus, students who have knowledge of phonetic principles can better develop decoding skills while reading.

Selecting Student Participants

Before selecting the students for your program, decide dates, times, and locations, as well as policy adoption for attendance and discipline, as examples. Criteria for warning notices and dismissal from the program can then be formed. Once the logistics are in place, student selection can begin.

First, the grade level(s) and number of students to be serviced by the program should be determined. Then academic criteria for selection of the candidates must be devised. Because our pilot school was a Federal Title I and a Florida Reading First School, the DIBELS and DRA were required to be administered throughout the year. These assessments were utilized for generating the list of students invited to participate in the program; for instance, to qualify for the pilot, our learners needed to have an intensive or strategic recommended level of instruction. Once your participants are identified, meet with the teachers, reading coach, site coordinator, and assistant principal to discuss all pertinent matters.

In addition, a consent form should be developed along with the invitation for participation. This letter informs parents as to why the program is being established, potential benefits to their child, schedule, and transportation information, as well as attendance, discipline, and dismissal policies. Parents who want their child to participate will need to sign the consent form. Obtain home and work addresses, email addresses, phone numbers, emergency contact information, and specifics regarding how the child will get home after hours. Include a date for the return of the form and provide the coordinator's contact information. With the permission slips in hand, confirm the student roster.

Securing Program Tutors

A tutor roster should also be formed. Early on, determine the population base of the tutors—college or secondary students, parents, professional groups, or community members. I suggest that background checks be conducted on all tutors before getting underway. Some school districts already require this procedure for classroom volunteers. If yours does not, you might want to work with local authorities to establish it.

A training schedule for the tutors also needs to be developed. Onsite training for the tutors should incorporate hands-on application of the materials to be used. A specialist, such as a reading coach, is the preferred leader for the training. If no specialist is available, try a teacher who is familiar with the instructional materials. Throughout the program, support and follow-up training are ideally provided for tutors. During the initial training, it is advisable to disseminate a calendar with the dates and times of future training.

In addition to the academic content, professional standards and conduct should be covered during tutor training. This area extends to attitude toward the role of tutor and respect toward students and adults. Tutors should know to expect professionalism and respect in turn. Additionally, "housekeeping" items should be addressed in the orientation. The pay schedule, appropriate attire, and the attendance policy might need review. It is advisable to require tutors to attend the entire duration of the tutoring sessions they are assigned. A contract can be developed that briefly outlines all pertinent expectations, complete with a signature section for tutors.

Tutors should be encouraged to share with one another and to develop a professional learning community. Creating a resource library on reading that includes materials specifically designed for tutors is an excellent strategy for providing assistance (Koralek & Collins, 2004). Program leaders, reading specialists, or classroom teachers should observe tutors in action. Solicit understanding from them as to where they were effective and where they can improve, and provide supportive, collegial feedback (Koralek & Collins, 2004; Schacter, n.d.). Unfortunately, this crucial element was not present in the pilot we studied, but it should be next time around.

Setting a Daily Schedule

To help your program operate smoothly, establish a daily schedule early on. Not only does this help with classroom management, but it also provides the necessary academic focus. As Koralek and Collins (2004) confirm, "A consistent structure helps both children and tutors to stay organized and focused on meeting individual goals. Children feel a sense of competence from being able to predict what comes next in each tutoring session" (para. 28).

As the schedule is determined, ask such important curricular questions as "What will the other students be doing while individuals are being tutored?" and "What literacy skills can be taught in the whole-group setting that will correspond to the one-on-one tutoring?" Once the whole-group activities have been decided, set the time frame for the tutoring. Transitions should be carefully considered when planning the schedule. If tutors will be working with individual students for, say, 30 minutes then classroom activities should accommodate that time interval. Good planning leads to fewer interruptions in classroom activities (see chap. 9). Continuity also helps tutored students feel part of the regular classroom activity.

Koralek and Collins (2004) find that individual instructional goals should be generated for each student tutored. These are best formed as a collaboration among the regular classroom teacher, tutor, and/or the reading specialist. This effort will guide the tutor when preparing daily activities. Daily log sheets should be completed for each student documenting activities and progress, as well as annotations on the progress made (e.g., did a particular skill prove easy or difficult?) and curricular plans for the next tutoring session.

Arranging the Tutoring Space

The environment in which the tutoring will occur can be overlooked when creating an after-school program. Because having a large group of students, tutors, and personnel in a single room makes for a very noisy environment, we recommend having as many rooms as possible set aside to accommodate the tutoring program. Tutors should have a space free from distraction, one that gives the students the freedom to express themselves. Students at the piloted school who received tutoring on picnic benches outside enjoyed their setting. Another idea is to have a room set up with tables or comfortable couches, chairs, pillows, and rugs. As a safety precaution, tutoring activities should *not* occur in a space closed off from school personnel.

Make these learning environments print rich, giving students access to books and other materials. The assortment of reading materials available can include books representing different genres and reading levels, magazines, kid-friendly sections of newspapers, posters, and student-created works. Not only does a print-rich environment expose students to a variety of literature, it is also motivating for those ready to explore curiosities and make new discoveries (Murphy, 2004). The value placed on reading should be visually evident within tutoring programs.

Finally, display students' work: This acknowledgment can be emotionally rewarding and it can promote student ownership over learning. Unfortunately, in SUPERKids, individual student work was not displayed, as classes utilized the tutoring rooms during the regular academic day.

Analyzing Performance Data

The final task involved in developing an after-school tutoring program in reading is determining the sources of data to be gathered and analyzed. If appropriate, use a preexisting instrument at your school. This could be a formal assessment, such as the DRA, DIBELS, DAR (Diagnostic Assessment of Reading), or a placement/beginning-of-the-year test designed by reading textbook publishers. Other forms of formal assessment involve collecting stakeholder input through such means as surveys and/or interviews (numerous examples of practitioner-developed instruments are available in Parts II and III of this book). Tutors' and tutored students' impressions of after-school programs, in addition to parents', teachers', principals', and coordinators', are all deserving of investigation. Informal assessments, such as running records (a standard informal reading assessment widely known in the teaching of reading) and student writing samples, can also be collected.

After deciding on the assessment instrument(s) and method(s) to be used, devise a timeline for implementation. Because the pilot program was considerably short (one semester long), I found it sufficient to collect pre- and posttest data only. For programs lasting an entire academic year, we recommend a beginning, middle, and end data collection schedule, as this provides for ongoing monitoring. As Chung (2000) reasons, "Continuous monitoring and shared understanding of program goals help staff maintain their focus, improve effectiveness and accountability, ensure parent and participant satisfaction, and identify necessary changes" (p. 14).

Select a qualitative or quantitative method for analyzing the data; mixed methods are ideal because they allow for statistical computations in addition to narrative explanations. Consult expert sources to guide your approach (e.g., Miles & Huberman, 1994) and share your results with others to verify your findings; based on feedback, you may want to adjust your plans.

Involving Parents

Throughout the tutoring program, parents or guardians should be invited to actively participate. Provide an orientation to the program—its setting, people, and materials—and extend continuous support to form connections between school and home (Schacter, n.d.). A monthly parent night in which families meet with tutors, discuss concerns, and learn reading skills to reinforce at home with their child is an asset to any tutoring program. When meeting with parents, have activities on hand to occupy the children and food. If you have a large English as a second language (ESL) population, as is the case of the SUPERKids program at the focus school, you might want to offer adult literacy as well. (I suggest opening up participation to all families at the school.) Adopt a slogan; "Teach the parent, reach the child" belongs to the National Center for Family Literacy (Cooter, 2004, p. 109).

CONCLUDING REMARKS

The wheel does not have to be reinvented when creating an after-school program, as many models can be consulted. Descriptions of effective after-school programs are available in Bond (2002), Chung (2000), Lauer et al. (2003), Miller and Snow (2004), Morris (1999), Morris, Shaw, and Perney (1990), Morrow and Woo (2001), Murphy (2004), and Schacter (n.d.). In addition to illustrating quality programs, researchers have highlighted steps that you may find useful for establishing, developing, and operating your own tutoring program (e.g., Koralek & Collins, 2004; Miller & Snow, 2004; Walker & Morrow, 1998; Walker, Scherry, & Morrow, 1999). When undertaking the challenging work of implementing an after-school tutoring program in reading, it seems wise to review the ideas and tips available.

During our journey of learning about after-school programs, we discovered tutoring benefits that exceed academics. Not only do successful remedial programs improve scores in reading, but they also increase students' attendance rates, reduce discipline referrals, and decrease dropout rates (Chung, 2000; Reading Rockets, 2004). When reading about literacy and crime, I had a flashback to the time a police officer disclosed that she dreaded the summer months. When I asked why, the officer replied that juvenile delinquency increases at this time. Not fully appreciating this comment until engaged in this project, I was relieved to learn that, as Chung (2000) contends, mentoring in the form of extramural tutoring helps to counter these grim statistics.

Currently, I am applying to grant agencies and soliciting local entrepreneurs for sponsorship of a year-long after-school tutoring program in reading for second-graders. If enough funding is granted, the program will be expanded to include first-graders for the second half of the school year. Documentation of student academic results, as well as feedback from students, parents, and teachers on the program's strengths and weaknesses will be collected. I will closely monitor the program to ensure that students experience continuous learning and gratification. This curriculum leader's hope is that permanent early literacy intervention will become a reality at every school. Perhaps my program will serve as a support to other elementary schools.

PRACTICAL, REFLECTIVE ACTIVITIES

- Conduct research using the Internet and assemble a list of extramural agencies (e.g., Boys and Girls Club of America and the YMCA). Identify the mission, objectives, purposes, and functions of each one. Contact any that you find personally intriguing and ask questions regarding the operation of the program.
- Visit an after-school organization in your community. Collect information and talk to the coordinators and participants at the site regarding programs in reading or any other area of interest.
- Volunteer to tutor in an after-school program for children, adolescents, or adults. Keep a log of your activities/tasks and reflect on any new learning. Do a presentation for the local community and/or write about your experiences. Share this information with local school boards, universities, businesses, or newspapers.

14

Curricular Effects of Looping for Students, Teachers, and Parents

Joseph C. Brown
Carol A. Mullen

OVERVIEW: WHAT IS LOOPING?

More formally known as teacher–student progression, *looping* refers to the multiyear practice whereby students stay with their teachers for 2 or more years as they get promoted to new grades (Forsten, Grant, Johnson, & Richardson, 1997; Gaustad, 1998; Laboratory at Brown University, 1997). The process, which allows teachers to move from one grade to the next with their students and repeat the cycle (e.g., Gaustad, 1998), has numerous benefits, notably higher academic achievement, improved attendance, and parental support. According to George and Lounsbury (2000), looping allows large schools to feel small by enabling students and teachers to stay together for multiple years. The Atlanta Journal-Constitution's 1999 study (as cited in George & Lounsbury, 2000) of 1,626 Georgia schools reinforces this claim: "The strongest point of the study is that the analysis was broad enough to show clearly that smaller schools are better for poorer kids than large schools" (p. 3).

A MIDDLE SCHOOL'S ADOPTION OF LOOPING

During the 2005–2006 school year, the urban Florida middle school at which I (Joseph Brown) am principal had 60 teachers and 700 students, with 60% qualifying for the free- or reduced-price lunch program. At this Title I school, almost 50% of the student population scored below proficiency on the Florida Comprehensive Achievement Test (FCAT). As the school's leader since 2001 (and before that, assistant principal and counselor), I faced a serious dilemma, not knowing at the time how educators in my building could help students succeed on the test.

During a district meeting with other principals in 2004, I suggested a plan to simultaneously implement a traditional and block schedule to help meet the needs of a low-achieving population. This system included six 50-minute periods, commonly referred to as a traditional schedule. A block schedule, on the other hand, consists of five 70-minute periods or four 90-minute periods. The block schedule structure allows for more class time and fewer classes, with the intention of improving achievement in those needed areas. My plan was to schedule low-achieving students in the block schedule, with the remaining student population following the traditional schedule.

After presenting the dual system to the subject-area leaders at my school, they asked why I was even looking at a block schedule, exclaiming that research has not shown block scheduling to be all that effective. One of the teacher leaders asked about effective school programs and research studies that have empirical results. I replied that positive results have been yielded for middle school teams that have implemented the looping model. Citing George and Lounsbury (2000), I explained that long-term teacher–student relationships may substantially add to the development of interpersonal relationships and thus to the quality and academic effectiveness of middle school education. The subject-area leaders, now curious, wanted to know more about looping, how this model might be implemented at our school, and what issues they could expect to confront at each stage of implementation.

Although I had prepared a school plan for a dual-time schedule, I was open to the desire expressed by the subject-area leaders to entertain a different curriculum model. Hence, I was not disappointed by their dismissal of my plan but rather encouraged by their ownership of our school's curriculum structure. It should also be noted that traditional or block scheduling is not exclusive of looping—looping can occur in concert with either structure. The subject-area leaders recognized the need, for the sake of our low-achieving students, to respond to the demands of the statewide assessment, but they all felt that block scheduling was not the most appropriate response. During this discussion, no decision was made to implement looping but only to pursue more information and continue the dialogue.

Change can be scary, as well as exciting: Educators and administrators know that some teachers will complain, and even threaten to leave, at the first mention of altering their school routine, so I asked the subject-area leaders to reflect on the rationale that would accommodate the looping model. When they responded, they clarified that any such decision would have to be based on what was best for students. A different group of team leaders was then questioned and invited to express concerns. Along with the teacher leaders, I agreed that before finalizing any decision it was important to visit schools where looping was already in place and share observations with the faculty. Before making visits outside the school, the school's administrators and teacher leaders weighed the various options of looping and studied the known benefits and drawbacks. And so our journey began.

TEACHER LEADERS AS CHANGE AGENTS

The district in which I work has a system in place for providing each of its middle schools with one Subject Area Leader (SAL) per core subject, including ESE. In addition to the SAL position, middle schools are allocated team leaders (the number is based on student enrollment) to coordinate the grade-level teams' efforts. A SAL receives a long-term assignment by the principal, but the principal appoints the team leader position annually. My middle school has 10 members (5 SALs and 5 team leaders) who comprise the teacher leadership team. As confirmed, the import and influence of a teacher leadership team at a school depends on the principal (Mullen, 2004a; Mullen & Graves, 2000), and at this school, these teachers are empowered with real decision-making authority.

As previously suggested, from the outset, the leadership team at my school demonstrated its influence in the transition to a looping model. Members were eager to learn about the research-based findings that both support and disprove the effects of looping. At that first meeting, they decided on the criteria on which to base the most promising arrangements for looping at our campus. They knew that teachers, including themselves, could be skeptical, questioning, and resistant, and that they would need to establish buy-in. These faculty leaders made all of the critical decisions involving such issues as who should be included in visits to schools that utilize the looping process, an invitation they extended to faculty not on the leadership team. In the decision-making process, they also included teachers who would not be affected by the change to looping (16 out of the 60 teachers at the schools would be affected).

After the visits to other schools, along with our review of the literature, the leaders and administrators together decided that our school would commit to looping in the 2005–2006 school year. The leadership team conducted discussions with the small grade-level teams. Because these faculty leaders were familiar with the research and had all participated in the consensus-building process, they were able to field the questions that fellow teachers and students asked. Due to the steadfast involvement of the leadership team in this change process, the members' vested interest in the quality and success of the program was evident.

As principal, I had the right to independently make the decision about this school reform model and to assign staff to their respective roles and responsibilities. Some teachers even commented that the leadership team had simply gone along with my own plans. However, the efforts of the teacher leaders proved contrary, as their engagement in the restructuring process underscored that they were, in fact, the primary force behind the change. Not only were they offended at the rumors being spread by their colleagues, but they also became vehement in their defense. A figurehead leadership team simply would not have bothered to expend this energy.

The intensive involvement of the leadership team in this change process fits with my leadership style. I know that I do not have all the answers to any complex problem, only the responsibility of the position itself. Although I have ideas that could certainly benefit the school and the students, these are no more objective than anyone else's. Placing the leadership team at the center of all core decision-making activates a creative conflict, I have found, enabling ideas that are better than my own to crystallize. I have learned to set aside my pride so I can be receptive to the ideas of others, even if these conflict with my own. The transition to the curricular–structural model known as looping is just one example of the creative process at work in this dynamic school.

BACKGROUND OF LOOPING: BENEFITS AND DRAWBACKS

Benefits

In 1913, under the name of *teacher rotation*, the U.S. Department of Education endorsed looping as a reform model for all levels of American schools (Forsten et al., 1997; Gaustad, 1998; George & Lounsbury, 2000). Today, looping is commonly found in American elementary schools, but although more and more middle schools are now using some form of looping, it is still considered relatively innovative, at least for this level (Forsten,

Grant, & Richardson, 1999). Literature has also documented the use of the looping model in Germany and Japan (Burke, 1996; George & Lounsbury, 2000). For instance, the famous Waldorf Schools, the worldwide result of a European movement, keeps students and teachers together for up to 8 years (Burke, 1997; Forsten et al., 1997).

Some American middle schools have implemented looping on a 2-year basis. A typical scenario features teachers inheriting a seventh-grade class with whom they "loop" through the eighth grade (George & Lounsbury, 2000). After completing this grade level, the teachers inherit a new class of seventh-graders. Notably, some benefits attributed to looping include higher academic achievement, fewer discipline issues, and improved parent–school communication (George & Lounsbury, 2000; Laboratory at Brown University, 1997). Ovalle (2004), an elementary teacher in Florida who participated in a 3-year loop, discovered that in the 3rd year of the loop, students outperformed their peers (who had not looped) by 21% in reading, 39% in writing, and 15% in math.

Another often noted benefit to the looping process is that teachers have more quality instructional time, especially at the beginning of the 2nd year (Crosby, 1998; Gaustad, 1998; Jordan, 2000). The first few weeks of school are typically spent acculturating students to the class rules, procedures, and expectations. Teachers also allocate time to reviewing material so they can determine students' individual and collective academic levels and abilities. As Gaustad (1998) explains, the longer contact spent with a class reduces the time teachers need to devote to diagnosing students' learning styles and strengths and weaknesses and "facilitates more effective instruction" (p. 1). By looping students, the loss of instructional time is regained—the teacher knows each student's level and ability, and the students are familiar with their teacher's style, and norms and rituals (Varholy, 2004).

Ovalle (2004) suggests that over the 3 years in which he looped, nearly 5 months of instructional time were gained. Because of looping, teachers obviously know what was taught the prior year and how it was taught, leading to less curriculum overlap (and second-guessing) the next year. Varholy (2004), a middle school educator who participated in a 2-year loop, agrees: "With looping I can be effective right from the start of the year" (p. 15). Teachers who loop spend the summer months planning to teach a familiar group of students; these summer activities, which maintain a year-round flow of learning, are commonly called the "summer bridge" (Forsten et al., 1999).

George and Lounsbury (2000), in *Making Big Schools Feel Small*, describe a situation involving a middle school in Connecticut wherein a team of seventh-grade teachers challenged the principal to allow them to stay with their students for eighth grade. The eighth-graders, who were in the 2nd year of the loop, scored 8th out of 163 schools in the state in writing, and 15th on the aggregate scores of reading, writing, and mathematics. In addition, according to George (2001), student improvement in writing increased from 41% in sixth grade to 79% in eighth grade, and students' scores in mathematics improved from 64% in sixth grade to 79% in eighth grade.

Furthermore, public middle schools in east Cleveland, Ohio, have partnered with Cleveland State University for the purpose of piloting a multiyear, teacher–student assignment (Burke, 1997). Results indicate that students participating in the program exhibited substantially higher reading and mathematics scores on standardized tests in the multiyear assignment than nonparticipants, even though the same teacher taught both groups. Because this study neutralized the teacher variable, it has helped accentuate the academic benefits of looping.

Similarly, Conyers Middle School in Conyers, Georgia, instituted a 3-year "progression team." At the end of this term, test data from the 53 students were compared with the school's other eighth graders. The progression team's academic growth on the Iowa Test of Basic Skills showed an average of 3.38 years, compared to 2.95 years for the other students. The progression team had a core total grade equivalent of 10.03, compared with the other eighth-graders' core total grade equivalent of 8.71. It is noteworthy that the progression team included both gifted and special education students (George & Lounsbury, 2000). The positive effects of looping appear to go beyond academic achievement to include improving attendance, discipline, and tolerance.

A generally held belief of educators is that students will not learn adequately if they are absent from school. The lack of emotional attachment to school is a major reason for truancy. School leaders face the challenge of promoting a caring environment in which all students feel they belong. Haslinger, Kelly, and O'Lare (1996) describe their school, in which 25 different languages are spoken among 610 students who represent 37 different countries, and with 87% of students qualifying for free or reduced price lunch. With such diversity, how can a school create an environment that welcomes all? Haslinger and colleagues (1996) offer looping as a solution for this dilemma: "As the classroom teacher and students develop a rapport with one another, stereotypes dissolve; the teacher sees children as unique, multi-talented individuals. This derails what is commonly a self-fulfilling prophecy" (p. 47). The authors also credit looping, along with incentive programs designed around looping, for helping their school attain an average daily attendance rate of 96%. They noted that looping helps to prevent any children from being lost in the crowd.

As studies attest, some of the most beneficial aspects of looping deal with socialization. According to the Laboratory at Brown University (1996), students reap benefits from time spent on developing social skills and cooperative group strategies in subsequent years. Varholy (2004) relates that looping results in decreased discipline problems, which means that students are receiving more instructional time. The Laboratory at Brown University (1996) also noted that looping fosters a sense of community and family. Because students are together for multiple years, they become accustomed to individual nuances and gain tolerance for differences in other students and cultures. Students also become caring of their peers, offering help and support if needed. For this reason, looping is conducive to the inclusive setting whereby exceptional education students are integrated into the general education classroom. Teachers who spend multiple years with special-needs students have the opportunity to develop a deep awareness of such individuals and can thus more effectively modify instruction as needed (see chap. 6).

Furthermore, this sense of classroom community helps reduce discipline problems and promote greater self-esteem and self-efficacy in students. Approximately 70% of the teachers involved in a looping program in Ohio reported that looping had a positive effect on classroom management (Burke, 1997). Lincoln (1998), a middle school principal in Connecticut, believes that looping can benefit one's school in numerous ways. Not only did looping lead to the improvement of classroom behavior in his school, as substantiated by the decrease in discipline referrals that occurred, problem-solving strategies were also strengthened, with students "encouraged to work out conflicts over a longer timeframe" (p. 58). In fact, it seems astounding that "there were fewer infractions for the looped eighth graders than for the non-looped control group, despite the fact that the looped students had incurred more behavioral infractions in the seventh grade" (Lincoln, 1998, p. 58).

It is also good news that parents tend to respond positively to their children being looped. Elliott and Capp (2003) relate that at Sierra Elementary School in Rocklin, California, 30 parents were randomly selected to complete a survey (using a 6-point Likert-type scale). Respondents rated this statement: "Compared to traditional grade-level grouping, I believe I have seen growth in my child across at least two years of looping that suggest to me looping is the best way for schools to be organized" (p. 36). Surprisingly, the school received 31 completed surveys (an enthused parent had copied the blank survey for a neighbor whose child was also in the program). Discounting the additional survey, the mean score was 5.78, with 22 parents marking 6 out of 6.

The Laboratory at Brown University (1996) also asserts that parents generally embrace looping once they understand how it can change the instructional environment for the better. George and Lounsbury (2000) attest that when 586 parents representing 33 different schools were asked to rate the statement, "Staying with the same teacher for more than one year has helped my child to be successful academically" (p. 76), 64% agreed. Of the same parent group, 67% viewed looping an effective way to organize a school; 81% also agreed that looping enabled the teachers to better know and accept their child. Varholy (2004) also relays support from parents, in addition to teachers and students:

> One advantage of looping is that the teacher knows each student's strengths and weaknesses, and is also very much informed of what students were taught the previous year. There is no wasted time, as in the repeating of review material, but rather a seamless continuation of instruction from one year to the next. (p. 7)

Drawbacks

In September 2005, Carol Mullen convened a focus group in Florida to ask the 10 seasoned teachers in attendance what they had found to be the benefits and drawbacks of looping. All had experienced the looping practice directly or indirectly in their schools, and the group ranged across all grade levels, with elementary, middle, and secondary representatives present. The attendees identified many of the advantages already covered.

Concerning drawbacks, they raised not obstacles so much as caveats and recommendations. As one pointed out, a minority of children and students thrives on or even needs a change each year. Although continuity from one year to the next with the same teacher is a good fit for most students, there are those who would prefer being exposed to a different leadership personality or style, or even peer group. Gaustad (1998) stresses that longer contact does not help a child who spends 2 or more years with an ineffective teacher, a concern expressed by parents whose children are looped. In addition, personality clashes between teachers and students have a greater chance of escalating in the looped classroom, along with problems arising from unreasonable parents, weaknesses displayed by teachers, and newcomers integrated into a looping class. Teaming teachers is one solution that Gaustad (1998) recommends for resolving or reducing these and other problems. Although looping is less expensive to implement than many other reforms, additional resources are needed, and further staff development is desirable (Simel, 1998).

This group also shared that students who are assigned to a different teacher every year may have a greater chance of being cognitively challenged, in that every educator has a unique perspective on various issues and possesses a particular set of beliefs and values. Those who have studied with a greater number of teachers may have also had the chance to extend their habits of mind, skills, and interests while widening their social network. Overall, however, the group readily endorsed looping for the instructional time saved, the continuity offered to students, and the support offered by parents.

Facilitative Curriculum Leadership

According to Moore (2004), facilitative (curriculum) leadership is a values-based system grounded in the concepts of collaboration, learning, and partnership and "helps people to better understand each other so that common goals can be established, agreed on, committed to, and reached" (p. 236). Before implementing looping at my middle school, the teacher leadership team utilized Moore's (2004) four components of facilitative leadership: valid information, free and informed choice, internal commitment, and compassion.

Valid information concerning a particular subject refers to that which is independently confirmable (Moore, 2004). A dialogue in which people share what they know, including assumptions and feelings, ensues. Moore (2004) explains that "an important element of this core value is to share the reasoning why one believes that the conclusions reached are valid and true" (p. 232). Free and informed choice relies inherently on the core value of valid information. If a person has relevant information at his or her fingertips, an impartial decision can be made. The individual believes that the decision made can be carried out with confidence because it was based on information or evidence.

Internal commitment is the natural progression for one who has made a free choice based on valid information. Hypothetically speaking, because the decision was evidence based, with knowledge of the possibilities and limitations, as well as of the potential consequences, the person owns the decision and willingly lives it. Internal commitment also refers to the dynamic process of verifying the information to support or refute the decision.

Compassion is the ability to temporarily suspend judgment when listening to others. Moore (2004) argues "that by doing this, the listener is able to demonstrate a genuine concern for and interest in what other people have to say" (p. 233). By showing compassion, other core values can be accessed or utilized.

In addition to employing the four core values Moore (2004) describes, the teacher leadership team at my school sought information through reading, research, dialogue, and observations. The leaders also embodied the attributes that Zollers, Ramanathan, and Yu (1999) describe as *adhocracy*, that is, a community that generates interdependence through collaborative decision making. This faculty group developed questions and a list of concerns that were addressed during its outside school visits, and the information was shared in writing and verbally among the teachers. The ensuing dialogue brought to light faculty's assumptions and feelings: All concerns were considered and weighed against the collected data. As partners, the teachers decided to implement looping throughout specific grade levels within the school: Eight teachers per grade level, 16 teachers in total, were affected by the implementation of the looping model. The process was a cooperative effort by which teachers relied on one another for ideas, feedback, and support. Once the decision was finally made, teachers felt that they had been heard, and so they accepted the decision to implement looping.

During their 1st year of the loop, teachers were supportive, positive, and determined to make looping successful. Their responsiveness can be attributed to the facilitative curriculum leadership style utilized by the teacher leadership team and, to some extent, the trust the principal had invested in his faculty and their ability to assume ownership of the issue. Although the majority of teachers affected by the looping model were enthusiastic about the change, not everyone was on board with it: Three teachers did not want to loop but decided to give it a try, and another teacher, who refused to participate in the discussions and information-sharing sessions, left education for a career in real estate. Although the school respected her decision to make a career change, the decision to remain silent kept her ideas and issues from becoming known. The self-alienation could have stemmed from her decision to change careers or the perception that her concerns would not have been respected. Because not all information was shared or tested for validity, our school community did not, consequently, fully experience the facilitative leadership process. Nonetheless, the facilitative process was effectively used by the community, and the final decision was based on the majority voice, as well as the best information available to us at the time.

INCLUSIVE EDUCATION AND LOOPING

The looping environment is considered to be conducive to inclusion. Zollers and coauthors (1999) and Gaustad (1998) agree that "the emotionally supportive environment and extra instruction time help to make inclusion successful" (Gaustad, 1998, p. 2). Inclusive education involves special education students learning alongside their peers in general education classrooms with appropriate support and aids. Though Zollers and colleagues (1999) studied a school that instituted inclusive education, their findings regarding school culture are also relevant to the process and implementation of looping.

These researchers indicate that some aspects of a school's culture are visible, such as training materials and the environment of the school. Invisible aspects include the factors that motivate its members and the sources of its behavioral norms. Aspects that promote an inclusive environment are inclusive leadership, a broad view of community, and shared language and values.

A top-down leadership style can effect a surface level change, but participatory leadership involves listening, understanding, and confronting assumptions, which can lead to long-term cultural changes (Zollers et al., 1999). These leadership styles are utilized to assist in school-wide change. Participatory leadership not only conveys respect for teachers but also potentially empowers them, thereby contributing to the success of change initiatives (Zollers et al., 1999). For these researchers, because participatory leadership includes all relevant stakeholders, it is really a form and process of inclusive leadership.

My school leadership team, similar to that portrayed in the Zollers and coauthors study, adopted a broad view of community that encompassed the staff (administrative, instructional, and noninstructional), students, parents, district, and neighborhood. Open communication lines were established at my site, with all groups sharing input, advice, and encouragement or expressing concerns. Taking a broad view of community generated support and excitement for the implementation of looping.

During the faculty-led discussions, shared understandings of terms had to be established to both frame and further the dialogue. For example, the first concept we grappled with was looping. It had to be made clear that we were focused on seventh-grade teachers and students moving together to eighth grade. Some teachers mistakenly assumed that we would be including sixth grade in the looping process or that teachers would be moved to the eighth grade and be given a different set of students. The leadership team also had to begin work on the issue of assessment and how best to evaluate the implementation process and outcomes.

Several areas of potential school progress will be reviewed when evaluating the success of the looping process. First, current year attendance and discipline records will be compared to the previous year's records. Second, current exam averages will be compared to previous averages on subject-area exams, which are administered the first and second semester. Finally, results from the statewide assessment will be utilized, weighing year-over-year growth against previous growth standards.

Through the process of inclusive leadership, in which the broad community was brought into the dialogue with shared meanings, the focus was always on achievement for all learners. Like the school in the Zollers and associates (1999) study, my own has in place an inclusive model in which special education students are supported by a general (mainstream) classroom teacher and a special education teacher. Both teachers assist all students. The looping model has been beneficial to the special education students, due in part to the relationship that develops between general and special education teachers, as well as the inclusive culture that evolves.

FINAL THOUGHTS

This case discussion honors the concept and practice of looping. Student achievement and connectedness, as well as parental support of schools, have all been associated with positive outcomes in a looping system. Students benefit from learning in a familiar social environment in which teachers build on prior knowledge. Even though academicians and policymakers may all support particular educational systems, it takes a team of leaders to successfully investigate, create, and implement a system. The leaders involved need to understand the theory behind the system, comprehend the research, and have a voice in the decision.

The teachers, administrators, and parents at the middle school we studied embraced looping as their new teaching/learning system. This whole-school change necessitated a deliberate fact-finding and discovery methodology. Teachers entered into dialogue with one another and in the process confronted biases and ignorance. They were the prime movers in the acceptance of the looping model. The faculty had studied the research on looping through skeptical eyes, with clarification of the process enacted through school visitations. The process at this middle school reflects the positive synergy that can be created when research, theory, and leadership all interact to generate new school-wide curriculum systems.

PRACTICAL, REFLECTIVE ACTIVITIES

- Visit a school in your district (or another) that uses the looping model. Observe teachers that loop and talk with those involved. Either formally or informally investigate the benefits and drawbacks of looping within this specific educational context. Share your results with your own school team.
- Invite a teacher or administrative team to your own school or graduate classroom, one that has a looping system in place. Ask questions and seek information but first read the relevant research in order to be as informed as possible.
- Do you think looping should be mandated by site-based administrators or initiated by enthusiastic volunteers? Explore this question by discovering the possibilities and pitfalls of each of these approaches for your own school or district.

15

Science Teachers as Curriculum Coaches of Language and Meaning-Making

Leila Amiri
Carol A. Mullen

DEVELOPING SCIENTIFIC HABITS OF MIND

In order to help students become comfortable with and succeed in science, teachers must provide tools that enable them to develop and adopt scientific habits of mind. In the Benchmarks for Science Literacy, the American Association for the Advancement of Science (AAAS; 2002) identified these habits as values and attitudes, computation and estimation, manipulation and observations, communication skills, and critical response skills. The scientific habits of mind ultimately begin and end with language.

Science as a discipline has been credited with having a unique culture, one deeply entrenched in accepted practices and based on the belief that scientists understand the natural world as it truly exists. Because language is an identifying characteristic of culture (Hill & Mannheim, 1992), it follows that science must have its own language. As a matter of fact, many of the words used in the science classroom are also used in everyday life, yet they take on a unique meaning in the context of science. Understanding the subtle differences between the common and science usage of these shared words is integral to the proper transfer of knowledge between the teacher and student.

For instance, in science education, *theory* is seen as a tool to explain a natural phenomenon—how and why things work as they do in the universe (Rhodes & Schaible, 1989). Theories are powerful generalizations that draw on multiple areas of investigation and link these with strong logic and inferences, often describing nonobservable entities that sometimes cannot be directly tested. In contrast to *theory*, *law* describes specific and observable aspects of the natural world. Theories and laws are different kinds of information—one does not lead to the other, and each is equally valid.

In everyday language, *theory* could imply a simple guess or hunch. A biologist understands that the theory of natural selection is based on thousands of observations and a logical explanation of evolution. A student may have a theory that the teacher likes the girls better than the boys because she was mean to him today. Scientifically, however, theories must be able to uphold the burden of truth. Students in the science classroom are expected to use the same words that they have used their entire lives but in a different way. They must understand that *theory* is only used for statements that are well supported and have great explanatory capability.

UNDERSTANDING THE SCIENTIFIC REGISTER AS SOCIAL ACTIVITY

As a science educator, I believe that the first step in becoming comfortable with the culture of science involves developing proficiency in the language used by successful scientists. Pimm (1987) discusses the existence of a mathematics register, a formal language that mathematicians use to share information. The science community, too, has a unique register. Science educators are in the position to introduce students to this register and coach them on its effective use. The specific components of this coaching develop in concert with each teacher's classroom experience and pedagogical style. In this context, each teacher becomes a curriculum leader and developer of science learning. Although textbooks contain definitions of science words, the teacher empowers students to think, behave, and communicate as practicing scientists, and students will have the opportunity to not only learn the language of science but also to use it effectively and appropriately.

Educational science researchers have described some of the challenges of language use in the science class. For example, Itza-Ortiz, Rebello, and

Zollman (2003) studied students' perceptions of the similarities between the everyday and physics meanings of *force, momentum,* and *impulse.* Those who were able to differentiate between the everyday and physics meanings of the term *force* performed better on exams. Attributing this superior performance to a better understanding of the concept of *force,* I concluded that teachers should strive to be more cognizant of students' common uses of specialized terms. The same results were not seen with the words *impulse* and *momentum,* however; students did not perform better on exams even though they exhibited the ability to differentiate between common and scientific uses of the words. Interestingly, different students showed enhanced understanding of different words. Not all students exhibited better conceptual understanding of all three words. That is, not all of the students were able to differentiate between the scientific and everyday uses of *force, impulse,* and *momentum.*

Similarly, in the United Kingdom, Johnstone and Selepeng (2001) examined the conceptual understanding of everyday words in a science context for native and non-native speakers of English in the first through sixth grade. They, too, found general misunderstandings among all of the learners, an even more serious problem with students for whom English is a second language.

In another study, Clerk and Rutherford (2000) administered a multiple-choice test designed to assay secondary students' misconceptions in physics, and students were prompted to explain the reasoning behind their answers. In many cases, students' responses reflected a misunderstanding of the question itself, not a misconception that the question was designed to target. We contend that language problems may sometimes masquerade as misconceptions. Teachers should thus avoid attributing all answers to a misconception, as miscommunication is sometimes the problem. Language, in this instance, takes on an integral role in the area of science instruction, not only as an information exchange medium but also as a diagnostic tool.

According to the linguistic relativity principle that Sapir and Whorf (as cited in Sapir, 1958) propose, language determines the items that we choose to ignore and attend to in our environment. The Sapir–Whorf hypothesis addresses the relationship between language and cognition, positing that cognition is dependent on language. In the most literal sense, language influences our ability to interpret life itself—words and their accepted meanings define reality. From this viewpoint, language determines our thoughts and behaviors simply because we do not think about and respond to those phenomena not spoken about. In the more modest and recent version of the Sapir-Whorf hypothesis, language does not specifically dictate cognition. Rather there are pluses and minuses in processing speed between different languages. An individual is able to think about those things that are not present in the native tongue—it just takes longer to process these items.

Languages are thus flexible enough to allow comprehension, but losses and gains can be expected as one shifts between them (Willingham, 2004).

Such terms as *theory, law, momentum,* and *pressure* used in everyday conversation take on new meaning in the context of science. These familiar and established patterns of language can function as barriers to comprehension when students neither internalize the alternative meanings nor see them as advantageous. The familiar and nonscientific use of a word can hinder comprehension because it does not fit in the context. Likewise, nonscientific meaning is out of context in a scientific text and is thus, at least as far as science conventions are concerned, incorrect. Take, for example, the statement "The boy jumped into the river from the bank." It is meaningless if we think of *bank* as a financial institution but not when *bank* is understood to mean embankment by a body of water. Similarly, science comprehension can suffer—if the specific meaning of the word as it relates to science context is not understood, the ideas that are being presented will not make sense. Although "not every student has a desire to learn science for the sake of learning science" (Woods, 2004, p. 370), scientific understanding benefits every adult's life (Dhingra, 2004).

Cognitive psychology addresses these issues of comprehension with the levels of processing theory (Craik & Lockhart, 1972; Craik & Tulving, 1975). Mere repetition of content prevents students from transferring the new knowledge to a different arena and does not necessarily promote better retention. Processing information at multiple levels aids in better retention, however, as in the instances of providing a textbook definition, inviting learners to provide their own definitions, using words in sentences, and comparing different meanings based on context.

Students gain from realizing that our current view of science recognizes a social dimension of knowledge that necessitates a meshing of data, theories, beliefs, views, creativity, consensus, and critique (McComas & Almazroa, 1998; Woods, 2004). Social perspective theories of knowledge acquisition propose that knowledge does not exist other than in a social context and that individual possession over which one assumes ownership is an antiquated idea. Consequently, you only know the meaning of *rain,* for example, because it has a prescribed connotation in the community to which you belong. Students of science must be given an opportunity to use science-specific meanings of words in ways that are both accurate and creative.

Science teachers are expected to model accepted word patterns and have students incorporate them into their vocabularies. In accordance with the notion of humans as pattern-processing beings, a teacher must first recognize a student's perspective or cultural use of words and then present the new pattern so it resonates with his or her existing pattern. This alternative and competing pattern must find a place in the existing language network so it will accommodate this addition. Hence, the adoption of each new concept and attention-worthy experience consumes energy and requires time for mental processing.

Michael (2003) suggests that concrete discursive practice impacts cognition and that communication among students allows for mutual and richer understandings to emerge. Social interactions with peers can allow students an opportunity to bridge the cultural gap between their actual world and the science world, without trading one for the other. Science learning depends, then, on social engagement and negotiation, and science education is subject to sociocultural and political realities. As critical science educator Woods (2004) reinforces, language, political forces, social needs, and other contextual factors significantly influence scientific progress and, hopefully, science education.

REACHING OUT TO UNIVERSITY NONSCIENCE MAJORS

Those participating in this pedagogical study were 25 freshmen (15 females, 10 males) registered in 2005 in the second semester of a course for nonscience majors at the University of South Florida in Tampa. Not all students in the course had completed the first semester of the sequence, and this study had no bearing on their final grades. At the time, I was a full-time, higher education instructor and doctoral student in science education.

Science That Matters (STM) is a two-part course that fulfills natural science general-education requirements for nonscience majors—elementary education majors were the target audience. During the Spring 2005 semester, students met twice weekly for 75 minutes at the university campus. Because the course was open to all majors, science pedagogical skills were not part of the curriculum. At this introductory level, education majors were exposed to the National Science Education Standards (NSES) and the Sunshine State Science (SSS) education standards, in addition to the major science topics that must be addressed in K–12 education based on these guidelines.

Data Collection

Two student worksheets were created as data sources for this study. The first introduced students to language and context, specifically the possibility of words having different meanings in science and nonscience contexts. The second worksheet, a reflective activity, was intended to aid in establishing the value of this meaning and context-based approach. The following questions were presented to students:

1. Without using any external sources, define the word *law*.
2. When would you use law? Provide a sentence using law that fits with your definition.
3. Provide the definition of law presented in class.
4. Is the definition you provided different than that given to you in class? (If yes, go to question 5. If no, go to question 6.)
5. Describe how the two definitions differ. (Proceed to question 6.)
6. Explain how the definitions are similar.
7. Write two sentences that show the different uses of law as you have defined and described them.

For questions 3 to 7, students were permitted to use the course text *Science that Matters* (Thomas, 2003).

The target words for this project were *law, hypothesis,* and *theory*. A separate worksheet was completed for each word. Students were asked to complete questions 1 and 2 and then put the worksheet aside. At that point, the scientifically approved definition was given, followed by their completion of the worksheet (within 15 minutes). After the individual seat-work was completed, students shared their sentences and definitions in small groups. The members then came together as a whole, at which time each group provided a representative sentence. Four weeks after the last word (*theory*) was presented, students tackled the second worksheet that read: "Think back to the writing/word use exercises you completed for this course and then respond to the following questions:

1. Do you feel the analysis (comparison and contrast) of the words *law, hypothesis,* and *theory* helped with your ability to understand the difference among the words? Please explain.
2. Do you feel the analysis has helped with your ability to use these words? Please explain.
3. Are you more comfortable now with the specific science meanings of the words? Please explain."

WHAT THE DATA RESULTS TELL US

Student understanding of the different definitions for a word was measured via two outcomes: the ability to produce a meaningful statement labeled "production" and the content of the statement—labeled "substance." *Production* was defined as student demonstration of the ability to produce a written artifact, a definition, sentence, or statement. Examining the content of the written text relative to students' ability to clearly articulate a definition, meaning, or analysis provided the basis for assessment of text substance. We analyzed each writing artifact independently and then made comparisons with prior writing examples from that student. Individuals' reflective comments were evaluated for content only.

All students showed improvement in the ability to create meaningful text. Initially, some students were not able to provide science context for the words. In response to the cue for constructing a sentence that exhibited science use they stated "nothing," "can't do it," and "would never use *law* in a science context." However, by the end of the three writing exercises, all students were able to provide meaningful sentences that exemplified both common and science-specific usages.

Furthermore, students' writing became progressively more complex. The first writing samples were short, whereas the latter ones were longer, more detailed, and more sophisticated. For example, when students started the writing activity with *hypothesis*, their response to the comparison of their definition with the book included such comments as "My definition is shorter than the book's definition," "The book's definition is just a little bit clearer than mine," and "I think of *law* as something you must obey, or you will go to jail." One person wrote, "In the science context, a law is something that is always true and cannot be broken. It is a natural law, whereas man-made laws can be broken but shouldn't be."

These comparisons do not reflect deep thought or even an accurate comprehension of the conceptual differences among the terms provided—they are merely a superficial analysis of definitions provided. However, subsequent analyses of the words *law* and *theory* reflected such thoughtful responses as "The everyday use of the word *law* is limited to self-imposed rules; we create these rules as a society, and the laws of nature just exist—they are out there." The second comparison reflects a deeper understanding that society creates laws and that natural laws are to be discovered. To this effect, one class member wrote:

> According to my definition, when the hypothesis is tested, that is the final answer. When a hypothesis is tested and found to be true, it is no longer studied. The book definition explains that a hypothesis is a testable prediction, and once it is proven, it brings the scientist one step closer to understanding the phenomenon under study.

Again, the student has taken the definition one step further than just a superficial comparison.

Hypothesis

The scientific and nonscientific definitions provided for *hypothesis* were similar. Students understood the word to mean "a question that needs to be proven" or "a testable statement." Their descriptions were essentially attempts to separate the colloquial and scientific uses by couching the word differently; however, the meaning and appropriate use of the word was the same in both contexts: "A prediction based on how you think a certain situation or experiment will turn out using your prior knowledge" was offered as a colloquial definition. The same student expanded, "A question posed in science; it is simply a part of the scientific method. Can be tested and proven correct or incorrect." "An educated guess" appeared several times for both colloquial and scientific definitions for hypothesis. The common and scientific uses of the word *hypothesis* are very close; adoption of the science-specific meaning only required a slight modification of the already existing concept.

Law

Several themes emerged from our interpretation of the students' definitions of the different words: Law proved the most succinct. The common use of the word related to governmental restrictions that must be obeyed; students agreed that human laws, developed to prevent chaos, did not reflect any natural phenomena. These laws can vary based on location, which is why they can change across cities, states, and countries. Hence, violating a man-made law would not have any natural consequences. The common use of law was thus related to restrictions created by society.

Scientific laws were seen as absolutes. The students explained that scientific laws describe reality and are not limited by society or technology. Interestingly, students had difficulty constructing a sentence without referring to a specific law, as in the case of these recurring examples: "The law of gravity is universally accepted" or "According to the law of gravity, what goes up must come down."

Theory

The word *theory* did not seem to hold significantly different meanings in nonscientific versus scientific contexts for the students—the word meant "explanation," regardless of the context in which it was used. *Theory* in a scientific context was relaying a factual explanation, whereas in a nonscientific context, it offered an explanation that was not necessarily true. The distinction between *theory* in the scientific register as opposed to the everyday register proved to be the most challenging part of the activity. For example, someone wrote "The scientific definition of *theory* is based more on explanations of aspects of the natural world than just everyday life. However, both definitions incorporate basing a theory on other factual information." This student clearly understands that theories must be backed by evidence; however, based on her sample sentences, the issue of evidence was not clear to her: "The mother had a theory that her daughter was still seeing a boyfriend that she disapproved of because her daughter would not tell her who she was going out with." Another sentence, "The scientist formulated a theory on the relationships between chimpanzees based on his observations," used *theory* in the science-specific sense.

In short, this student used the word *theory* to connect two apparently unrelated phenomena. She did not differentiate between the validity of the relationships that were being established. In everyday usage, a theory is simply an opinion and does not necessarily need strong support. In contrast, in the world of science, a theory is only valid based on verifiable support.

More Student Learning

The results of the reflective activity indicated that almost all of the students (90%) found the writing exercises beneficial. The following responses typified their answer to the question asking if the exercises had enhanced understanding, affirming that new awareness had occurred on the whole:

> Yes, because when you compare two words it helps in the retaining process. By comparing the words, you utilize them in a way other than just reading the definition, so the words are more familiar to you.
> I do feel that analyzing the words helped me to better understand their definitions. Before, I had blurred them all together. I had thought words like theory and hypothesis were basically the same thing and carried the same meaning.
> Once I started to compare and contrast the words, I noticed subtle differences across the definitions, making each word easier to remember.

Students reported that the analysis we conducted with regard to examining similarities and differences between the scientific and nonscientific meanings aided in their ability to use the words appropriately. The in-class exercises apparently made them more confident with their everyday usage of the words: "When I use the words now, I have a clear understanding of what they mean, unlike before," "I can use the words in a way that makes sense, which gives me a confident feeling," and "Because I've learned how these words differ from each other, I can use them correctly."

Students for whom no benefit was evident also deserve acknowledgment. Regarding the classroom exercises, two individuals wrote, "I memorized the definitions without really knowing what I was saying," and "The different uses of the words were fairly similar to me. I had encountered these words throughout my earlier science courses many times." A minority (3 out of 25 individuals) did not find the exercises helpful for understanding scientifically accepted uses of the three words. Perhaps they were already familiar with the science-specific uses or were simply not receptive to the activity. Typical responses to the question of whether the activities had expanded their capacity to use the words in the two different contexts were "I could probably better use the words now, but they are not part of my daily life" and "My ability to use the words correctly may have changed. However, because I most often use the words in their general social context, my use remains largely unchanged."

INSIGHTS INTO TEACHING
SCIENCE EDUCATION

This pilot study illustrates how a science teacher at the K–12 or university level can function as a language coach (curriculum leader) in the classroom. The students in this action research study were introduced to the role of language in understanding and specifically of words in different contexts. The activities highlighted in this chapter are an example of how university instructors can address the significance of context in the process of meaning-making in the world of science. Younger students can also benefit from similar practice and analysis of word meaning as it relates to different contexts. Teaching students to communicate in science-minded ways should begin in the early years, which can influence their decision to pursue science in college. Dhingra (2004) adds the crucial point that

> whether or not [a student] practices science professionally, she recognizes the sig-
> nificance of the role played by such issues as human cloning, abortion rights, stem-
> cell research, and so forth and of her own role in voting on these issues. She is
> aware that her increased access to a vast array of information, with the develop-
> ment of new technologies over recent years, puts her in a position to evaluate state-
> ments and ideas with much more insight than in the past. (p. 363)

With practice, my freshmen students became more adept at creating science contexts for everyday words that have specific science meaning. Over the course of the writing activities, they developed an ability to use the target words in both common and science-approved contexts. As the self-reports for the majority revealed, students' understanding, familiarity, and comfort with everyday words that have a science meaning can expand.

The students that reported lack of benefit from the activities lend insight for further development and strengthening of this pedagogical approach. This group revealed a persistent reliance on prior knowledge. Even in cases where students identified advantages to having participated in the activities, definitions acquired earlier (in this case, high school courses) were still present. For example, several had defined *hypothesis* as "an educated guess" even though this had not been used in class as an appropriate science definition. This association, a remnant of high school science, is potentially a barrier in comprehending *hypothesis*. The reliance on past knowledge reminds us that students enter our classroom with prior knowledge and beliefs that we as curriculum developers must be prepared to address. However, it is impossible for curriculum to address all aspects of an academic area; hence, individual teachers will have to focus on the unique needs of each student population (Woods, 2004).

The same three students decided that they would not need to use the new definitions at anytime, and they chose to limit their vocabulary. If there is no need to use a word, then it becomes obsolete. A shortcoming of the study is that the target words were not specifically used in the course, so after initial presentation and discussion, they did not reappear. The words most likely lost value for the students, and so, in their eyes, the activities did not provide them with any new and usable skills.

FINAL THOUGHTS

The scientific definitions of the words *hypothesis*, *law*, and *theory* were discussed with the student group, but their common definitions were not. Thus, students did not have the opportunity to analyze the nonscientific meanings. With this practical shortcoming in mind, more activities can be designed that would allow students to further process meaning in science and also develop better coaching skills. For example, students can be asked to display their newly developed comfort with using science words. The exercises briefly discussed here focused entirely on the definitions and simple usage of science words. Students were not asked to transfer the skills to a more complex activity. More complicated processing could involve exploring the specific factors that contribute to the development of a scientific theory, such as asking students to develop a theory based on their daily observations and why those elements are so crucial to its survival.

Unlike such deeply rooted beliefs as gravity, a controversial or unbelievable theory could initiate students into the role of scientist for whom supporting data and evidence is necessary for backing up claims. A more in-depth learning approach could provide students with the opportunity to better process and understand the relevant science terms and, more importantly, processes that back scientific claims. Rather than asking students to find support for a theory, they could construct arguments for and against the theory. Once again, they would have to evaluate information for compatibility with science-approved definitions of fact and theory.

PRACTICAL, REFLECTIVE ACTIVITIES

- Arrange your science class into small groups and have each conduct an Internet search of different scientific words. As a follow-up activity, engage your teams in identifying applications or examples of each of the terms. Assemble a directory of terms, definitions, and examples for the class to which new installments can be added (drawings and figures may be included).
- Ask your students to play teacher at home. Have them ask a sibling or parent to describe a science term and bring those definitions back to class. As a group, ask them to share the responses they brought from home and compare them to the scientifically accepted definitions.
- Invite students to develop sentences using specific words in science and nonscience contexts and to display their work.
- Engage students in scientific debate over a controversial issue such as evolution, human cloning, abortion rights, and stem-cell research. In order to establish a feeling of safety and climate of openness, this exercise can begin on an individual basis with essay writing. Build up to small group discussion and finally a whole-class debate.

III

University-Based Curriculum Leadership Exercises

16

A Guide for Instructors, Coaches, and Future School Leaders

Carol A. Mullen

This curriculum leadership guide complements the practical, reflective activities provided in Parts I and II and can be modified for master's or doctoral courses in curriculum and leadership or used for professional development. Instructors, coaches, and students will find these time-tested exercises helpful for experimenting with curricular concepts and practices. Adjust them to reflect your own pedagogical tastes and suit your purposes, aims, and contexts. No particular sequence exists, although the warm-up activities are first.

I developed these original activities for my introductory and advanced graduate courses in curriculum and leadership, refining them over time. One goal is to have teachers embrace an image of themselves as curriculum leaders, not strictly as staff or administrators. Another is to enable their appreciation of curriculum leadership as a multifaceted, multidimensional construct that affects their daily lives. A final goal is to expose students to artistic and scientific ways of interpreting curriculum through pedagogical approaches that reflect an open attitude.

WARM-UP ACTIVITIES

Introductions

In addition to the usual information students provide when introducing themselves to a new group, such as their name, location of work, and reason for taking the course, solicit course-specific information that will get them thinking about curriculum. Students should introduce themselves by referring to the curriculum roles they play at their schools or elsewhere (e.g., chair of an accreditation committee) and by identifying the various curricular responsibilities they perform (e.g., interpret test score data). (The introductions can also be handled in pairs, with newcomers learning about one another, taking notes, and then introducing their partners. Although this process takes more time, it tends to spark lasting feelings of camaraderie.)

As everyone introduces him- or herself, record individual roles and responsibilities. This list can serve as a further introductory activity: Invite students to discuss the range of roles and duties they collectively represent, with reflection on those they share and those that are more unusual and why.

Defining Key Terms

Secure to the wall (or arrange on easels) large sheets of paper and place magic markers nearby.

On one side of the room, the following headings should appear (one per sheet):

- Define *curriculum.*
- List major curriculum theories.
- List major curriculum practices.

On the other side of the room, include the following headings (also, one per sheet):

- Define *leadership.*
- List major leadership theories.
- List major leadership practices.

Invite everyone to record associations on each sheet of paper as they enter the room for the first session. (This assignment can also be adjusted to the distance-learning environment, with assignment templates, chat rooms, peer groups, threaded discussion, and other techniques.)

Once the activity is complete (it can be carried out while the syllabus is discussed, introductions are made, or something else), invite students to discuss their meanings of curriculum and leadership and to reflect on the patterns they see among the definitions and statements (which can be handled as part of the discourse or recorded in journals). Also have them look for anomalies (ideas that do not fit): Be sure to allocate sufficient reflective time for this.

Next, post a sheet of paper with "Curriculum Leadership" at the top. At this point, it is probably best to move students into cooperative groups and/or allow time until the next class to think about what this concept and practice means. Later in that same class or the following one, discuss everyone's definitions of and associations with *curriculum leadership*. Ask the students to search for patterns again. This particular concept is less familiar than the other two and will likely take longer for them to mull over. (Definitions, ideas, and practices are provided throughout this book.)

Type the ideas recorded on the large sheets of paper and distribute photocopies (or an electronic file). Further reflection can ensure at this point.

Creating a Venn Diagram

Related to the previous activity, ask students to draw a basic Venn diagram (or fill in an activity sheet) that contains two large, intersecting circles. Beside one circle, they should write "curriculum" and, beside the other, "leadership," at the intersection, "curriculum leadership." In each circle, have them list all of their major associations with each of these concepts.

This activity can be completed solo, in pairs, or in groups. Prompt students to take time to share with the large group and pay particular attention to how curriculum leadership is described. A typed-up, collective list of the three definitions can be distributed to the class, serving as the basis for further reflection.

Initiating Curriculum Leadership

Students can take the opportunity to demonstrate curriculum leadership in meaningful and unique ways, either solo or in pairs. Invite them to decide ways for performing curriculum leadership right in the classroom. Ideas include bringing in informed guest speakers; sharing curriculum documents from schools and states; and discussing relevant Internet sites and other materials. Document what has been accomplished that forwards collective learning about curriculum, leadership, and curriculum leadership.

IN-CLASS ACTIVITIES

Reflecting on Key Terms

During a review session of the course (or periodically), ask students to reflect on the previously generated definitions of curriculum, leadership, and curriculum leadership. They may refer to the photocopied definitions, as well as their Venn diagrams. What new insights do they have about these concepts? What research, cases, or stories have they read that broaden the early definitions and associations? Have them record their growth statements in their journals and discuss them aloud in small groups and/or as a whole group.

Devising Curriculum Timelines

What catalytic movements occurred throughout public schooling and American society that have had a profound effect on curriculum? Educational textbooks provide master timelines for the curriculum field that typically begin with the 1950s and move through the various decades, ending with the current one. For an up-to-date, searchable master timeline that moves through 1700, 1800, 1900, and 2000, consult "Roots in History Master Timeline," part of the PBS documentary *School: The Story of American Public Education* (2001).

This activity is the more traditional approach taken to constructing a master timeline for curriculum. Alternatives include doing a theme-based timeline that focuses on school reform, scholarly leadership, or any other topic. Regarding school reform, ask students to consider the major federal actions that have had an impact on curriculum reform since 1950 (e.g., Goals 2000—Educate America Act, U.S. Department of Education, 1994; Walker [2003] provides just such a chart; see p. 100). Regarding scholarly leadership, students can identify the key curriculum thinkers and the breakthrough ideas for which they are known that changed the study of curriculum (consult Table 3.1).

These last two activities can be combined: Request that students create two separate timelines, merge them, and in the meantime do extra reading. In this instance, they will have created a reform-based curriculum scholarship timeline. In the final analysis, students should ask themselves what they have learned and what they still need to learn.

Changes to Curriculum

Ask students to select from or add to the following list of major changes that are currently affecting the curriculum of K–12 public schools. First, they should consider the consequences to curriculum (possibilities and pitfalls) as each of these reforms or initiatives gains acceptance. Second, students can reflect on how the very idea of curriculum itself will be affected by the changes. Have them record their responses in their journals.

Alternative schooling:

- Home schooling
- Charter schools
- Magnet schools
- Mentoring
- Tutoring
- Specialized centers and sites
- Training by corporations

Out-of-school experiences:

- Internships
- Fieldwork
- Independent study
- Overseas experience
- Technology

Technology:

- Chat rooms and learning with "virtual" strangers
- Learning directly from experts
- Student know-how
- Accessing information as needed
- Course and program delivery via distance education

Validation:

- Performance instead of seat-work
- Portfolios, not letter grades
- Life experiences

Organizational change:

- Daily attendance optional
- No fixed schedule
- Students create own study paths

- No required courses
- Outsiders function as resources in classroom
- No grouping by age or gender
- Peer coaching replaces whole-class instruction
- Mandated mentoring policies
- Mentoring support from National-Board–Certified (and other) teachers (this activity is a variation on McNeil's [2003] activity; see pp. 8–9).

Journaling a Philosophy of Curriculum

Journal writing is widely established as a means of reflecting on experiences and key relationships, ideas, events, and issues. Through journaling, curriculum leaders cultivate their effectiveness and capacity to lead: "The ability to lead depends, in part, on the leader's ability to understand his or her own desires and those of the members of the organization and to translate these desires into action that produces a desired shape of events" (Rallis & Goldring, 2000, p. 93). Use journaling as a tool for enhancing your professional life. There are at least two types of journals that aspiring leaders can use to aid in their growth: self-reflective (individual) and dialogue (partnership; Mullen, 2004a).

Self-Reflective Journal. Instruct students to start a journal and regularly record their thoughts. Have them write freely or use categories that will help to elicit and organize their ideas, feelings, and desires. They can analyze their journals for themes about their own philosophies of curriculum and development as curriculum leaders; they can also write an overview of what they have learned and share it with colleagues to initiate a dialogue. Areas of curriculum that could be addressed include integrated units, student learning needs, instructional decision making, diversity, developmentally appropriate curriculum, inclusion, grouping strategies, student involvement and empowerment, assessment formats, achievement gaps, and standardized testing.

Suggest that students think of themselves as cameras "photographing the present" "and [their] response to this process" (Pinar, 1995, p. 26). As a two-step process, students will first photograph the present, observing and recording their memories or associations. Here, they are describing, not interpreting, their reactions to such questions as: What is my present role and reality as a curriculum leader? What aspects of curriculum leadership attract and repel me? What is my orientation to curriculum—as a discrete set of tasks or as a holistic enterprise? Next, students begin interpreting their responses and understanding of the present context using intellectually demanding questions, such as What are the fundamental biographic themes of curriculum that shape my thoughts and work? What concepts, events, or problems are recurring? How are the past and future influencing my present reality? What personal beliefs and values about education inform my present and shape my future?

Dialogue Journal. This type of journal involves interactive writing, or at least sharing reflections with others. It extends the use of a self-reflective journal to include mutual reflection and sharing. More is learned about events and ideas by writing and talking about them with others than keeping ideas strictly to oneself. As writers take risks, and develop trust and self-acceptance, they become more open and questioning of their experience. Administrators or other key players can keep a joint journal or write individually and share accounts, even undertake meta-analyses in a third journal. In addition to growth, accountability is monitored for any professional when they take the time to write and share their thoughts. School leaders can revisit decisions and look for better, more informed options. Events will be more accurately tracked, and their ability to recall salient details will improve. If their documentation is used at any point to clarify or resolve difficult situations, they will be relieved to have had it on hand.

Analyzing Student Data

As part of an individual/group assignment or as a whole-class activity, ask students to locate student results on federally mandated tests and/or other relevant data. The following steps can be taken to enhance their ability to analyze data and help focus the school community's efforts on important knowledge and skills. Based on one or more of these activities or variations on them, students can prepare a brief report that describes their results. They can benefit from sharing it with the class and, ideally, their colleagues and school district.

1. Obtain and then examine data reflecting student achievement levels of academic standards from your school or another. Instead of focusing on recent information only, look at chronological data for a specified period (e.g., 3 years). Of course, you can study your own students' scores, reflecting growth over time, as well as the test data provided on particular skill sets per class period (i.e., vocabulary skills in period 1). In Florida, for example, these reports are available online at the FDOE Web site: http://www.fldoe.org/Default.asp?bhcp=1.

Insights gained from such data analysis activities might provide clues about whether new curricular strategies are truly effective. Use standardized test data to study the progress of individual students in reading and math. One caution, some state tests, such as the FCAT, use mean scaled scores (MSS) for the norm-referenced test and Developmental Scaled Scores (DSS) for the standards-based test. Comparing scores over years may be misleading. This can be tricky if you do not understand how the test is designed and scored. Worse, you could end up thinking regression or no gains have occurred when the DDS may have in fact jumped a whole grade level. For example, a 7th-grade student who scores a DSS of 1930 in reading and, the next year, scores 1875, will appear to have made no academic gains when, in actuality, the grade levels have different score ranges. You will need to refer to the Chart of FCAT Achievement Levels and FCAT Scores to accurately assess this student's progress. States often use a version of the SAT 10th Edition (this acronym now stands on its own, as "aptitude" is considered controversial, see http://people.howstuffworks.com/sat.htm), which uses MSS. Again, look over the test documentation for accurate interpretation.

2. Another good activity involves taking reading scores from your school (e.g., for the third grade) and comparing them to the district and state levels for all grades and subjects. As an eye opener, record the data using bar graphs (e.g., graph percentage of all Level 1 students, 2 students, and so forth, for reading by school, district, and state) and interpret the patterns.

3. Make a list of all the sources in your school where reliable data on student achievement can be found. This may include "hard" (test) data that is usually quantified, as well as "soft" data (e.g., observations, anecdotal, information requests). Ask yourself: Are the testing data reliable? What additional data sources might add value to reliability? Study individual students in which the subtests of reading and math are displayed. This information is usually only given to parents, teachers, and school administration, but districts have the ability to disaggregate student information/data (i.e., to separate or break down) by subgroups (e.g., disabled, economically disadvantaged, migrant, race/ethnic group). Identify which subgroups are in a particular school and compare the gains of each subgroup to identify areas of need. For example, see if the mean gains of migrant students are the same as the total population of the school.

4. Alternatively, try understanding what the test scores mean for your school or district (or another) and how the test designers intended

them. This would require reading, for instance, the "Understanding FCAT Reports 2005" state printout, which is a 44-page document that reveals and interprets test results. (Count on having to simplify the information.)

Turn to relevant Internet sites to consult test score and related data postings. Your particular school district and state department of education should have the standardized data results publicly available, as part of state or federally mandated data collections. For example, the Wisconsin Department of Public Education (2006) and the Florida Department of Education (2006) display test data results for school districts and all schools.

5. In addition to studying data over time and in a form that is returned to the school, look at other, similar but more successful schools or districts in your state (or another state). Investigate what curricular initiatives have been implemented to attain their success levels.

Practitioners find this Internet site to be an invaluable learning tool: http://www.greatschools.net. GreatSchools.net, a nonprofit organization, provides information on elementary, middle, and secondary schools and about public, private, and charter schools for all 50 states; detailed school profiles are available for Arizona, California, Colorado, Florida Illinois Texas, New Jersey, New York, Pennsylvania, and Washington. Use this Web site to search any state by typing the name of a city, then hitting "go." On the next page, click on "Public Elementary" and then the school you want to search (a list of schools will appear); next, click on "Compare This School." A list of schools appears with which to compare your original choice. The tabs at the top let you see the standardized score comparisons for school grades, ethnicity, and more. The information is understandable even if you are not from the state you are researching.

6. Locate other standards-based evidence of student learning from your district. No single test or indicator can tell us whether students have learned everything that is important for them to learn, so examine student portfolios, for instance, which contain reading levels from district-mandated assessments, math assessments, and so forth. For example, you can investigate student performance indicators highlighting promotion: What percentage of students advanced to the next level at your school? Note that promotion does not always indicate evidence of meeting standards. (For Florida, only in third grade must a basic education student achieve a required score on state tests or pass a rigorous portfolio evaluation to be promoted. Promotion at

other grades, at the time of publication, is not dictated by test scores.)

7. Learn about school performance on statewide tests (e.g., school grades) by consulting the relevant databases. Now that you know the grade of your school and the typical range for your district, how can you constructively use this information to empower the players at your own site? What are the strengths and weaknesses of using a school grading system for evaluating and comparing sites? Can you think of an alternative?

Developing a Curriculum Map

Analyzing student test data from the end of a unit or a high-stakes test will prompt questions about whether any changes need to be made to the curriculum. Students can support the teachers or administrators in their schools, and the success of students, by designing a grade- or subject-specific curriculum map. (Educator Heidi Hayes Jacobs [1989] is the recognized pioneer of curriculum mapping.) Instruct students to work with peers (or teachers) on drafting a preliminary map that addresses the basic elements of curriculum:

- What is taught
- How instruction occurs
- When instruction is delivered

Importantly, students will want to involve the teachers on their team in cocreating this map. Teachers who together map out who is teaching what and when learn about overlaps, redundancies, and gaps—missed opportunities in instruction. One faculty team discovered from this process that the mathematics text they were using did not cover many of the standards on the state test, prompting the teachers to make curricular changes (Murphy & Datnow, 2003). Another curriculum committee at a different school decided it was time to address the widespread apathy of teachers toward science by involving the faculty in creating a 2-year curriculum map for science:

> Staff training on science curriculum mapping ensued after we received administrative support and funding, and the entire teaching staff participated in the training on an inservice day. The teachers, organized into teams, worked on various aspects of the curriculum map, with ongoing efforts that followed to solicit the teachers' contributions as curriculum experts. (Anonymous, master's course paper, 2005)

As Gabriel (2005) explains, this guide "[outlines] the essential knowledge for a particular grade level, [suggests] various activities and learning extensions, and [offers] a plan on how to organize [the] year" (p. 129). Students probably wish that they had been handed a curriculum map when they started out as teachers, as guidance with built-in flexibility can prove invaluable.

With the colleagues in the class and especially their teacher cohorts, also have students map out the curriculum by addressing the following (and any other) questions:

- What do students need to know at the end of a semester- or year-long unit?
- What questions do we need to ask that will guide our focus and student interest?
- What other areas or topics might we want to cover that will support this unit's goals?
- What are the main objectives of this unit?
- How will our own goals of student learning be assessed?
- What materials are needed for student and teacher success?
- How much time is needed to cover this unit?
- How will the curriculum be organized? Thematically? Chronologically? Other?
  (paraphrase of Gabriel's [2005] list, pp. 130–131.)

Students should make their school-based curriculum maps public as an "expression of community accountability" (Murphy & Datnow, 2003, p. 73) or collective promises (Sergiovanni, 2000, 2005). They can revisit and revise the map—a living text—over time and as needed.

Web-based applications (and consultants) are available for assisting with curriculum mapping (see, e.g., Rubicon Atlas, 2006). What follows is the sequence used in general for creating school-based curriculum maps:

- Identify a theme or topic and subtopics that support established state-level standards.
- Decide specific goals and objectives for each subtopic.
- Sequence the introduction of standards and topics on a timeline.
- Choose materials (e.g., core novel, science text, social studies text) that support the goals.
- Create lessons and assessments for topic areas.

Table 16.1 is a curriculum map depicting the integrated science/social studies/ language arts theme, how living things interact. Instruction is aimed at the fourth- to fifth-grade reading level (4.0–5.0). The curriculum map, that two special-education elementary teachers who work in Florida designed, is

TABLE 16.1
Curriculum Mapping of How Living Things Interact

Unit: How living things interact
Week 1: How does the topography and climate of the region effect the way people live, work, and play?

Resources: Blake's (1997) *Akiak: A Tale from the Iditarod* plus globe, maps, various picures of Alaska and Iditarod Race, Florida's Sunshine State Standards (SUNSHINE STATE STANDARDS), 3rd–5th grade.

Day 1
1. *Picture walk*: Students read the story, predicting characters, plot, and potential vocabulary.
2. *Geography orientation*: Students locate Alaska on globe, world map, and map of the United States.

Sunshine State Standards:

1. Students use a table of contents, index, headings, captions, illustrations, and major words to anticipate or predict content and purpose of a reading selection.
2. Students use maps, globes, charts, graphs, and other geographic tools, including map keys and symbols, to gather and interpret data and to draw conclusions about physical patterns.
3. Students know how regions are constructed according to physical criteria and human criteria.

Day 2

1. *Prior knowledge activation activities*: Students view pictures of various Alaskan terrain, cities, outdoor activities, and dog sled racing.
2. *Vocabulary preview: Examples*: rugged, vowed, decent, blizzard, borrowed. Through class discussion, students generate language for definitions, draw pictures, and, when applicable, put definitions on a continuum (e.g., flurry to blizzard).
3. *Geographic orientation*: students locate Anchorage, Nome, Kuskokwim, and Takotna on a map and document findings.

Sunshine State Standards:

1. Students use a table of contents, index, headings, captions, illustrations, and major words to anticipate or predict content and purpose of a reading selection.
2. Students use maps, globes, charts, graphs, and other geographic tools.

Day 3

1. *Author's intent and plot development*: Whole-class instruction to complete graphic organizer that follows plot.
2. *Vocabulary preview*: Examples: blizzards, checkpoints, courageous, experienced, musher, refuge
3. *Climate study*: Students use text and Internet search to compile descriptors of Alaska's climate during the Iditarod.

(Continued)

240

TABLE 16.1
(Continued)

Sunshine State Standards:
1. Students identify the author's purpose in a simple text.
2. Students understand the development of plot and how conflicts are resolved in a story.
3. Students read text and determine the main idea or essential message, identify relevant supporting details and facts, and arrange events chronologically.
4. Students learn that natural events are often predictable and logical.
5. Students understand how the physical environment supports and constrains human activities.

Day 4

1. *Summarization*: Whole-class discussion to identify interesting details versus important ideas. Sort information from text into interesting or important. Using the information in the columns, a summarizing statement is generated. Teacher uses scaffolding to assist students in writing summarization statements.
2. Climate study: students compare Alaska and Florida's winter climate.

Sunshine State Standards:
1. Students clarify understanding by rereading, self-correction, summarizing, checking other sources, and via class or group discussion.
2. Students understand how the physical environment supports and constrains human activities.
3. Students will compare and contrast regions.

Day 5

1. *Inferential comprehension*: Students complete comprehension questions in heterogeneous groups of 2 to 3.
2. *Cause and effect*: Students record three results identifying the causes using graphic organizer.
3. Students write summarization of daily events of story.

Sunshine State Standards:
1. Students recognize cause-and-effect relationships
2. Students clarify understanding by rereading, self-correction, summarizing, checking other sources, and class or group discussion.
3. Students understand how the physical environment supports and constrains human activities.

Notes. From Blake, R. J. (1997), "Akiak: A tale from the Iditarod." In J. D. Cooper and J. J. Pikulski (Eds.), *Houghton Mifflin reading: A legacy of literacy* (Florida teacher's edition, pp. 26–51). Boston. MA: Houghton Mifflin Company. Copyright © 1997 by Houghton Mifflin. Adapted with permission.
Grade-level expectations for the Sunshine State Standards, language arts Grades 3 to 5 (see http://www.firn.edu/doe/curric/prek12/frame2.htm).
The standards used in this unit are also modified from a Florida county's elementary curriculum, 2004–2005.

currently in use for a 1-week period out of an 8-week unit. Resources used for the map are specified in Table 16.1 (see sources), along with the following justification criteria for choosing the Akiak story:

- Interesting biome with strong focus on climate and social structure.
- Story/narrative structure adaptable to elementary instruction.
- Emotionally engaging, inspiring story for learners.
- Vocabulary and language use that promote learning and more general application.
- Materials available for lessons (e.g., globe, maps, pictures of Alaska and Iditarod Race).

Conducting Action Research

Instruct students to conduct an action research study and write a paper on one (or more) of the curricular areas highlighted in this book: administrator coaching, curricular interruptions, high-stakes testing, literacy leadership, magnet academies, student progression, teacher certification, technology leadership, transitional leadership, school culture, and special education. Or have them select a different curricular topic that is of interest to them.

The following case study model has guided the action research of many groups of aspiring school leaders at various universities in the United States. Students can follow or adapt these six field-tested steps:

1. Describe the school administrative issue, problem, or trend you are studying with the open mind of a researcher.
2. Give relevant background information to provide context for the issue represented in the case and your rationale for the selection.
3. Discuss connections and associations you have with the case and the issue, site, and key players involved. Share a relevant educational story.
4. Probe beneath the surface to examine the complex issues involved and provide details using narrative description. Consider how the issue is being addressed, by whose point of view, and for what purpose or end.
5. Analyze the case by discussing the issue/dilemma involved. Ask what you are learning from this study and whether your paper is shedding light on existing problems/issues in education.
6. Offer conclusions based on your analysis of the case. What can you recommend that might help others address the issue or problem that you have studied? Make suggestions for practitioners and researchers (Mullen, 2004a, 2004b).

Drawing Curriculum as an Image

Distribute paper and markers so students can draw and label a figure. Note that this is a conceptual, not an artistic, exercise. (When adjusted for online learning, basic draw programs can be provided to assist with this exercise.)

Ask students to imagine curriculum as an animal, machine, solar system, garden, or something else and identify each element (e.g., arm, bolt, planet, fertilizer) in curricular terms (e.g., equipment, program, project, test, interaction, experience). (In the preface for this volume, the analogy of an octopus depicts a multifaceted view of curriculum.)

Based on students' images, probe the insights of the class into curriculum. How have the members imagined curriculum? What can they surmise about the role they perform at the school, or any underlying forces in their socialization, that may have shaped their thoughts? What development might be anticipated in their drawing or thinking as they reach toward the formal role of curriculum leader (e.g., department head, assistant principal, principal, district office supervisor)? Responses to these questions can be reflected on and/or recorded in students' journals.

Next, have students share their drawings and reflections with the whole group. All of the drawings can be displayed on the wall (or somewhere else) so meaning-making can occur as the members study and discuss the works. As a group, have them identify the similarities and differences among these educational texts and the possibilities and limitations of the images of curriculum selected.

Curriculum as House Metaphor

Invite students to imagine curriculum metaphorically as a house: What factors and materials would they have to consider? Prompt them to journal an elaborate response that takes into account such factors as site, foundation, shape, lighting, heating, and building materials. Request that students develop a blueprint (e.g., packages of curriculum materials developed by publishers and curriculum groups) with other workers. Remind them to consider the structure. For example, will the (curriculum) foundation consist of a basement? If so, will it be constructed of poured concrete, treated wood, or something else? They should also account for treatment, waterproofing, and drainage, as well as insulation.

Highlight good construction techniques that reduce energy losses (e.g., caulking around windows), and advise them to maximize solar gains and protection from cold nights. What can they plant or build for wind protection and shade?

Exterior walls (e.g., wood-frame) should be considered—different types and thicknesses of insulation can be added.

Landscaping and gardening are additional aspects to consider to prevent greenery from growing wild. What (curricular) arrangements of bushes, flowers, and so forth might work best for their climates? What suits their tastes and the particulars of the house (e.g., color, style, accents)?

Students can ask themselves, How has the curriculum been imagined and re-imagined through this activity?

Meditating on Curriculum

Read the poem "A Pedagogue's Poetic Meditation" (Fig. 16.1; Mullen, 2002a, pp. 16–17), which creates a meditative space.

Choral reading can alternatively be set up with volunteers from the class or someone with a theatrical voice. Set the scene before the reading begins: Soft jazz (or other music) can be played at a low volume, and the lights should be dimmed (if the lights in your classroom cannot be dimmed, use flashlights or candles). Spread various media around—everything from bins (with small items), markers, and magazines to clay, paints, and fabrics and provide each station with large paper, canvases, plastic, or some other surface on which to create.

Request that students practice meditation as a group before beginning. As you slowly read the poem (students will have not seen it previously or talked about images of growth and decay), listeners are to enter into a meditative state. As individuals feel ready, they can reach for the medium (media) of expression at their station that they already decided on. They can slowly engage with the medium, creating spontaneous and intuitive images. (The point of this activity is not art-making per se, but rather reflection.) Allow ample time for this process to unravel.

Once everyone has completed the process, direct students to prop up their work so all can see it and share the images that came to mind as they heard the words and music. After the turn-taking is complete, the group can discuss any patterns involving growth and decay that have emerged from this activity, relating the images to curriculum and leadership and cycles and life. What can they infer about curriculum, leadership, and curriculum leadership from this particular activity? Again, students can converse as a whole or reflect on this question in their journals.

This exercise (Fig. 16.1) is a tribute to John Dewey's philosophy and images of growth as poetically described in *Experience and Education* (1938). Once the activity is complete, students can read this text and with greater appreciation. Another option is to consult chapter 3's synopsis of Dewey's contributions to curriculum theory. It is best to leave any such intellectual engagement until afterward so students will trust their spontaneous, image-making processes.

Imagine yourself in a place
Where everything is growing
You can see everything growing
You can hear everything growing
You can feel everything growing
See Hear Feel the growth
Move toward this growth
Get closer to that which is growing
Kneel down
Look closely
Reach and touch
REACH
TOUCH
STRETCH with all your might
What's so special about this growth?
Look again more closely
Notice that the growth is growing
How is it growing, this growth?
Up and down and around
A moving force.
Follow the pattern of the growth
Notice its texture, density, depth.
Can growth enable conditions for more growth?
See how the growth makes the ground fertile
How it cultivates a life system
And depends on that which exists.
Just look at this spectacular growth!
A momentum energized by its own force
Stimulated by external stimulants to grow.
Watch how this persevering force moves
Over the ground
Under the soil
Through the land
Working the ground with its muscles
Winding Seamless Patterned
Activity without beginning or end
Notice how entangled and plush
Is this thick brush of growth
Thickened from plasmatic juices of creativity,
It lives, this intoxicating growth of leak green.

(Continued)

Look over and away from this growth
See another growth in the distance
Move toward it
See how it grows
Hear how it grows
Touch how it grows
Ahh, this growth is different!
It grows too, this sight before me
But very differently—
The ground, sucked up,
Moves away from itself
Repulsed at its own sight.
Depriving soil of nutrients and minerals
This place is swollen with poisonous froth
A vacuum suction of negativity
What living form of life is this?!
Growth, but not harmonious and glowing
Like a pulsating wire that carries no current
A solipsistic sun shunning bright suns
This growth feeds upon itself
With a stranglehold upon the world
Bent toward its own use
Extracting, depleting, wilting, decaying
A growth spreading feverishly,
Suckers turned away from eternity.

Look away from this contaminated sight
And while turning, absorb the negative energy
Turning still, transform it into bright light
Of spiral shooting tendrils.
Hold the warm sinewy tendrils
Winding around your porous hand
Up through and inside your tendons
A tendril rooting, spreading, filling, thriving.
Balmy breezes of the seashore
Blowing hayseed of the inland prairies
The felt-radiance of s/he next to you.
This growing growth, caresses
Absorbs and replenishes
Replenishes and absorbs
A timeless cycle of creation
Boundaryless Boundless Bountiful
A growing growth that is YOU.

FIG. 16.1.   Meditation on curriculum as growth and decay.

References

Adler, M. J. (1982/2004). The Paideia Proposal. In D. J. Flinders & S. J. Thornton (Eds.), *The curriculum studies reader* (2nd ed.; pp. 159–162). New York: Routledge.

Altmann, E. M., & Trafton, J. G. (2004). *Task interruption: Resumption lag and the role of cues.* Proceedings of the 26th annual conference of the Cognitive Science Society Chicago, IL (pp. 1–6). Retrieved March 30, 2005, from http://interruptions.net/literature.htm

American Association for the Advancement of Science. (AAAS). (2002). *Benchmarks for science literacy.* Retrieved October 3, 2005, from http://www.project2061.org/tools/benchol/ ch12/ch12.htm

American Association of University Women [AAUW] (1992/2004). How schools short-change girls: Three perspectives on curriculum. In D. J. Flinders & S. J. Thornton (Eds.), *The curriculum studies reader* (2nd ed.; pp. 205–228). New York: Routledge.

American Library Association. (1989). *Presidential committee on information literacy: Final report.* Retrieved July 9, 2005, from http://www.ala.org/ala/acrl/acrlstandards/informationliteracycompetency.htm#f1

Amrein, A., & Berliner, D. C. (2002). High-stakes testing, uncertainty, and student learning. *Education Policy Analysis Archives, 10*(18), 1–20. Retrieved April 10, 2005, from http://epaaasu.edu/epaa/v10n18

Anderson, M., Cavert, C., Cain, T., & Heck, T. (2005, June). *Teambuilding puzzles.* Brockport, NY: Fundoing Publications.

Apple, M. W. (1986/2004). Controlling the work of teachers. In D. J. Flinders & S. J. Thornton (Eds.), *The curriculum studies reader* (2nd ed.; pp. 183–197). New York: RoutledgeFalmer.

Archbald, D. A. (2004, October). School choice, magnet schools, and the liberation model: An empirical study. *Sociology of Education, 77*(4), 283–310.

Austin, V. L. (2001). Teachers' beliefs about co-teaching. *Remedial and Special Education, 22*(4), 245–255.

Bailey, B. P., Konstan, J. A., & Carlis, J. V. (2000, April). *Measuring the effects of interruptions on task performance in the user interface.* Paper presented at the Institute of Electrical and Electronics Engineers Conference on Systems, Man and Cybernetics, Nashville, TN. Retrieved May 6, 2005, from http://orchid.cs.vivo.edu/publications/ieee-smc-2000.pdf.

Baker, E., Wang, M., & Wallberg, H. (1994). The effects of inclusion on learning. *Educational Leadership, 52*(4), 33–35.

Barth, R. S. (2002). The culture builder. *Educational Leadership, 59*(8), 6–11.

Beninghof, A. M. (1996). Using a spectrum of staff development activities to support inclusion. *Journal of Staff Development, 17,* 12–15.

Bernhardt, R., Hedley, C. N., Cattaro, G., & Svolopoulos, V. (Eds.). (1998). *Curriculum leadership: Rethinking schools for the 21st century.* Cresskill, NJ: Hampton Press.

Blasé, J., & Blasé, J. (2004). *Handbook of instructional leadership: How successful principals promote teaching and learning* (2nd ed.). Thousand Oaks, CA: Corwin.

Bobbitt, F. (1918). *The curriculum.* Cambridge, MA: Riverside Press.

Bobbitt, F. (1918/2004). Scientific method in curriculum-making. In D. J. Flinders & S. J. Thornton (Eds.), *The curriculum studies reader* (2nd ed.; pp. 9–16). New York: RoutledgeFalmer.

Bolman, L. G., & Deal, T. E. (1993). *The path to school leadership: A portable mentor.* Newbury Park, CA: Corwin.

Bolman, L. G., & Deal, T. E. (1997). *Reframing organizations: Artistry, choice, and leadership.* San Francisco, CA: Jossey-Bass.

Bond, S. (2002). *Introductory guide for implementing and evaluating volunteer reading tutoring programs: A SERVE special report.* (Contract #ED-01-CO-0015). Washington, DC: U.S. Department of Education.

BPS Press Office. (2005). British psychological society. Retrieved April 3, 2005, from http://www.bps.org.uk/media-centre/press-releases/releases

Bravo, M. L., Gilbert, L. A., & Kearney, L. K. (2003). Interventions for promoting gender equitable technology use in classrooms. *Teacher Education Quarterly, 30*(4), 95–109.

Brubaker, D. L. (2004). *Creative curriculum leadership: Inspiring and empowering your school community* (2nd ed.). Thousand Oaks, CA: Corwin.

Bruning, R. H., Schraw, G. J., Norby, M. M., & Ronning, R. R. (2004). *Cognitive psychology and instruction* (4th ed.). Upper Saddle River, NJ: Pearson Education.

Buell, M. J., Hallam, R. A., & Gamel-McCormick, M. (1999). A survey of general and special education teachers' perceptions and inservice needs concerning inclusion. *International Journal of Disability, Development, and Education, 46*(2), 143–156.

Burke, D. (1996). Multi-year teacher/student relationships are a long-overdue arrangement. *Phi Delta Kappan, 77,* 360–361.

Burke, D. (1997). *Looping: Adding time, strengthening relationships.* (Report no. EDO-PS-97-25). (ERIC Document Reproduction Service No. ED414098)

Carnegie Task Force on Teaching as a Profession. (1986). *A nation prepared: Teachers for the 21st century.* New York: Carnegie Corporation. (ERIC Document Reproduction Service No. ED268120)

Carter, R. A. (2004). Visual literacy: Critical thinking with the visual image. In J. L. Kincheloe & D. Weil (Eds.), *Critical thinking and learning: An encyclopedia for parents and teachers* (pp. 291–296). Westport, CT: Greenwood.

Chen, E., Heritage, M., & Lee, J. (2005). Identifying and monitoring students' learning needs with technology. *Journal of Education for Students Placed At Risk, 19*(3), 309–332.

Chung, A. (2000, June). *After-school programs: Keeping children safe and smart.* (Contract # ED-00-PO-1771; pp. 1–24). Washington, DC: U.S. Department of Education. Retrieved November 12, 2005, from http://www.ed.gov/pubs/afterschool/afterschool.pdf.

Clandinin, D. J., & Connelly, F. M. (1992). Teacher as curriculum maker. In P. W. Jackson (Ed.), *Handbook of research on curriculum* (pp. 363–340). New York: Macmillan.

Clandinin, D. J., & Connelly, F. M. (1995). *Teachers' professional knowledge landscapes.* New York: College Press.

Clandinin, D. J., & Connelly, F. M. (2000). *Narrative inquiry: Experience and story in qualitative research.* San Francisco, CA: John Wiley & Sons.

Clerk, D., & Rutherford, M. (2000). Language as a confounding variable in the diagnosis of misconceptions. *International Journal of Science Education, 22*(7), 703–717.

Conant, J. B. (1959). *The American high school today.* New York: McGraw-Hill.

Connelly, F. M., & Clandinin, D. J. (1988). *Teachers as curriculum planners: Narratives of experience.* New York: Teachers College Press.

Cook, B. G., Semmel, M. I., & Gerber, M. M. (1999). Attitudes of principals and special education teachers toward the inclusion of students with mild disabilities: Critical differences of opinion. *Remedial and Special Education, 20*(4), 199–207.

Cooter, R. (Ed.). (2004). *Perspectives on rescuing urban literacy education: Spies, saboteurs, and saints.* Mahwah, NJ: Lawrence Erlbaum Associates.

Covey, S. J. (1989). *The 7 habits of highly effective people: Powerful lessons in personal change.* New York: Fireside.

Craig, B. (n.d.). *My recipe for school improvement: Walkthrough observations on a handheld Computer.* Retrieved May 15, 2005, from http://www.pes-sports.com/The%20Administrative%20Observer.pdf

Craik, F. I., & Lockhart, R. S. (1972). Levels of processing: A framework for memory research. *Journal of Verbal Learning and Verbal Behavior, 11,* 671–684.

Craik, F. I., & Tulving, E. (1975). Depth of processing and the retention of words in episodic memory. *Journal of Experimental Psychology, 104*(3), 268–294.

Cranston, N., Tromans, C., & Reugebrink, M. (2002). *Forgotten leaders? The role and workload of state secondary school deputy principals in Queensland.* Retrieved June 6, 2005, from http://www.nswsdpa.asn.au/files/June04/ForgottenLeaderyDeputy.pdf

Crosby, P. (1998). Looping in the middle school: Why do it? *Teaching PreK–8, 29*(3), 46–47.

Cunningham, W., & Cordeiro, P. (2003). *Educational leadership: A problem-based approach.* Boston, MA: Pearson Education.

Curriculum Leadership Institute. (2005). *The CLI model: Pathways to school improvement.* Retrieved October 15, 2005, from http://www.cliweb.org/index.htm

Curtis, D. (2005). National edtech plan puts students front and center. *Edutopia,* 1–2. Retrieved July 2, 2005, from http://www.glef.org

Daane, C., Beirne-Smith, M., & Latham, D. (2000). Administrators' and teachers' perceptions of the collaboration efforts of inclusion in the elementary grades. *Education, 121*(2), 331–339.

D'Alonzo, B. J., Giordino, G., & Vanleeuwen, D. M. (1997). Perceptions by teachers about the benefits and liabilities of inclusion. *Preventing School Failure, 42,* 4–11.

Danielson, C., & McGreal, T. L. (2000). *Teacher evaluation to enhance professional practice.* Alexandria, VA: ASCD.

Daresh, J. C. (2004). *Beginning the assistant principalship: A practical guide for new school administrators.* Thousand Oaks, CA: Corwin.

de Alba, A., González-Gaudiano, E., Lankshear, C., & Peters, M. (2000). *Curriculum in the postmodern condition.* New York: Peter Lang.

Dewey, J. (1929/2004). My pedagogic creed. In D. J. Flinders & S. J. Thornton (Eds.), *The curriculum studies reader* (2nd ed.; pp. 17–23). New York: RoutledgeFalmer.

Dewey, J. (1938). *Experience and education.* New York: Macmillan Publishing.

Dhingra, K. (2004). Science: Critical thinking and the teaching of science. In J. L. Kincheloe & D. Weil (Eds.), *Critical thinking and learning: An encyclopedia for parents and teachers* (pp. 363–367). Westport, CT: Greenwood.

Dick, M. H. H. (2005, October). *Principals' experience of mentoring: Narrative portraits.* Unpublished doctoral dissertation, University of Alberta, Canada.

Donham, J., Bishop, K., Collier Kuhlthau, C., & Oberg, D. (2001). *Inquiry-based learning: lessons from library power.* Worthington, OH: Linworth.

Douzenis, C. (1994, September). *Evaluation of magnet schools: Methodological issues and concerns.* Retrieved September 21, 2005, from http://www.proquestumi.com

Downey, C. J., Steffy, B. E., English, F. W., Frase, L. E., & Poston, W. K. (2004). *The three-minute classroom walk-through: Changing school supervisory practice one teacher at a time.* Thousand Oaks, CA: Corwin.

Downing, J. E., & Eichinger, J. (2003). Creating learning opportunities for students with severe disabilities in inclusive classrooms. *Teaching Exceptional Children, 36*(1), 26–31.

Effective Teams. (2005a). *Lesson from geese,* 1–2. Retrieved September 4, 2005, from http://www.teams.org.uk/geese.htm

Effective Teams. (2005b). *Team health check,* 1–2. Retrieved September 4, 2005, from http://www.teams.org.uk/hcheck.htm

Eisenberg, M., & Johnson, D. (1996). *Computer skills for information problem-solving: Learning and teaching technology in context.* (ERIC Document Reproductive Service No. ED392463)

Eisner, E. W. (1991). *The enlightened eye: Qualitative inquiry and the enhancement of educational practice.* New York: Macmillan.

Eisner, E. W. (1996). Is 'the art of teaching' a metaphor? In M. Kompf, W. R. Bond, D. Dworet, & R. T. Boak (Eds.), *Changing research and practice: Teachers' professionalism, identities, and knowledge* (pp. 9–19). London: Falmer.

Eisner, E. W. (2001/2004). What does it mean to say a school is doing well? In D. J. Flinders & S. J. Thornton (Eds.), *The curriculum studies reader* (2nd ed.; pp. 297–305). New York: Routledge.

Elliott, D., & Capp, R. (2003). The gift of time. *Leadership, 33*(2), 34–36.

English, F. W., & Hill, J. C. (1990). *Restructuring: The principal and curriculum change.* Reston, VA: National Association of Secondary School Principals.

English, F. W., & Larson, R. L. (1996). *Curriculum management for educational and social service organizations* (2nd ed.) Springfield, IL: Charles C. Thomas.

English, F. W., & Steffy, B. E. (2005). Curriculum leadership: The administrative survival skill in a test-driven culture and a competitive educational marketplace. In F. W. English (Ed.), *Sage handbook of educational leadership: Advances in theory, research, and practice* (pp. 407–429). Thousand Oaks, CA: Sage.

Erwin, E. J. (1993, Winter). The philosophy and status of inclusion. *Envision: A publication of The Lighthouse National Center for Vision and Child Development,* pp. 1, 3–4.

Farmer, L. S. J. (2001). *Teaming with opportunity: Media programs, community constituencies, and technology.* Englewood, CO: Libraries Unlimited.

Farmer, L. S. J. (2003). *Student success and library media programs: A systems approach to research and best practice.* Westport, CT: Libraries Unlimited.

Fennick, E., & Liddy, D. (2001). Responsibilities and preparation for collaborative teaching: Co-teachers' perspectives. *Teacher Education and Special Education, 24*(3), 229–240.

FLEX: Foreign Language Experience Programs. (1996). *ERIC/CLL Minibib.* Retrieved October 1, 2005, from http://www.cal.org/ericcll/minibibs/FLEX.html

Flinders, D. J., & Thornton, S. J. (2004a). Preface and introduction. In D. J. Flinders & S. J. Thornton (Eds.), *The curriculum studies reader* (2nd ed.; pp. xi–xiv). New York: RoutledgeFalmer.

Flinders, D. J., & Thornton, S. J. (2004b). Looking back: A prologue to curriculum studies. In D. J. Flinders & S. J. Thornton (Eds.), *The curriculum studies reader* (2nd ed.; pp. 1–8). New York: RoutledgeFalmer.

Flinders, D. J., & Thornton, S. J. (Eds.). (2004c). *The curriculum studies reader* (2nd ed.). New York: RoutledgeFalmer.

Florida Department of Education, Divisions of Assesment & School Performance/Education Information & Accountability/Evaluation & Reporting. (2006). Retrieved January 3, 2006, from http://www.firn.edu/doe/eias

Florida State University Schools. (2005). *New Millennium High Schools,* 1–8. Retrieved October 16, 2005, from http://fsus.fsu.edu

Florida Virtual School. (2004). *Florida Virtual High School stakeholders survey* (FLVS), 1–2. Retrieved October16, 2005, from http://www.flvs.net/general/school_data.php

Forsten, C., Grant, J., Johnson, B., & Richardson, I. (1997). *Looping: 72 practical answers to your most pressing questions.* Peterborough, NH: Crystal Springs Books.

Forsten, C., Grant, J., & Richardson, I. (1999). Multiage and looping: Borrowing from the past. *Principal, 78*(4), 15–16.

Franklin, L. L. (1999). Becoming seamless: Dynamic shifts in a mentoring commitment. In C. A. Mullen & D. W. Lick (Eds.), *New directions in mentoring: Creating a culture of synergy* (pp. 104–115). London, England: Falmer.

Gabriel, J. G. (2005). *How to thrive as a teacher leader.* Alexandria, VA: Association for Supervision and Curriculum Development.

Gallagher, M. (1998, December 1). Fatherless boys grow up into dangerous men. *Wall Street Journal*, A22.

Gandara, P. (1995). *Over the ivy walls: The educational mobility of low-income Chicanos.* Albany, NY: State University of New York Press.

Gardner, H. (1991). *The unschooled mind: How children think and how schools should teach.* New York: Basic Books.

Gaustad, J. (1998, December). *Implementing looping.* (ERIC Digest #123), 1–6. Retrieved August 6, 2005, from http://eric.uoregon.edu/publications/digests/digest123.html (ERIC Reproduction Service No. EDO-EA-98-7)

George, P., & Lounsbury, J. (2000). *Making big schools feel small: Multiage grouping, looping, and schools-within-a-school.* Westerville, OH: National Middle School Association.

George, P. (2001, December). Priorities and barriers in high school leadership: A summary of findings. *Principal Leadership, 2*(4), 50–52. Retrieved September 8, 2005, from http://www.findarticles. com/p/articles/mi_qa4002/is_200112/ai_n9016067

Gerke, W. (2004, November). More than a disciplinarian. *Principal Leadership*, 1–2. Retrieved June 10, 2005, from http://www.findarticles.com/p/articles/mi_qa4002/is_200411/ai_n9463787

Gettinger, M. (1989). Effects of maximizing time spent and minimizing time needed for learning on pupil achievement. *American Educational Research Journal, 26*(1), 73–91.

Glatthorn, A. A. (2000). *The principal as curriculum leader: Shaping what is taught and tested.* Thousand Oaks, CA: Corwin.

Goldring, E. B., & Smrekar, C. (2002, September/October). *Magnet schools: Reform and race in urban education.* Retrieved December 3, 2005, from http://www.findarticles.com/p/articles/mi_hb3428/is_200209/ai_n8268416

Goldring, E. B., Smrekar, C. (2005). *Shifting from court-ordered to court-ended desegregation in Nashville: Student assignment and teacher resources.* Retrieved December 3, 2005, from http://www.ccpr.ucla.edu/isarc28/Final%20Papers/School%20SegregationGamoranAn.pdf

Gonazalez, C., Llenza, E., Seligman, A., Vnuk, K., & van Loveren, R. (2004, December). *Needs assessment: SUPERKids initiative for the University of South Florida Board of Trustees.* Presented at the monthly meeting for the USF Board of Trustees, Tampa, FL.

Goodlad, J. I. (1984). *A place called school.* New York: McGraw-Hill.

Goodlad, J. I. (1999). Flow, eros, and ethos in educational renewal. *Phi Delta Kappan, 80*(8), 571–578.

Goodlad, S. J. (2004). Democracy, schools, and the agenda. *Kappa Delta Pi Record, 41*(1), 17–20.

Gottesman, B. (2000). *Peer coaching for educators* (2nd ed.). Lanham, MA: Scarecrow Education.

Gross, S. J. (1998). *Staying centered: Curriculum leadership in a turbulent era.* Alexandria, VA: Association for Supervision and Curriculum Development.

Hammel, A. M. (2004). Inclusion strategies that work. *Music Educators Journal*, 90(5), 33–37.

Hargreaves, A., & Fullan, M. (2000). Mentoring in the new millennium. *Theory Into Practice*, 39(1), 50–56.

Hartzell, G. (2002). *Why should principals support school libraries?* (ERIC Document Reproductive Service No. ED470034)

Haslinger, J., Kelly, P., & O'Lare, L. (1996). Countering absenteeism, anonymity and apathy. *Educational Leadership*, 54, 47–49.

Hausfather, S. (1996). Vygotsky and schooling: Creating a social context for learning. *Action in Teacher Education*, 18, 1–10.

Heathfield, S. M. (2005). *How to build a teamwork culture: Do the hard stuff*, 1–3. Retrieved June 9, 2005, from http://humanresources.about.com/cs/involvementteams/1/aa/12200la.htm

Heflin, L. J., & Bullock, L. M. (1999). Inclusion of students with emotional/behavioral disorders: A survey of teachers in general and special education. *Preventing School Failure*, 43(3), 103–111.

Hendershot, G. (2001, December 12). *Internet use by people with disabilities grows at twice the rate of non-disabled, yet still lags significantly behind.* Retrieved July 6, 2005, from http://www.nod.org/content.cfm?id=682

Henderson, J. G., & Hawthorne, R. D. (2000). *Transformative curriculum leadership* (2nd ed.). Columbus, OH: Merrill.

Henning, M. B., & Mitchell, L. C. (2002). Preparing for inclusion. *Child Study Journal*, 32(1), 19–29.

Hill, J. H., & Mannheim, B. (1992). Language and world view. *Annual Review of Anthropology*, 21, 381–406.

History of Curriculum. (2002, Fall). *EDUC640: Curriculum & instructional leadership, Loyola Marymount University.* Retrieved March 10, 2005, from http://myweb.lmu.edu/mryan

Hootstein, E. (1998). Differentiation of instructional methodologies in subject-based curricula at the secondary level. *Exceptional Children*, 60(3), 249–261.

Hoover, J. J., & Patton, J. R. (2004). Differentiating standards-based education for students with diverse needs. *Remedial and Special Education*, 25(2), 74–78.

Hopkin, M. (2004). *Early man had mining in mind.* Retrieved August 10, 2005, from http://www.bioedonline.org/news/news.cfm?art=978

Horn, R. A. (2002). Differing perspectives on the magic of dialogue: Implications for a scholar-practitioner leader. *Scholar–Practitioner Quarterly*, 1(2), 83–102.

Hoyle, J. R. (1995). *Leadership and futuring: Making visions happen.* Thousand Oaks, CA: Corwin.

Hudson, M. B. (n.d.). *Differences in administrating magnet schools: Implications for practitioners and professors of educational administration.* Retrieved December 2, 2005, from http://www.hehd.clemson.edu/SRCEA/YrBkv1n1/Hudson.htm

Huling, L. (2001, November). *Teacher mentoring as professional development.* (ERIC Document Reproduction Service No. ED460125)

Itza-Ortiz, S. F., Rebello, S., & Zollman, D. (2003). The vocabulary of introductory physics and its implications for learning physics. *The Physics Teacher*, 41(6), 330–346.

Jackson, L., Ryndak, D. L., & Billingsley, F. (2000). Useful practices in inclusive education: A preliminary view of what experts in moderate to severe disabilities are saying. *Association for Persons with Severe Handicaps*, 25(3), 129–141.

Jackson, P. W. (1990/2004). The daily grind. In D. J. Flinders & S. J. Thornton (Eds.), *The curriculum studies reader* (2nd ed.; pp. 93–102). New York: Routledge.

Jacobs, H. H. (Ed.). (1989). *Interdisciplinary curriculum: Design and implementation.* Alexandria, VA: Association for Supervision & Curriculum Development.

Janesick, V. J. (2003). *Curriculum trends: A reference handbook*. Denver, CO: ABC–CLIO.

Johnstone, A. H., & Selepeng, D. (2001). A language problem revisited. *Chemistry education: Research and practice in Europe, 2*(1), 19–29.

Jordan, D. (2000). Looping: Discovering the difference. *Teaching Pre-K–8, 30*(6), 58–59.

Kamens, M. W., Loprete, S. J., & Slostad, F. A. (2003). Inclusive classrooms: What practicing teachers want to know. *Action in Teacher Education, 25*(1), 20–26.

Kavale, K., & Forness, S. (2000). History, rhetoric, and reality: Analysis of the inclusion debate. *Remedial and Special Education, 21*(5), 279–296.

Kealy, W. A. (2004). Media literacy. In J. L. Kincheloe & D. Weil (Eds.), *Critical thinking and learning: An encyclopedia for parents and teachers* (pp. 287–291). Westport, CT: Greenwood.

Kenyon, G. M. (1996). Meaning/value of personal storytelling. In J. Birren, G. Kenyon, G. E. Ruth, J. Schroots, & T. Svensson (Eds.), *Aging and biography: Explorations in adult development* (pp. 39–60). New York; Springer.

Kincheloe, J. L., & Weil, D. (Eds.). (2001). *Standards and schooling in the United States: An encyclopedia*. Santa Barbara, CA: ABC–CLIO.

Kliebard, H. M. (1975/2004). The rise of scientific curriculum-making and its aftermath. In D. J. Flinders & S. J. Thornton (Eds.), *The curriculum studies reader* (2nd ed.; pp. 37–46). New York: Routledge.

Koralek, D., & Collins, R. (2004). Developing a tutoring program. *Reading Rockets*, 1–8. Retrieved July 14, 2005, from http://www.readingrockets.org/article.php?ID=166

Kovalik, S. (1994). *Integrated thematic instruction: The model* (3rd ed.). Kent, WA: Books for Educators.

Laboratory at Brown University. (1997). *Looping: Supporting student learning through long-term relationships*. Providence, RI: Northeast Islands Regional Educational Laboratory.

Lance, K. (1994). *The impact of school library media centers on academic achievement*. (ERIC Document Reproduction Service No. ED372759)

Lance, K. (2001). *Proof of the power: Recent research on the impact of school library media programs on the academic achievement of U.S. public school students*. (ERIC Document Reproduction Service No. ED456861)

Lankshear, C., & Knobel, M. (2004). Infusing critical thinking into the sociocultural view of literacy. In J. L. Kincheloe & D. Weil (Eds.), *Critical thinking and learning: An encyclopedia for parents and teachers* (pp. 281–287). Westport, CT: Greenwood.

Lauer, P., Akiba, M., Wilkerson, S. B., Apthorp, H. S., Snow, D., & Martin-Glenn, M. (2003). *The effectiveness of out-of-school-time strategies in assisting low-achieving students in reading and mathematics: A research synthesis*. (Regional Educational Laboratory Contract #ED-01-CO-0006) http://www.mcrel.org/pdf/schoolImprovementReform/5032RR-RsostresearchBrief.pdf

Lincoln, R. (1998). Looping in the middle grades. *Principal, 78*(1), 58–59.

Lind, S. (2003, November). *Teachers' perceptions of culture in low and high attrition schools*. Unpublished doctoral dissertation, University of South Florida, Tampa.

Lipskey, D. K., & Gartner, A. (1996). Inclusion, school restructuring, and the remaking of American society. *Harvard Educational Review, 66*(116), 762–796.

Llewellyn, P. E. (2004). Will I be ready as an administrator for school emergencies? *International Journal of Educational Reform, 13*(2), 118–125.

Lortie, D.C. (1998, Summer). Teaching educational administration: Reflections on our craft. *Journal of Cases in Educational Leadership, 1*(1), 1–12. Retrieved May 6, 2005, from http://www.ucea.org/cases

Loucks-Horsley, S. (1995). The Concerns-Based Adoption Model (CBAM): A model for change in individuals. *National Academy of Sciences*. Retrieved October 2, 2005, from http://www.nationalacademies.org/rise/backg4a.htm

Marsh, C. J., & Willis, G. (2003). *Curriculum: Alternative approaches, ongoing issues* (3rd ed.). Upper Saddle River, NJ: Merrill/Prentice-Hall.

Marshall, K. (1996, January). How I confronted HSPS (Hyperactive Superficial Principal Syndrome) and began to deal with the heart of the matter. *Phi Delta Kappan, 77*(5), 336–343

Marshall, K. (2003, May). Recovering from HSPS (Hyperactive Superficial Principal Syndrome): A progress report. *Phi Delta Kappan, 84*(9), 701–708.

Marshall, K. (2005, June). It's time to rethink teacher supervision and evaluation. *Phi Delta Kappan,* 86(10), 727–735.

Maslow, A. H. (1954). *Motivation and personality.* New York: Harper & Brothers.

Maynard, T. (2000). Learning to teach or learning to manage mentors? Experience of school-based teacher training. *Mentoring & Tutoring, 8*(1), 17–30.

McCann, I., & Radford, R. (1993). *Mentoring for teachers: The collaborative approach.* London: Falmer.

McCarthy, M. M. (1999). How are school leaders prepared? *Educational Horizons, 77*(2), 74–81.

McComas, W. F., & Almazroa, H. (1998). The nature of science in science education: An introduction. *Science & Education, 7,* 511–532.

McLesky, J., & Waldron, N. L. (2002). Inclusion and school change: Teacher perceptions regarding curricular and instructional adaptations. *Teacher Education and Special Education, 25,* 41–54.

McNeil, J. D. (1965). *Curriculum administration: Principles and techniques of curriculum development.* New York: Macmillan.

McNeil, J. D. (2003). *Curriculum: The teacher's initiative* (3rd ed.). Upper Saddle River, NJ: Merrill Prentice-Hall.

Merriam, S. B. (1998). *Qualitative research and case study applications in education.* San Francisco, CA: Jossey-Bass.

Michael, L. (2003). Reformulating the sapit-whorf hypothesis: Discourse, interaction and distributed cognition. In G. I. Hey, G. Pizer, H-Y Su, + Szmania (Eds), *Proceedings of the 10th Annual Symposium about Language and Society, 45,* 107–116. Austin, TX: Texas Linguistic Forum.

Miles, M. B., & Huberman, A. M. (1994). *Qualitative data analysis: An expanded source-book* (2nd ed.). Thousand Oaks, CA: Sage.

Miller, K., & Snow D. (2004). *Noteworthy perspectives: Out-of-school time programs for at-risk students.* Aurora, CO: Mid-continent Research for Education and Learning.

Moir, E., & Bloom, G. (2003). Fostering leadership through mentoring. *Educational Leadership, 60*(8), 58–60.

Monahan, R. G., Marino, S. B., & Miller, R. (1996). Teacher attitudes toward inclusion: Implications for teacher education in schools 2000. *Education, 117,* 316–320.

Moon, T., Tomlinson, C., & Callahan, C. (1995). *Academic diversity in the middle school: Results of a national survey of middle school administrators and teachers.* (Research Monograph 95124). Charlottesville, VI: National Research Center on the Gifted and Talented, University of Virginia. Retrieved May 1, 2005, from http://www.wfcnetwork.org/content/view/242/5 (1998, January)

Moore, C. (1998). *Educating students with disabilities in general education classrooms: A summary of the research.* Research Monograph TAA#AK-03-INCL Eugene, OR: Western Regional Resource Center.

Moore, T. I. (2004). Facilitative leadership: One approach to empowering staff and other stakeholders. *Library Trends, 53*(1), 230–237.

Morrill, S., & Ryan, P. (2004). *The elements of magnet schools.* Retrieved April 13, 2005, from http://tiger.towson.edu/~smorri2/research/paper.htm#Advantagesofmagnetschools

Morris, D. (1999). *The Howard Street tutoring manual: Teaching at-risk readers in the primary grades.* New York: Guilford.

Morris, D., Shaw, B., & Perney, J. (1990). Helping low readers in grades 2 and 3: An after-school volunteer tutoring program. *Elementary School Journal, 91*(2), 134–150.

Morrow, L., & Woo, D. (2001). *Tutoring programs for struggling readers: The America reads challenge.* New York: Guilford.

Mullen, C. A. (2001). Disabilities awareness and the preservice teacher: A blueprint of a mentoring intervention. *Journal of Education for Teaching: International Research and Pedagogy, 27*(1), 39–61.

Mullen, C. A. (2002a). A pedagogue's poetic meditation. *Teacher Education Quarterly, 29*(4), 16–17.

Mullen, C. A. (2002b). Guest editor of "Teacher Activism in Education Reform." *Teacher Development: An International Journal of Teachers' Professional Development, 6*(1), 1– 128.

Mullen, C. A. (2002c). The original ten: A multisite case study of Florida's millennium high school reform model. *Educational Policy Analysis Archives, 10*(40), 1–23. Retrieved November 6, 2005, from http://epaa.asu.edu/epaa/v10n40.html

Mullen, C. A. (2003). What is a *scholar-practitioner?* K–12 teachers and administrators respond. *Scholar-Practitioner Quarterly: A Journal for the Scholar-Practitioner Leader, 1*(4), 9–26.

Mullen, C. A. (2004a). *Climbing the Himalayas of school leadership: The socialization of early career administrators.* Lanham, MA: Scarecrow Education.

Mullen, C. A. (2004b). Mapping a landscape of leadership: Cultivating scholarly-practical inquiry. *International Journal of Educational Reform, 13*(2), 101–107.

Mullen, C. A. (2005a). Doctoral cohort experimentation at a distance. In C. A. Mullen (Ed.), *Fire and ice: Igniting and channeling passion in new qualitative researchers* (pp. 197–238). New York: Peter Lang.

Mullen, C. A. (2005b). Scholar practitioner. In C. A. Mullen (Ed.), *Fire and ice: Igniting and channeling passion in new qualitative researchers* (pp. 47–57). New York: Peter Lang.

Mullen, C. A. (2005c). *The mentorship primer.* New York: Peter Lang.

Mullen, C. A. (with Kohan, A. R.). (2002). Beyond dualism, splits, and schisms: Social justice for a renewal of vocational–academic education. *Journal of School Leadership, 12*(6), 640–662.

Mullen, C. A. (with Sullivan, E. C.). (2002). The New Millennium High School: Tomorrow's school today? *International Journal of Leadership in Education, 5*(3), 273–284.

Mullen, C. A., & Cairns, S. S. (2001). The principal's apprentice: Mentoring aspiring school administrators through relevant preparation. *Mentoring & Tutoring, 9*(2), 125–152.

Mullen, C. A., & Farinas, J. (2003). What constitutes a "highly qualified" teacher? A review of teacher education standards and trends. *Teacher Education and Practice, 16*(4), 318–330.

Mullen, C. A., & Graves, T. H. (2000). A case study of democratic accountability and school improvement. *Journal of School Leadership, 10*(6), 478–504.

Mullen, C. A., & Johnson, W. B. (in press). Accountability–democracy tensions facing democratic school leaders. *Action in Teacher Education.*

Mullen, C.A., Kealy, W.A., & Sullivan, A. (2004, Fall). National technology standards for K–12 schools: A case studty of unresolved issued in public relations. *Journal of School Public Relations, 25*(4), 340–363.

Mullen, C. A., & Lick, D. W. (Eds.). (1999). *New directions in mentoring: Creating a culture of synergy.* London: Falmer.

Murphy, J. (2004). *Leadership for literacy: Research-based practice, pre-K–3.* Thousand Oaks, CA: Corwin.

Murphy, J., & Datnow, A. (Eds.). (2003). *Leadership lessons from comprehensive school reforms.* Thousand Oaks, CA: Corwin.

National Board for Professional Teaching Standards [NBPTS]. (2002, August). *What teachers should know and be able to do*, 3–4. Retrieved August 15, 2005, from www.nbpts. org

National Board for Professional Teaching Standards [NBPTS]. (2004a, August). *State & local support & incentives*, 1–4. Retrieved August 15, 2005, from www.nbpts.org

National Board for Professional Teaching Standards [NBPTS]. (2004b, August). *Why America needs National Board Certified Teachers*, 1–11. Retrieved August 15, 2005, from www.nbpts.org

National Commission on Excellence in Education [NCEE]. (1983, April). *A nation at risk: The imperative for educational reform*. Washington, DC: U.S. Department of Education. Retrieved July 3, 2005, from http://www.ed.gov/pubs/NatAtRisk/findings.html

National Education Technical Plan. (2004). *The national education technology plan: The future is now*, 16–17. Retrieved March 15, 2005, from http://www.nationaledtechplan. org/default.asp

National Parks Conservation Association. (2005). *Giant Pacific Octopus*. Retrieved March 30, 2005, from http://www.npca.org/marine_and_coastal/marine_wildlife/octopus.asp

National Policy Board for Educational Administration [NPBEA]. (2002, January). *Standards for advanced programs in educational leadership for principals, superintendents, curriculum directors, and supervisors*, 1–18. Retrieved May 9, 2005, from http://www. npbea.org/ELCC/ELCCStandards%20_5-02.pdf

National Policy Board for Educational Administrators for the Educational Leadership Constituent Council. (1995). *Technology Standards for School Administrators (TSSA)*. Retrieved October 10, 2005, from http://cnets.iste.org/tssa.

Neill, J. (2005). *Outdoor education evaluation and research center*. Retrieved April 18, 2005, from http://www.wilderdom.com/experiential/ExperientialDewey.html

Oakes, J., Selvin, M., Karoly, L., & Guiton, G. (1992). *Educational matchmaking: Academic and vocational tracking in comprehensive high schools*. Berkeley, CA: National Center for Research in Vocational Education.

Office of the Attorney General of Florida. (2005, September). Florida government-in-the-Sunshine Law. Retrieved March 8, 2005, from http://myfloridalegal.com/sunshine

Office of Superintendent of Public Instruction. (n.d.). *What makes a school successful: Effective School leadership*. Retrieved September 21, 2005, from http://www.k12.wa.us/ SchoolImprovement/Leadership.aspx

Oleson, M. (2005, April). *Curriculum leadership then and now*, 1–3. Retrieved April 2, 2005, from http://iowa.ascd.org/documents/curriculumleadersandcathedrals.doc

Oliver, R. (2003). Assistant principal job satisfaction and desire to become principals. *NCPEA Education Leadership Review, 4*(2), 38–46.

Oliver, R. (2005). Assistant principal professional growth and development: A matter that cannot be left to chance. *Educational Leadership and Administration, 17,* 89–100.

Olson, L. (2003, January 15). Ed. Dept. OKs first accountability plans. *Education Week, 22*(18), 1–2. Retrieved October 10, 2005, from http://www.edweek.org/ew/index.html

Olson, M. R., Chalmers, L., & Hoover, J. H. (1997). Attitudes and attributes of general education teachers identified as effective inclusionists. *Remedial and Special Education, 18,* 28–35.

O'Shea, D. J. (1999). Making uninvited inclusion work. *Preventing school failure, 43*(4), 179–181.

O'Shea, D. J., & O'Shea, L. J. (1998). Learning to include. *Teaching Exceptional Children, 31*(1), 40–48.

Ovalle, R. (2004). Why isn't looping a more common practice? A leadership case study. *International Journal of Educational Reform, 13*(2), 136–142.

Paquette, B. S. (2004). Are today's beginning school administrators prepared for their jobs? A case study. *International Journal of Educational Reform, 13*(2), 111–117.

Perie, M., & Baker, D. P. (1997, August). *Job satisfaction among America's leaders: Effects of workplace conditions, background characteristics, and teacher compensation.* Retrieved March 11, 2004, from http://nces.ed.gov/pubsearch/pubs info.asp?pubid=97471

Peterson, K. D., & Deal, T. E. (1998). How leaders influence the culture of schools. *Educational Leadership, 56*(1), 28–30.

Pew Internet and American Life Project Report. (2004). *Pew Internet project surveys.* Retrieved August 10, 2005, from http://pew Internet.org/ppf/r/148/report_display.asp

Piaget, J. (1951). *Play, dreams, and imitation in childhood.* New York: Norton & Company.

Piaget, J. (1952). *The origins of intelligence in children.* New York: International Press.

Pimm, D. (1987). *Speaking mathematically: Communication in mathematics classrooms.* London: Routledge.

Pinar, W. F. (1978/2004). The reconceptualization of curriculum studies. In D. J. Flinders & S. J. Thornton (Eds.), *The curriculum studies reader* (2nd ed.; pp. 149–157). New York: Routledge.

Pinar, W. F. (1995). *Autobiography, politics, and sexuality: Essays in curriculum theory 1972–1992.* New York: Peter Lang.

Pinar, W. F. (1995/1996). *Preface and acknowledgements.* In W. F. Pinar, W. M. Reynolds, P. Slattery, & P. M. Taubman (Eds.), *Understanding curriculum: An introduction to the study of historical and contemporary curriculum discourses* (pp. xiii–xviii). New York: Peter Lang.

Pinar, W. F. (2005a). From statesmanship to status: The absence of authority in contemporary curriculum studies. *Journal of the American Association for the Advancement of Curriculum Studies, 1,* 1–37.

Pinar, W. F. (2005b). The problem with curriculum and pedagogy. *Journal of Curriculum and Pedagogy, 2*(1), 67–82.

Pinar, W. F., & Irwin, R. L. (Eds.). (2005). *Curriculum in a new key: The collected works of Ted. T. Aoki.* Mahwah, NJ: Lawrence Erlbaum Associates.

Pinar, W. F., Reynolds, W. M., Slattery, P., & Taubman, P. M. (1995/1996). *Understanding curriculum: An introduction to the study of historical and contemporary curriculum discourses.* New York: Peter Lang.

Poeske, L. D., Stober, S. S., Dyson, J. C., & Cheddar, L. A. (2005). Traditional curriculum versus hidden curriculum. In J. P. Shapiro & J. A. Stefkovich (Eds.), *Ethical leadership and decision making in education: Applying theoretical perspectives to complete dilemmas* (2nd ed.; pp. 44–58). Mahwah, NJ: Lawrence Erlbaum Associates.

Ponticell, J. (2005, June). *Culture, symbols, risk organizational "soul."* Presentation at Gifts by the Sea VIII: The leadership challenge: Integrating Key Strategies for Success, Clearwater, FL.

Popham, W. J. (1972/2004). Objectives. In D. J. Flinders & S. J. Thornton (Eds.), *The curriculum studies reader* (2nd ed.; pp. 71–84). New York: Routledge.

Portner, H. (Ed.). (2005). *Teacher mentoring and induction: The state of the art and beyond.* Thousand Oaks, CA: Corwin.

Posner, G. (1992). *Analyzing the curriculum.* New York: McGraw-Hill.

Rallis, S. F., & Goldring, E. B. (2000). *Principals of dynamic schools: Taking charge of change.* Thousand Oaks, CA: Corwin.

Reading Rockets. (2004). *Evidence that tutoring works, 1.* Retrieved May 11, 2005, from http://www. readingrockets.org/article.php?ID=92

Rees, L. (2003). *Benefits of mentoring, 1–2.* Retrieved April 3, 2005, from http://www. prepcenter.org/ pt_m_rsch_bom.htm

Reick, W. A., & Wadsworth, D. E. (2000). Inclusion: administrative headache or opportunity? *NASSP Bulletin, 84*(618), 56–62.

Research Points. (2005, Summer). Teaching teachers: Professional development to improve student achievement. *Research Points, 3*(1), 1–4. Washington, DC: American Educational Research Association. Retrieved July 28, 2005, from http://www.aera.net/uploaded Files/Journals_and_Publications/Research_Points/RP Summer05.pdf

Rhodes, G., & Schaible, R. (1989). Fact, law, and theory: Ways of thinking in science and literature. *Journal of College Science Teacher, 18,* 228–232.

Riley, K. L., Wilson, E. K., & Fogg, T. (2000, October). *Transforming the spirit of teaching through wise practice: Observations of two Alabama social studies teachers.* Retrieved February 10, 2005, from http://stac.highbeam.com/s/socialeducation/ocotber012000/ transformingthespiritofteachingthroughwisepractices

Robbins, P., & Alvy, H. (2004). *The new principal's fieldbook: Strategies for success.* Alexandria, VA: Association for Supervision and Curriculum Development.

Robertson, J. (2005). *Coaching leadership: Building educational leadership capacity through coaching partnerships.* Wellington, NZ: New Zealand Council for Educational Research.

Rogers, C. R. (1961). *On becoming a person.* Boston: Houghton Mifflin.

Rouse, E. R. (1998, March). *Schools and student achievement: More evidence from the Milwaukee Parental Choice Program.* [Online]. Available: http://www.ny.frb.org/ research/epr/98v04n1/9803rous.pdf

Rowley, J. B. (1999, May). The good mentor. *Educational Leadership, 56*(8), 20–22.

Rubicon Atlas. (2006). *Atlas curriculum mapping.* Retrieved July 30, 2005, from http://www.rubiconatlas.com/AtlasCurriculumMapping.html

Sapir, E. (1958). The status of linguistics as a science. In E. Mandelbaum (Ed.), *Culture, language, and personality* (pp. 207–215). Berkeley, CA: University of California Press.

Schacter, J. (n.d.). *Reading programs that work: A review of programs for pre-kindergarten to 4th grade* (pp. 40–48). Santa Monica, CA. Retrieved May 14, 2005, from http://www.mff.org/pubs/ME279.pdf

Schermer, D. G. (2005, April). Cathedral building and curriculum leadership. *Iowa ASCD Educational Leadership,* 1–5. Retrieved October 8, 2005, from http://iowa.ascd.org/documents/curriculumleadersandcathedrals.doc

Schirduan, V., & Case, K. (2004). Mindful curriculum leadership for students with Attention Deficit Hyperactivity Disorder: Leading in elementary schools using multiple intelligences theory (SUMIT). *Teachers College Record, 106*(1), 87–95.

School: The Story of American Public Education. (2001, September 3–4). "Roots in history master timeline," part of the Public Broadcasting Service (PBS) documentary entitled School: The PBS Series. Retrieved November 14, 2005, from http://www.pbs.org/kcet/publicschool/roots_in_history/testing.html

Schumaker, D., & Sommers, W. (2001). *Being a successful principal: Riding the wave of change without drowning.* Thousand Oaks, CA: Corwin.

Schwab, J. (1969). The practical: A language for curriculum. *School Review, 78,* 1–23.

Scruggs, T. E., & Mastropieri, M. A. (1996). Teacher perceptions of mainstreaming/inclusion, 1958–1995: A research systhesis. *Exceptional Children, 63,* 59–74.

Sergiovanni, T. J. (2000). *The lifeworld of leadership: Creating culture, community, and personal meaning in our schools.* San Francisco, CA: Jossey-Bass.

Sergiovanni, T. J. (2001). *The principalship: A reflective practice perspective* (4th ed.). Toronto, ON: Allyn and Bacon.

Sergiovanni, T. J. (2005). *Strengthening the heartbeat: Leading and learning together in schools.* San Francisco, CA: Jossey-Bass.

Shade, R. A., & Stewart, R. (2001). General education and special education preservice teachers' attitudes toward inclusion. *Preventing School Failure, 46*(1), 37–41.

Shapiro, J. P., & Stefkovich, J. A. (2005). *Ethical leadership and decision making in education: Applying theoretical perspectives to complete dilemmas* (2nd ed.). Mahwah, NJ: Lawrence Erlbaum Associates.

Simel, D. (1998). Education for *bildung*: Teacher attitudes toward looping. *International Journal of Educational Reform, 7*(4), 330–337.

Skinner, B. F. (1953). *Science and human behavior.* New York: Macmillan.

Slattery, P. (1995). *Curriculum development in the postmodern era.* New York: Garland.

Sloan, K., & Sears, J. T. (Eds.). (2001). *Democratic curriculum theory & practice: Retrieving public spaces.* Troy, NY: Educator's International Press.

Smith, J. B. (1995). *Achieving a curriculum-based library media center program: The middle school model for change.* Chicago, IL: American Library Association.

Smith, M. K. (1996/2000). *Curriculum theory and practice.* Retrieved April 16, 2005, from www.infed.org/biblio/b-curric.htm

Smrekar, C. E. (2004). Magnet schools. The Gale Group. Retrieved September 9, 2005, from http://encyclopedias.families.com/magnet-schools-573-574-ecc

Southwest Educational Development Laboratory [SEDL]. (1995) *Inclusion: The pros and cons. In Issues … about Change,* 4(3). Retrieved April 4, 2005, from http://www.sedl.org/change/issues/issues43.html

Speier, C., Valacich, J., & Vessey, I. (1997). *The effects of task interruption and information: Presentation on individual decision making,* 1–15. Retrieved March 1, 2005, from http://interruptions.net/literature/Speier-ICIS97-p21-speier.pdf

Stainback, S., & Stainback, W. (1985). *Integration of students with severe handicaps into regular schools* (Report No. E468). (ERIC Document Reproduction Service No. ED255009)

St. Cloud Area School District 742, Minnesota. (2005). Retrieved May 24, 2005, from http://www.stcloud.k12.mn.us

Steeves, K. B., & Browne, B. C. (2000). *Preparing teachers for National Board Certification: A facilitator's guide.* New York: Guilford.

Terry Sanford Institute of Public Policy: Duke University. (2004, September). *Documentation of unitary status, 100 districts in South and Border; for Clolfelter, Ladd, and Vigdor: Federal oversight, local control, and the specter of "resegregation" in southern schools,* 1–69. Retrieved December 18, 2005 from http://www.pubpol.duke.edu/people/faculty/clotfelter/summaryunitarystatus.pdf

Thomas, K. A. (2003). Science is easier than you think. In G. Meisels & R. L. Potter (Eds), *Science that matters* (pp. 10–47). Dubuque, IA: Kendall/Hunt.

Thomas, T. P., & Schubert, W. H. (2001). Reinterpreting teacher certification standards. In J. K. Kincheloe & D. Weil (Eds.), *Standards and schooling in the United States: An encyclopedia, 1* (pp. 229–243). Santa Barbara, CA: ABC–CLIO.

Thorndike, E. L. (1911). *Animal intelligence: Experimental studies.* Darien, CT: Hafner.

Thornton, C., & Lowe-Parrino, G. (n.d.). *Hands-on teaching (H.O.T.) strategies for using math manipulatives: A teacher resource binder.* Vernon Hills, IL: ETA.

Thornton, S. J. (2003/2004). Silence on gays and lesbians in social studies curriculum. In D. J. Flinders & S. J. Thornton (Eds.), *The curriculum studies reader* (2nd ed.; pp. 307–313). New York: Routledge.

Tomlinson, C. A., Brighton, C., & Hertberg, H. (2003). Differentiating instruction in response to student readiness, interest, and learning profile in academically diverse classrooms: A review of literature. *Journal for the Education of the Gifted, 27*(2/3), 119–145.

TSSA Collaborative. (2001). *TSSA: Technology standards for school administrators.* North Central Regional Technology in Educational Consortium. Retrieved September 23, 2003, from http://cnets.iste.org/tssa

Tyler, R. W. (1949). *Basic principles of curriculum and instruction.* Chicago: University of Chicago Press.

Tyler, R. W. (1949/2004). Basic principles of curriculum and instruction. In D. J. Flinders & S. J. Thornton (Eds.), *The curriculum studies reader* (2nd ed.; pp. 51–59). New York: Routledge.

Umphrey, J. (2004, November). Take some "me" time. *Principal Leadership, 5*(3), 6. Retrieved October 18, 2005, from http://www.findarticles.com/p/articles/mi_qa4002/is_200411/ ai_n9463780.

U.S. Department of Education. (1994). *Goals 2000—Educate America*. (H.R. 1804). Retrieved November 9, 2005, from http://www.ed.gov/legislation/GOALS2000/TheAct/index/html

U.S. Department of Education. (1989, February). Planning and local initiative are crucial: Developing magnet programs. *Education Digest, 54*(6), 22–24.

U.S. Department of Education. (1999). *NAEP inclusion policy: The nation's report card*. Washington, DC: Institute of Education Sciences (IES National Center for Education Statistics). Retrieved October 18, 2005, from http://nces.ed.gov/naep3/about/inclusion.asp

U.S. Department of Education. (2002, January 8). *No Child Left Behind Act of 2001*. Washington, DC: Office of Elementary and Secondary Education. Retrieved May 1, 2005, from http://www.ed.gov/policy/elsec/leg/esea02/107-110.pdf

U.S. Department of Education. (2003). *Policy and Program Studies Service: Evaluation of the Magnet Schools Assistance Program, 1998 grantees*, 1–228. (Final report: Doc #2003-15). Washington, DC: America Institutes for Research. Retrieved December 18, 2005, from http://www.ed.gov/rschstat/eval/choice/magneteval/finalreport.pdf

U.S. Department of Education. (2004, September). *Creating successful magnet schools programs*, 1–68. Retrieved March 11, 2005, from http://www.ed.gov/admins/comm/choice/magnet/report.pdf

U.S. Department of Education. (2005). *Title I—Improving the academic achievement of the disadvantaged*. [Online]. Retrieved April 8, 2005, from http://www.ed.gov/policy/elsec/leg/esea02/pg1.html

Varholy, J. (2004, April). *Looping—a curriculum race winner?* Unpublished manuscript.

Villa, R. A., & Thousand, J. S. (2003). Teaching all students. *Educational Leadership, 61*(4), 6–17.

Villa, R. A., & Thousand, J. S. (Eds.). (2005). *Creating an inclusive school* (2nd ed.). Alexandria, VA: Association for Supervision and Curriculum Development.

Walker, B., & Morrow, L. (Eds.). (1998). *Tips for the reading team strategies for tutors*. Newark, NJ: International Reading Association.

Walker, B., Scherry, R., & Morrow, L. (1999). *Training the reading team: A guide for supervisors of a volunteer tutoring program*. Newark, NJ: International Reading Association.

Walker, D. F. (2003). *Fundamentals of curriculum: Passion and professionalism* (2nd ed.). Mahwah, NJ: Lawrence Erlbaum Associates.

Werts, M. G., Wolery, M., & Snyder, E. D. (1996). Teachers' perceptions of the supports critical to the success of inclusion programs. *Journal of the Association for Persons with Severe Handicaps, 21*, 9–21.

Wikipedia, the Free Encyclopedia. (2005, July 23). *Columbine High School massacre*. Retrieved August 8, 2005, from http://en.wikipedia.org/wiki/Columbine_High_ School_ massacre.

Wiburg, K. M. (2003). Technology and the new meaning of educational equity. *Computers in the Schools, 20*(1–2), 113–128.

Wiles, J. (1999). *Curriculum essentials: A resource for educators*. Toronto, ON: Allyn and Bacon.

Willingham, D. T. (2004). *Language in cognition: The thinking animal*. Upper Saddle River, NJ: Pearson-Prentice Hall.

Wisconsin Department for Public Instruction, Office of Educational Accountability. (2006). *School Performance Report*. Retrieved July 6, 2005, from http://www.dpi.state.wi.us/spr/index.html

Wood, C. (2005, April/May). High school.com. *Eudtopia*, 32–37. Retrieved September 9, 2005, from http://www.edutopia.org/magazine/ed1article.php?id=Art_1270&issue=apr_05

Woods, C. S. (2004). Science education. In J. L. Kincheloe & D. Weil (Eds.), *Critical thinking and learning: An encyclopedia for parents and teachers* (pp. 368–371). Westport, CT: Greenwood.

Yonkers Public School District. (2005). *Yonkers public schools: Our district.* Retrieved May 26, 2005, from http://www.yonkerspublicschools.org /Inside_pages/about_ourdistrict.htm

Yu, C. M. & Taylor, W. (1997, Spring). (Eds.). Difficult choices: Do magnet schools serve children in need? *Report of the Citizens' Commission on Civil Rights* (1–113). Washington, DC: Citizens' Commission on Civil Rights. Retrieved April 22, 2005, from http:// www.cccr.org/images/magnet.pdf

Zepeda, S. J. (2003). *Instructional supervision.* New York: Eye on Education.

Zollers, N. J., Ramanathan, A. K., & Yu, M. (1999). The relationship between school culture and inclusion: How an inclusive culture supports inclusive education. *Qualitative Studies in Education, 12*(2), 157–174.

About the Contributors

Carol A. Mullen, PhD, is an associate professor of educational leadership at the University of South Florida (USF), Tampa, and a graduate of the Ontario Institute for Studies in Education, University of Toronto. She specializes in curriculum leadership, mentorship and collaboration, and graduate student development. Mullen is editor of the refereed international journal *Mentoring & Tutoring: Partnership in Learning* and the faculty mentoring coordinator of USF's College of Education New Faculty Mentoring Program (NFMP). She teaches master's and doctoral courses and supervises the Writers in Training (WIT), a thriving doctoral cohort she founded. Mullen is the recipient of the 2005 Florida Association for Supervision and Curriculum Development (FASCD) Teaching and Research Excellence Award in instructional supervision. Her authorships include more than 130 articles, book chapters, and other works and, as guest editor, 12 special issues of journals, in addition to 10 books, most recently *A Graduate Student Guide: Making the Most of Mentoring* (2006). Others include *Fire and Ice: Igniting and Channeling Passion in New Qualitative Researchers* (2005), *The Mentorship Primer* (2005), and *Climbing the Himalayas of School Leadership: The Socialization of Early Career Administrators* (2004). *Breaking the Circle of One: Redefining Mentorship in the Lives and Writings of Educators* (1997/2000) received the Exemplary Research in Teacher Education Award from the American Educational Research Association (Division K).

Leila Amiri, MA, is a doctoral student in science education and a health professions advisor at the University of South Florida. She has 10 years of teaching experience at the K–12 and undergraduate levels. Her high school teaching experience was focused on science; at the undergraduate level, she teaches research methods, general science, and elementary science education. She holds a bachelor's degree in biology and a master's degree in cognitive and neural science.

Joseph C. Brown, MEd, is pursuing a doctorate degree in educational leadership from the University of South Florida. He earned a master's degree in counselor education and another in educational leadership and became a middle school administrator after working as a counselor in the Hillsborough County School District, Florida. He served as an assistant principal for 4 years and has been a principal since 2001. In 2002, he was nominated for the state of Florida's Assistant Principal of the Year. His dissertation focuses on the implementation of concept-based curriculum in schools, and his work in such areas as teachers' grading systems has appeared in *Principal Leadership*. In 2005, he was awarded the Berbecker Scholarship from USF's College of Education.

Darlene Y. Bruner, EdD, is an associate professor of educational leadership at the University of South Florida, Tampa, who has extensive experience as a school principal and district supervisor. She teaches courses in leadership, law, and curriculum. Her research interests concern the work culture of schools, the principalship, curriculum, and school reform issues. Coauthored articles have appeared in such journals as *Education Policy Analysis Archives* and *Essays in Education*.

Kristy L. Cantu, MEd, is pursuing a doctoral degree in educational leadership from the University of South Florida. She teaches the emotionally handicapped at the intermediate elementary level and has taught in the Pinellas County school district for the past 8 years. Her bachelor's degree is in specific learning disabilities, with varying exceptionalities and educational leadership added more recently. Her research interests include the intersection among disabilities, curriculum, and school culture.

Annie Hunter Clasen, MA, is the lead instructor for the Customer Service Academy at Aparacio-Levy Adult Technical Center in Tampa. She has 17 years of teaching and 13 years of business experience and is completing an educational leadership certificate. Clasen has a master's degree in educational leadership and another in marketing education, as well as a bachelor's of art in business administration. Recognized in 2004 with the President's Award from the Florida Association of Career Technical Educators, Clasen serves on state and national curriculum development committees. She coauthored a school-to-work activity book.

Cindy Dowdy, MEd, received her degree in early childhood education from Brenau University in Gainesville, Georgia. She is a reading coach at Cimino Elementary and Buckhorn Elementary in Valrico, Florida. Her 18 years in the public school system include being a classroom teacher, reading specialist, and media specialist. She has specialized in working with both the struggling reader and the reading teacher. She holds master's degrees in early childhood education and educational leadership.

Kayla English, MA, holds a master's degree in educational leadership and a bachelor's degree in elementary education from the University of South Florida. For the past 7 years, she has taught in Florida's Hillsborough County School District. In 2003, she was nominated Teacher of the Year; in 2004, she was named a Better Educated Students and Teachers (BEST) Career Ladder mentor teacher.

Valorie L. Fish, MEd, has been teaching at the primary level for the last 9 years. In 2005, she received $10,000 in grants to fund an after-school tutoring program in reading for second-grade students. She has received another substantial grant to enhance instruction in her classroom and at her school. Fish is currently pursuing an education specialist degree in educational leadership at the University of South Florida. She earned, from the University of Florida, a master's degree in elementary education.

Janice L. Hutinger, MEd, is an educational leadership doctoral student at the University of South Florida with a master's degree in this discipline and a bachelor's degree in special education. Her experience includes more than 19 years as an elementary teacher in both basic and special education. Hutinger also worked as a professional circus performer, and finds the skills she learned there valuable for working in the public education system. In 2005, she was awarded the Berbecker Scholarship from USF's College of Education.

Robert M. Jordan, BS, has an undergraduate degree in English education from the University of South Florida. He is studying educational leadership in a master's program. His certifications are K–12 English, middle-grades English, and English for speakers of other languages. For 6 years he taught eighth-grade language arts in Florida and currently holds the position of administrative supervisor at USF, where he also serves on the College of Education's Academic Grievance Committee for the master's degree.

Susan King, MA, has more than 25 years of classroom experience in both public and private schools and 11 years as a district administrator. She is the supervisor of Magnet Schools for Hillsborough County Public Schools and holds a BSE in English, a master's degree in counselor education, and reading certification. She is the chairperson of the Hillsborough Advocates for Public Education and serves on district-level committees. She is also the founder and president of a Gasparilla Krewe, Les Belles Femmes. King is completing the educational leadership program at the University of South Florida.

Jennifer McCrystal, MA, is a third-grade teacher at Valrico Elementary in Valrico, Florida, who holds a master's degree in educational leadership from the University of South Florida. McCrystal has 15 years experience as a classroom teacher and serves as a district trainer in reading and cooperative learning.

James Osborn, MA, has a master's degree in educational leadership from the University of South Florida. He completed a master's degree program in music education at the same institution. Osborn holds K–12 certifications in music education and exceptional student education. Currently in his 14th year of teaching, he is teaching a self-contained intermediate class of students that are trainably mentally handicapped. In 1999 he was selected by the Tampa Chapter of the Council for Exceptional Children as the Outstanding Special Service Individual and was recently nominated for the Human Development Center's Praeceptor Educator Award.

Mary Schmitz-Phillips, BA, is certified in early childhood education and English for speakers of other languages. She has taught first and second grade and is currently team teaching third grade at Pizzo Elementary, Tampa, Florida, as a part of the continuous progress model. She is a member of the Parent– Teacher Association, chairs schoolwide committees, and is completing a master's degree in educational leadership at the University of South Florida.

Scott M. Smith, MEd, received his master's in education leadership from the University of South Florida and is an honors economics and government instructor at J. W. Mitchell High School in New Port Richey, Florida.

Robin Snyder, BA, has 18 years of classroom experience in both public and private schools. She is a fourth-grade teacher at Valrico Elementary in Valrico, Florida, and specializes in writing instruction. She has worked with the Hillsborough County School District as a writing trainer through the Tampa Bay Writing Project and is pursuing a master's degree in educational leadership at the University of South Florida.

Cameron Spears, MS, is a doctoral student and graduate teaching assistant in instructional technology at the University of South Florida. He taught at the undergraduate and graduate levels for 6 years. Before beginning his pursuit of his doctoral degree, he spent 19 years in the computer industry, leading design and development efforts for both commercial and defense applications. His bachelor's and master's degrees are in computer science, and he holds four U.S. patents for computer technology-related inventions. Most recently, he was the instructional technology recipient of the University Fellowship Grant within USF's College of Education.

Michael Tabor, MEd, holds a bachelor's of science in mathematics education and is completing a master's degree in education leadership at the University of South Florida. Tabor teaches mathematics at C. Leon King High School in Tampa, Florida.

Jennifer E. Varholy, MEd, is pursuing an educational specialist degree in educational leadership at USF. In 1999 she completed a master's degree in education at the University of South Florida. She holds certification in English (grades 6–12 and 5–9), as well as elementary education. She is an experienced eighth-grade language arts teacher in Florida who has achieved National Board Certification. In 2002, she was selected as Teacher of the Year at her school and serves in various leadership roles. Her main research interest is in teacher leadership at the middle school level.

Author Index

A

Adler, M. J., 86
Akiba, M., 200
Almazroa, H., 217
Altmann, E. M., 117
Alvy, H., 61
Amrein, A., 23
Anderson, M., 112, 113
Apple, M. W., 39
Apthorp, H. S., 200
Archbald, D. A., 166
Austin, V. L., 88

B

Baker, D. P., 133
Baker, E., 85
Bailey, B. P., 117
Barth, R. S., 99, 110
Beime-Smith, M., 90
Beninghof, A. M., 89
Berliner, D. C., 23
Billingsley, F., 92
Bishop, K., 81
Blasé, J., 74
Bloom, G., 137, 138
Bobbit, F., 12, 17, 32, 40
Bolman, L. G., 62, 64, 100
Bond, S., 200
Bravo, M. L., 182
Brighton, C., 90
Browne, B. C., 134, 139, 140
Brubaker, D. L., 12, 13, 14, 24, 25

Bruning, R. H., 117, 118
Buell, M. J., 88, 89
Bullock, L. M., 85, 90
Burke, D., 206, 207, 208

C

Cairns, S. S., 8, 59
Cain, T., 112, 113
Callahan, C., 91
Carlis, J. V., 117
Carter, R. A., 72, 73
Case, K., 17, 92
Cavert, C., 112, 113
Chalmers, L., 93
Cheddar, L. A., 6
Chen, E., 21, 177, 186
Chung, A., 188, 193, 199, 200
Clandinin, D. J., 4, 7, 11, 12, 13,
      14, 25, 28
Clerk, D., 216
Collier Kuhlthau, C., 81
Collins, R., 194, 195, 197, 198, 200
Conant, J. B., 34
Connelly, F. M., 4, 7, 11, 12, 13, 14, 25, 28
Cook, B. G., 85, 87
Cordeiro, P., 178
Covey, S. J., 64
Craig, B., 151
Craik, F. I., 217
Cranston, N., 63
Crosby, P., 206
Cunningham, W., 178
Curtis, D., 177

D

Daane, C., 90
D'Alonzo, B. J., 85
Danielson, C., 157
Daresh, J. C., 66
Datnow, A., 238, 239
Deal, T. E., 62, 64, 100
de Alba, A., 11
Dewey, J., 17, 33, 40
Dhingra, K., 217, 223
Dick, M. H. H., 22
Donham, J., 81
Douzenis, C., 165
Downey, C. J., 149, 150, 152, 154,
    155, 156, 157, 158, 159
Downing, J. E., 92
Dyson, J. C., 6

E

Eichinger, J., 92
Eisenberg, M., 71
Eisner, E. W., 14, 17, 34
English, F. W., 3, 13, 23, 149, 150,
    152, 154, 155, 156, 157, 159
Erwin, E. J., 84

F

Farinas, J., 134, 142
Farmer, L. S. J., 71, 81
Fennick, E., 87, 88
Flinders, D. J., 14, 16, 18, 26, 29, 31,
    32, 35, 38
Fogg, T., 169
Forness, S., 85
Forsten, C., 202, 205, 206
Franklin, L. L., 75, 77, 82
Frase, L. E., 149, 150, 152, 154, 155, 156,
    157, 159
Fullan, M., 3

G

Gabriel, J. G., 238, 239
Gallagher, M., 188
Gamel-McCormick, M., 88, 89
Gandara, P., 188, 190

Gardner, H., 7
Gartner, A., 90
Gaustad, J., 202, 205, 206,
    209, 211
George, P., 63, 202, 203, 205,
    206, 207, 208
Gerber, M. M., 85, 87
Gerke, W., 67
Gettinger, M., 118
Gilbert, L. A., 182
Giordino, G., 85
Glatthorn, A. A., 13, 19, 20, 22,
    23, 24, 25, 73
Goldring, E. B., 10, 162, 234
Gonazalez, C., 189
González-Gaudiano, E., 11
Goodlad, J. I., 36
Gottesman, B., 89, 136, 137, 155, 158
Grant, J., 202, 205, 206
Graves, T. H., 112, 204
Gross, S. J., 18, 20, 24
Guiton, G., 86

H

Hallam, R. A., 88, 89
Hammel, A. M., 85, 90
Hargreaves, A., 3
Hartzell, G., 81
Haslinger, J., 207
Hawthorne, R. D., 12, 17, 20, 24, 25
Heathfield, S. M., 112
Heck, T., 112, 113
Heflin, L. J., 85, 90
Hendershot, G., 70, 78
Henderson, J. G., 12, 17, 20, 24, 25
Henning, M. B., 86
Heritage, M., 21, 177, 186
Hertberg, H., 90
Hill, J. C., 23
Hill, J. H., 214
Hootstein, E., 91
Hoover, J. H., 92, 93
Hopkin, M., 27
Horn, R. A., 4
Hoover, J. J., 93
Hoyle, J. R., 62
Huberman, A. M., 199
Hudson, M. B., 169, 171
Huling, L., 137, 138

I

Irwin, R. L., xii
Itza-Ortiz, S. F., 215

J

Jackson, L., 92
Jackson, P. W., 14, 85
Jacobs, H. H., 238
Janesick, V. J., 14
Johnson, B., 202, 205, 206
Johnson, D., 71
Johnstone, A. H., 216
Jordan, D., 206

K

Kamens, M. W., 89, 93
Karoly, L., 86
Kavale, K., 85
Kealy, W. A., 70, 72, 73
Kearney, L. K., 182
Kelly, P., 207
Kenyon, G. M., 7
Kliebard, H. M., 17
Knobel, M., 72
Kohan, A. R., 74, 86, 87
Konstan, J. A., 117
Koralek, D., 194, 195, 197, 198, 200
Kovalik, S., 117, 118

L

Lance, K., 70, 72, 73
Lankshear, C., 11, 72
Larson, R. L., 3, 13, 14
Latham, D., 90
Lauer, P., 200
Lee, J., 21, 177, 186
Liddy, D., 87, 88
Lincoln, R., 208
Lind, S., 100, 101, 107, 109, 138
Lipskey, D. K., 90
Llenza, E., 189
Llewellyn, P. E., 59
Lockhart, R. S., 217
Loprete, S. J., 89, 93

Lortie, D. C., 8
Loucks-Horsley, S., 89
Lounsbury, J., 202, 203, 205, 206, 207, 208
Lowe-Parrino, G., 113

M

Mannheim, B., 214
Marino, S. B., 95
Marsh, C. J., 6, 7, 11, 14, 16, 26
Marshall, K., 150, 151, 155
Martin-Glenn, M., 200
Maslow, A. H., 36
Mastropieri, M. A., 93
McCann, I., 136
McCarthy, M. M., 22, 23
McComas, W. F., 217
McGreal, T. L., 157
McLesky, J., 93
McNeil, J. D., 24, 234
Merriam, S. B., 7
Michael, L., 218
Miles, M. B., 199
Miller, K., 188, 200
Miller, R., 95
Mitchell, L. C., 86
Moir, E., 137, 138
Monahan, R. G., 95
Moon, T., 91
Moore, C., 99
Moore, T. I., 210
Morrill, S., 162, 163, 165, 176
Morris, D., 200
Morrow, L., 200
Mullen, C. A., xiii, 4, 5, 7, 8, 16, 18, 22, 23, 40, 41, 59, 60, 62, 63, 65, 68, 69, 70, 74, 77, 81, 84, 86, 87, 91, 100, 111, 112, 114, 134, 136, 137, 142, 154, 178, 179, 180, 181, 182, 185, 186, 188, 204, 234, 244
Murphy, J., 74, 84, 87, 88, 187, 188, 193, 195, 196, 198, 200, 239

N

Neill, J., 33
Norby, M. M., 117, 118

O

Oakes, J., 86
Oberg, D., 81
O'Lare, L., 207
Oleson, M., 12, 21, 85
Oliver, R., 22
Olson, L., 93
Olson, M. R., 93
O'Shea, D. J., 90, 93, 95
O'Shea, L. J., 90, 93
Ovalle, R., 206

P

Paquette, B. S., 59, 64, 65
Patton, J. R., 92
Perie, M., 133
Perney, J., 200
Peters, M., 11
Peterson, K. D., 100
Piaget, J., 35
Pimm, D., 215
Pinar, W. F., xii, 12, 14, 16, 18, 24,
    29, 33, 35, 41, 234
Poeske, L. D., 6
Ponticell, J., 100
Popham, W. J., 16
Posner, G., 23
Poston, W. K., 149, 150, 152, 154, 155,
    156, 157, 159

R

Radford, R., 136
Rallis, S. F., 10, 234
Ramanathan, A. K., 210
Rebello, S., 215
Rees, L., 137
Reick, W. A., 89, 95
Reugebrink, M., 63
Reynolds, W. M., 14, 16, 18, 33
Rhodes, G., 215
Richardson, I., 202, 205, 206
Riley, K. L., 169
Robbins, P., 61
Robertson, J., 4
Rogers, C. R., 37
Ronning, R. R., 117, 118
Rouse, E. R., 164
Rowley, J. B., 9

Rutherford, M., 216
Ryan, P., 162, 163, 165, 176
Ryndak, D. L., 92

S

Sapir, E., 216
Schaible, R., 215
Schermer, D. G., 3, 20, 21
Scherry, R., 200
Schirduan, V., 17, 92
Schraw, G. J., 117, 118
Schubert, W. H., 134, 135
Schumaker, D., 61, 64, 74,
    81, 157, 166, 171
Schwab, J., 19, 22
Scruggs, T. E., 93
Selepeng, D., 216
Seligman, A., 189
Selvin, M., 86
Semmel, M. I., 85, 87
Sergiovanni, T. J., 7, 74, 88, 239
Shade, R. A., 86
Shapiro, J. P., xiv
Shaw, B., 200
Simel, D., 209
Skinner, B. F., 30, 37
Slattery, P., 14, 16, 18, 33
Slostad, F. A., 89, 93
Smith, J. B., 71
Smith, M. K., 30, 33
Smrekar, C. E., 162, 164
Snow, D., 188, 200
Snyder, E. D., 84
Sommers, W., 61, 64, 74, 81, 166, 171
Speier, C., 117
Stainback, S., 99
Stainback, W., 99
Steeves, K. B., 134, 139, 140
Steffy, B. E., 149
Stefkovich, J. A., xiv
Stewart, R., 86
Stober, S. S., 6
Sullivan, A., 70
Sullivan, E. C., 179, 180, 181

T

Taubman, P. M., 14, 16, 18, 33
Taylor, W., 164
Thomas, K. A., 219

Thomas, T. P., 134, 135
Thorndike, E. L., 38
Thornton, C., 113
Thornton, S. J., 14, 16, 18, 26, 29,
    31, 32, 35, 38
Thousand, J. S., 87, 88, 90, 92, 99
Tomlinson, C. A., 90, 91
Trafton, J. G., 117
Tromans, C., 63
Tulving, E., 217
Tyler, R. W., 16, 32, 88

U

Umphrey, J., 67

V

Valacich, J., 117
Vanleeuwen, D. M., 85
van Loveren, R., 189
Varholy, J., 206, 208, 209
Vessey, I., 117
Villa, R. A., 87, 88, 90, 92, 99
Vnuk, K., 189

W

Wadsworth, D. E., 89, 95
Wang, M., 85

Waldron, N. L., 93
Walker, B., 200
Walker, D. F., 13, 20, 23
Wallberg, H., 85
Werts, M. G., 84
Wilburg, K. M., 185
Wiles, J., 29
Wilkerson, S. B., 200
Willingham, D. T., 217
Willis, G., 6, 7, 11, 14, 16, 26
Wilson, E. K., 169
Wolery, M., 84
Woo, D., 200
Wood, C., 182
Woods, C. S., 217

Y

Yu, M., 164, 210

Z

Zepeda, S. J., 157
Zollers, N. J., 210
Zollman, D., 215

Subject Index

A

Accountability (*see also* Democratic accountability), ix, x, 14, 18, 24, 56, 91, 161, 199, 235, 237, 239
Action research(ers), xiii, 4–5, 8–9, 114, 131, 223, 242
Administrator walk-through (model), 23, 67, 149–155, 157–161
 Administrator/Teacher Mentor Walk-Through Reflection Sheet (Table), 153
 Classroom Walk-Through Checklist (Table), 160
Aspiring leaders, 5–6, 29, 61, 63, 65, 177, 234
Assessment, 4–5, 14, 18–19, 21–23, 72, 75, 87, 92–94, 110, 114, 121–124, 135, 137–138, 140–141, 150, 158, 166, 168, 189, 191–194, 196, 199, 203, 212, 220, 234, 237, 239

C

Coaching, 5, 22–23, 87, 135, 139, 150, 152, 155, 158–159, 215, 217, 219, 221, 224–225, 234, 242
 coaches, 64, 155–156, 160–161, 229
Cases, xiv, 3, 5–7, 9, 19, 24–25, 232
 case study, xiv, 7 (defined), 9, 131, 140, 142 (case study model)
Change, xii, 3, 10, 13, 18–19, 21, 23, 25, 28, 32–35, 38, 41, 45–46, 53, 60–63, 65, 67–68, 74, 77–79, 81–82, 84, 87–89, 95–96, 99–100, 119, 129–130, 154, 163, 166–167, 171–173, 175, 177–179, 181–182, 185, 192, 199, 204–205, 208–209, 211, 212–213
 changes to curriculum, 232–234
 school-wide change, 157–158, 212
Collaboration
 teacher collaboration, 77, 87–88, 94, 98
 collaborative teaching, 87 (defined)
Curriculum, ix, xi–xiii, 4–41, 69, 73–74, 77, 82, 85, 87, 89–92, 97–100, 102–103, 114, 124, 126, 133, 135, 137, 140, 149–150, 154–155, 159, 162–169, 174–185, 193–195, 203, 206, 213, 218, 224, 229, 234–235, 238–239, 241, 243–244
 collaborative curriculum, 19
 continuum, 22, 31, 38–39, 51, 240
 curricular collaboration, 113 (described)
 curricular interruptions, 5, 116, 242
  Factors that Interfere With Instruction (Table), 121–122
 field, 26, 28–30, 35, 41, 51, 88, 232
 inner curriculum, xii, 12, 25
 leader, 3, 5, 17, 18, 73, 74, 75, 88, 151
 leader(ship), ix, x–xiii, 3, 10, 18, 60, 62, 64, 67–69, 73–75,

81–82, 84–86, 88, 95–96, 100, 103, 112, 118–119, 133–134, 136, 147, 150–151, 154–155, 159–162, 164, 167, 177–178, 183, 200, 210–211, 215, 223, 229–232, 234, 243–244
conceptions and types, 23–25, 210
guide, 229–246
map/mapping, 238–242
  Curriculum Mapping of How Living Things Interact (Table), 240–241
theory, 30, 35, 246
thinkers, 28–56
  Key Thinkers in Curriculum Studies (Table), 42–56
  process-leaning, 29, 31–35, 38–41
  product-learning, 29, 31–32, 37, 34–35, 38–41
instructional curricular tools, xiii, Part III
looping, 202–213
  defined, 202
  meditating on curriculum, 244–246
origins, definitions, and types, 11–26

D

Democracy, x, 46, 73, 86
  social justice, 70, 166
Diversity, 13, 20, 23, 56, 90–91, 112–113, 162, 165–166, 171, 207, 234

E

Educational Leadership Constituent Council (ELCC) standards, 63, 177

F

Florida Comprehensive Assessment Test (FCAT), 72, 76, 203, 236–237

H

High-stakes testing, 5, 14, 18, 25, 33, 242

I

Inclusion, 7, 19, 48, 87–96, 98, 113–114, 211, 234
  Concerns-Based Adoption Model (CRAM), 89
  definitions and frameworks, 84–86
  differentiated instruction, 87, 90–92, 94–95
  Exceptional Student Education (ESE), 97, 99, 102, 104, 107, 110, 268
  Individuals with Disabilities Education Act (IDEA), 85
  special education, 5, 84–85, 88, 94–95, 140, 207, 211–212, 242
  students (children) with disabilities, 6, 84–91, 93–94, 96, 99

L

Literacy
  Benchmarks for science literacy, 214
  critical literacy, 73
  information literacy, 6, 70–74, 81, 187
    definitions and frameworks, 71–74
  media literacy, 83

M

Magnet school, 162–176, 233
  administrator, 171
  description, 162–166
Mentoring, xii, xiv, 135–137, 139, 161
  (see mentor, as in board, lead, and teacher)
  teacher mentoring, 22, 137–138, 147

N

National Board Certification (NBC), 126, 135, 140, 142
National Board (certified) teacher/ curriculum leader/educator, 133, 136, 141–143, 147–148, 234

National Board for Professional Teaching
Standards (NBPTS), 133–134, 136
New Millennium High School(s)
(NMHSs) (*see also* Career
academy) 178–179 (overview),
181–184
No Child Left Behind Act of 2001
(NCLB), 12, 16, 21, 25, 91,
96, 116, 164, 187, 195

S

Science education, 215, 218, 223
Scholar practitioner, 4, 9
School culture, 5–7, 61–62, 99–100
(described), 101–102, 104–107,
110, 114, 159, 169–170, 211, 242
Administrator School Culture
Interview protocol, 101
School Culture Survey of
Teachers' Perceptions
(Table), 105–107
Site-based curriculum leadership, 12, 19,
96, 102, 151, 160, 183, 185, 213
administration/management,
4–5, 9, 166
Student learning, 15, 19, 22, 24, 41, 74,
81, 91, 117–118 (impact on
student learning), 133–136
(NBPTS-focused), 151, 164, 169,

193, 222–223 (science writing
context), 234–235 (vis-à-vis
self-reflective journal), 237, 239

T

Teacher leader(ship), 10, 24, 139,
203–204, 204–205 (as change
agents), 210–211
Technology, 8, 19, 56, 70, 98,
168, 171, 177–178,
183–185, 221, 233
communication technology, 167
informational technology, 180
National Education
Technology Plan, 177
infusion, 23, 97, 177
issues and challenges, 181–182
leadership, 5, 7, 18, 242
magnet, 172
technology-related
legislation, 177–178
specialists, 98, 121–122
Technology Standards for School
Administrators (TSSA), 177
Tutoring, 188, 190–191, 193, 197–198,
233 (*see also* Tutor)
After-school tutoring program(s),
188, 194, 199–200
program(s), 195, 198–200